GW00786314

Painted Lady

Richard Masefield is married with three children. Born in 1943, a cousin of John Masefield the poet, he has worked variously as a repertory actor, a journalist, a salesman, an advertising executive and a dairy farmer, before concentrating his energies on historical fiction.

Also in Pan Books by Richard Masefield

Brimstone
Chalkhill Blue

Richard Masefield

PAINTED LADY

Pan Books
London, Sydney and Auckland

First published 1988 by William Heinemann Ltd
This edition published 1989 by Pan Books Ltd,
Cavaye Place, London SW10 9PG
9 8 7 6 5 4 3 2
© Richard Masefield 1988
ISBN 0 330 30721 5

Printed and bound in Great Britain by
Cox and Wyman Ltd, Reading, Berkshire

This book is sold subject to the condition that it
shall not, by way of trade or otherwise, be lent, re-sold,
hired out, or otherwise circulated without the publisher's prior
consent in any form of binding or cover other than that in which
it is published and without a similar condition including this
condition being imposed on the subsequent purchaser

FOR LEE

A lady who needs no paint

Prelude
London, 1861

Mr Wilberforce Brown – of the firm of Eustace, Smithson and Brown, Solicitors – consulted his watch by the light of the gas flares of the Army and Navy club on the corner of Pall Mall and St James's Square. It was ten minutes past four, and a little early still for his appointment – precisely as intended; for, as an attorney of orderly inclination and punctual habit, he hated above anything to be late. Brown paused for a moment beneath the flares, frowning his disapproval of the intrusive barrel-organ across the street while he snapped shut the chronometer again and fumbled it back into his fob pocket.

'Unlucky choice,' he thought as he turned northward into the square to the strains of the *Traviata* waltz. Half of England in mourning since the great bell of St Pauls had tolled the news of Prince Albert's death. The Prince himself barely cold in his grave, and the fellow chose to light upon an air like this for his recital! Wilberforce Brown sighed and rebuttoned his overcoat against the cold. It was Christmas Eve. The previous day the entire city had come to a standstill out of respect for the Prince Consort and his funeral at Windsor; even the Exchanges had closed. Tomorrow and on Boxing Day it would do so again for the seasonal religious festival. Which gave Brown but a single opportunity, this afternoon, in which to conclude his business in the square.

As he advanced up the pavement in the direction of Number Fifteen, a scattering of recent snow lay untrampled still before him. In the gathering dusk it illuminated the square's central enclosure with reflected light, investing its statue of King William III as a Roman emperor with an additional mantle of white. A

1

deliberately imperial theme which was echoed in the façades of the mansions that overlooked it – in the pediments of Number Twenty-One where the Bishop of Winchester resided when in town, and in the fluted Corinthian pilasters of Sir Watkin Williams Wynne's establishment next door.

'Palaces fit for the dwellings of noblemen and persons of quality,' was the intention with which these town houses of St James's had first been constructed in the flurry of building work that accompanied the Restoration of the monarchy. And now almost two centuries later, and despite certain traitorous tendencies amongst the rich and the fashionable to move westward into Knightsbridge and Belgravia, it was very much the function they still performed. Within the walls of Norfolk House on the far side of the square the future King George III had been born. Number Seventeen accommodated his daughter-in-law, the unfortunate Queen Caroline, during the House of Lords inquiry into her alleged adultery. From the balcony of Number Sixteen next door, as Mr Brown pacing beneath it was very well aware, her husband, the Regent, had caused the great victory of Waterloo to be announced to a waiting crowd. Over the years a number of individual houses had been given over to gentlemen's clubs. One or two had even descended to commerce of one kind or another – to banking, insurance or other such indispensable services for the wealthy. But in 1861 the majority remained faithful still to their original intention. And although Wilberforce Brown might only have guessed at the statistics of the matter, it was a fact that on the afternoon of his perambulation along its western perimeter, two bishops, three dukes, five earls and a countess were all of them officially resident in St James's Square.

And so to Brown's anticipated destination of Number Fifteen. A house with its own illustrious history. It was here that Frances Stuart, Duchess of Richmond, had once lived – the celebrated Restoration beauty who'd lent her face and figure to her country's coinage in the role of its 'Britannia'. Later, in a rebuilt and fashionably classical version of the mansion, a Prime Minister, a Lord Chief Justice and a Postmaster-General successively resided, before Lord Southbourne had purchased the freehold from Lord Lichfield for a sum approaching £11,000.

Wilberforce Brown considered Number Fifteen's imposing

Ionic pillars and triangular pediment, the façade of an Athenian temple grafted to a London town house, and again he unbuttoned his coat to haul on his watch-chain. He was still a little premature, yet not unreasonably so, he thought. He smoothed his already smooth Crimean whiskers and straightened his already level silk top hat. Then he mounted the six marble steps that spanned the area, to make his presence known.

"Good afternoon, Martha. Is your mistress at home?" A formality merely, the answer already known to him.

"Yes, Sir, you are expected."

The maid who relieved him of his hat, his coat and gloves was at some pains, he noticed, to avoid his eyes. "If you would care to walk into the small drawing-room, Sir," she said, "Milady will be down directly."

The girl knew him, naturally. And she knew the nature of his errand too. It could hardly be otherwise. But whatever she might venture on the subject to her cronies below stairs, she'd been too well schooled to reveal her natural interest to his face. She followed him silently into the room to turn up the gas, then closed the double doors behind her without a backward glance.

The small drawing-room at Number Fifteen was similar in all essentials to the Duchess's at Number Twelve or to Lady Cowper's at Number Four across the square – with wealth and status, those twin gods of the Victorian Age, manifest in every furnishing and ornament. Polished rosewood, velvet plush and Indian carpeting, all as red as good port wine – gasoliers of gilded bronze, silk, porcelain, alabaster and marble to invite admiring comment and furtive valuation.

Brown, who already knew the room, did neither. Remaining standing, he searched instead for its more revealing aspects – for the real treasures of the place – humming to himself the infectious tune of the street organ and feeling absurdly awkward. To the right of the doorway and its velvet *portières* stood a flourishing palm tree in an antique brass container, and above it Boucher's 'Portrait of Louisa'. A copy in oils, and rather a free one. On a wall beside the window were three small Italian watercolours – three views of an exquisite little island floating on the surface of some calm sub-Alpine lake – but too delicate of execution in Brown's opinion for their heavy walnut frames. Near the marble chimney-piece, on

3

either side, Victoria and her consort posed self-consciously in medieval dress; poor Albert, as a latter-day King Arthur, draped comprehensively in black. On the mantel itself between a pair of Staffordshire figures was an inlaid Buhl clock, with the legend '*Tempus fugit*' engraved above its face. And propped beside this loudly ticking timepiece, where its owner had drawn attention to it once before, an ivory miniature of a dark and Byronesque young man in a dashing open shirt: the archetypal romantic hero (and in fact Lord Southbourne in his youth). Beside him, Brown's own reflection in the chimney glass appeared remote and stiffly formal, every inch the man of law. Regretfully he turned back to the glass bell-jars on the tables. Stuffed birds, wax flowers and fruit, predictably. But one apart and close to Milady's chair, that broke the decorative pattern. A child's doll, featureless and tattered, slumped gracelessly against the glass, its shiny scalp quite innocent of hair.

"Why Mr Brown, how very punctual you are!" Her voice a rich contralto in keeping with the décor of her drawing-room. Her dress though, as he turned to greet her, something of a disappointment. Black craped silk, tightly buttoned from businesslike collar and tie to plain cut-steel belt buckle, and then descending in a cascade of scolloped flounces to cover the hive-shaped cage of her crinoline.

"But what sad happenings since last we met, Sir," she said by way of an explanation for her dreary weeds, and holding out her hands to him. Both hands, as if they were friends only, with no business to settle between them. "Our dear Prince taken from us, Mr Brown, and the Queen to spend her Christmas now in mourning, poor lady."

"Indeed Ma'am, a severe loss to the nation," Brown murmured, catching the gleam of her wedding-ring as he bowed over her hands. That and her silver drop ear-rings the only jewelry that she wore. He felt the awkwardness of his position – longed to expedite the business that had summoned him. But that was not to be allowed, it seemed. At least not yet.

"Octavia, I fear, is less punctual than yourself, Sir," his hostess was saying. "You must let me entertain you while we wait. Have you taken tea?"

The width of her crinoline as she swept over to the bell-pull was

4

flattering to a figure tending now to stoutness. Yet for a large woman she moved with grace – her stays too expensively well made to creak, despite their burden. The black, moreover, showed off the vibrant colour of her hair, oiled with Macassar and smoothly netted in its heavy chignon against her neck. "Do sit down, Sir, please. Let us be comfortable by all means while we wait.

"Sugar, Mr Brown, and milk?" she enquired a little later. "We have it fresh each day, you know, from the cowkeeper's in Coventry Court across the Haymarket."

Seated beside the lady on the sofa, her attorney marvelled at the smooth perfection of the face she turned towards him as he took the cup. A woman of three-score years or more, born in the last century and in the reign of George III, with scarce a visible line to mar her plump and rosy cheeks. The gas hissed softly and the clock ticked steadily away throughout the silence in their conversation. Conscious suddenly that he was staring, Brown took a gulp of tea – a beverage he'd never personally cared for. Then, having burned his lips and tongue, plunged recklessly into speech again. In the past he'd often remarked the child's doll in that jar beside her chair, he told her inconsequentially. He wondered at its history. Was it her own originally? Did it have a name?

"*Jemima* – she is named Jemima; and yes, she's mine. I'm so glad now I never parted with her. Throw anything away, Mr Brown, and, to be sure, the day will come when you wish you had it back again." The lady smiled and rose in a perfumed swish of silk to lift the glass bell from the doll, jerking her own hoops back into place as she did so. "As a matter of fact, Jemima has a very entertaining history. You might even say that our stories run parallel, mine and this shabby little muppet's!" Carefully she lifted the doll from its velvet cushion and returned with it to the sofa, cradled like a baby against her tight black bodice. "That I suppose is partly why I've kept Jemima by me all these years, to remind me of how far I have come. Of what I once was, and of what I might have been today if things chanced differently."

The gentleman's cup clattered noisily in its saucer, and the lady smiled again. Her smile a wide and vivid curve of carmine. A far cry indeed from the adenoidal rosebud mouths the widowed Queen herself had set the fashion for, and one that no amount of *prunes and prisms* would reduce. "Come now, Mr Brown," she

5

chided, "is that a look of disapproval I detect? And are you perhaps of Lord Southbourne's opinion in such affairs? Do you believe at heart, as he did, that the follies of our past are best forgotten, despite all we have to learn from them?"

"The very contrary, my dear Madam, I do assure you . . ."

But she was too generous a woman deliberately to embarrass him. "No, Sir," she said reflectively, coming to his rescue with another broad and brilliant smile across her silver teapot. "No, indeed, I do believe I'd sooner part with all my Chelsea Derby and half the silver in the house than my disreputable little Jemima here. She is the one thing, you see, that I still have of my childhood. My mother gave her to me on my ninth birthday. I remember it as clearly as if it were only last week . . .

" 'See here, Sary sweetheart – see what Mamma has brought ye!' " Her rendering of the rural accent was surprising in its accuracy. "I can see her dear face now, Mr Brown. Such beautiful blue eyes she had. And Jemima as she then was – I can see her too. All spanking new, all painted up, with coloured feathers in her bonnet and a red velvet Spanish vest – the very latest thing. The very picture of a little lady! You'd scarcely think it, would you, to behold her now?"

BOOK 1

(1807–1819)

Chapter One

"See 'ere, Sary sweetheart – see what your Ma 'as brung ye!"

She'd heard it in her mother's strong Sussex voice as she ran out to her from school behind the others. Her mother's large hand on the sleeve of Fred Snudden's scarlet tunic, and holding up the doll for all to see. "Came up from Cuckmere 'Aven in the Lower's boat this morning – and over from France afore that I daresay, if truth be told." Her mother winked at Snudden. "And Freddie 'ere, 'e says, 'That's Sary's,' just like that – Lor' bless the man! So there ye are then, duck, 'tis all for you."

And Sary could remember now the shriek of joy she'd given. A smuggled Paris doll! A perfect little *dame de qualité* with painted porcelain face and curls and feathers, and everything! And not only that, but awarded to her here before the village school and with half the little girls of Alfriston to see it! The girls who'd pinched her and called her 'whore's brat', now pea-green with envy, every one! In all her lifetime to that moment Sary Snudden had never known such perfect triumph.

Born in a downland farmhouse but a few miles along the coast from Cuckmere Haven, Sary's name was first recorded in the Sellington parish register as 'Sarah Ann', with her mother's maiden name of 'Ashby' appended in want of any other, before the b for bastard. And although Ann Ashby had refused point-blank to swear the natural father before a magistrate, there'd been others in Sellington village ready enough to guess his name. The young master-smuggler, Aaron Corbyn, had spoiled her shape for a fact, they said, before that red-haired rogue seduced his brother's wife and led her on to conviction as an accessory to his felonies. Transported to Botany Bay, the pair of them, in splendid notoriety! And when Ann Ashby left her father's house to take her baby girl to Aaron Corbyn's brother, and to set up with him in place of the wife he'd lost, the village gossips knew they'd guessed the bastard's parentage aright.

Not that the buzz of scandal that surrounded her in the household of her Corbyn uncle had any power to harm a child of Sary's age and character. However they might resent Ann Ashby and her easy ways, the maidservants and scullions of Mr Rafe Corbyn's manor house of Chalkdean could bear no lasting grudge against her chance-born daughter.

"For recollect, the child would 'ardly choose to make 'er entrance to this world through bastardy, now would she?" the stout nursemaid, Mrs Henshaw, regularly and most reasonably avowed to anyone who'd lend an ear. "Not she, the precious mite!"

And Sary's own recollections of those early years at Chalkdean were still shot through with the perpetual sunshine of any happy infancy. Sunshine and laughter, and the images of shiny-faced kitchenmaids who scooped her up to set her on the dresser while they worked. Footmen who let her splash her little pink toes in the pantry sink, and grooms who bore her shoulder-high across the yards to see the horses in their stalls. Memories of her half-cousin, Lizzie – all silk and fluffy curls – sharing in her lessons, and in games of hunt-the-slipper in the Chalkdean schoolroom. A picture even of her sad-faced Uncle Corbyn, succumbing like the others to the charms of the imp with the monkey grin and carrot-coloured topknot; stooping to tickle his brother's little by-blow in her nursery cot, until she wriggled out of it and jumped up into his outstretched arms.

Yet even the best of things must end, or so her mother told her. And, before her seventh birthday, Sary had exchanged the light and freedom of her life at Chalkdean Manor for the reduced circumstance of a dark little house at Blatchington, near Seaford on the coast. And for a different 'soldier uncle', a captain of dragoons, who divided his time between her mother's lodgings and the great military barracks up the lane. For the child, to whom the motives of adult men and women were still a puzzling mystery, the

10

move had been as incomprehensible as it was unwelcome. But with the fatalistic commonsense of youth she'd soon adjusted to the variety of uniforms that crossed their door-stoop – and to the procession of military uncles who'd succeeded the first within the curtains of her mother's bed. They brought her lollipops and sugarplums and coloured ribbons for her hair besides, which made her like them very well. And when the latest, 'Uncle Jack', invited Annie and her daughter to follow him to summer training exercises, over the downs in Alfriston, Sary this time had gone willingly enough.

"Life brings us choices, Sary Ann, regular as spring and autumn. All we 'ave to do is take 'em," was the way her mother saw it. They'd paused to catch their breath amongst the grazing sheep at the summit of Hindover Hill – with Blatchington and Seaford and the glittering expanse of the English Channel at the back of them, the steep track down to Frogfirle combe ahead, and open downland all around. A huge empty landscape which a child accustomed to the lanes and cottages of Blatchington must find daunting. ('Too much sky,' was how the little girl described it to herself.)

"That's Ashby land," her mother told her, pointing backward to a distant brow above the river mouth, "the place where I was raised. And over there, d'ye see?" She crouched down beside her daughter to show her where to look. "See where that pointy little spire pokes up above the hill? There's where you and I'll be living next, down with Uncle Jack, in Alfriston.

"Choices," Annie Ashby reiterated. "Up they pops, and all without our asking. One path or another – we only 'ave to choose the one as looks most likely, and follow where it leads, see? No kind of trick to it, my pet." With which she smiled the broad and blue-eyed smile that always served to light up Sary's world, her fair hair blowing round her face. Then she straightened up to shoulder her burden and reach for her daughter's hand again. To stride on down the hill to Alfriston and the waiting Uncle Jack.

The rupture of the short-lived Peace of Amiens in 1803, and resumption of hostilities with France, brought greater threats than ever of an invasion by Buonaparte's *grande armée* bivouacked across the Channel. With a good glass, the French encampment at

Boulogne could be clearly seen from the Kent coast. And neutral travellers brought reports to England of thousands of flat-bottomed transports already in construction. Others credited Buonaparte with plans for digging a tunnel beneath the Channel; or for marching troops across from Calais on a pontoon bridge, with directions issued by their officers from the baskets of Blanchard gas balloons! In the words of the popular rhyme:

> Some say in wooden house he'll glide,
> Some say in air balloon,
> E'en those who airy schemes deride
> Agree his coming soon.

In fact he didn't come. But even after Trafalgar – even in 1806, the year that Sary and her mother had crossed the hill from Blatchington, the possibility of a French invasion was still considered a real one. Reinforced Martello towers with gun platforms from which invasion beaches could be swept with grapeshot were built along the Sussex shore. Auxiliary forces – regular 'defencibles', militiamen and volunteers – were concentrated in large numbers still in the southern counties of England. And in the summer months all of Sussex, it seemed, was drilling to repel the enemy. In the lower Cuckmere valley, to north and south of the village of Alfriston, acres of cone-shaped white tents now stood where cattle had been wont to graze the water-meadows. Further down the river, alongside the old sea battery at Cuckmere Haven, a temporary barracks had been constructed from prefabricated sections sent around the coast from Woolwich. And in Alfriston itself cottages, cowsheds and barns were licenced by the War Office to accommodate the officers and their mounts. On the village green a gunroom was established and in the market square a quartermaster's store – with the old cattle pound behind it gravelled over for a parade-ground, where regulars like 'Uncle Jack' were set to train the raw recruits.

To little Sary Ann, already well accustomed to the sight of blazoned uniforms, to the sounds and smells of men and horses in great numbers, Alfriston had seemed at first a bustling and a friendly kind of place. In the Star Inn taproom, at her mother's knee, her red hair and precocious taste for ale were universally admired. And as the only offshoot then in evidence amongst the female *convenients* and followers of the troops, she soon found herself an object of indulgence in the taverns and the back-street billets of the village.

At the end of the summer, the conscripted militia regiments sent down for training from the Midlands and from other southern counties had departed for their winter quarters. And when Jack was also returned to his troop of Sussex Fencibles at Blatchington, Sary's mother had replaced him in the way of military 'uncles' with one Sergeant Frederick Snudden – a veteran of the Duke of York's unsuccessful army of the Netherlands, who now ran the local quartermaster's stores. A big balding guardsman with a battlefield limp and a powerful taste for Sussex ale; and one who was not at all averse to housing Annie Ashby and her little girl within his cottage billet. Annie preferred the Cuckmere village, patently, to Blatchington. Despite continuing visitations from the local militia and yeomanry volunteers, there was a settled rural quality about the place that no barrack-town could offer. Respectability she'd never coveted for herself, but her daughter's was another case. Without the unnecessary embarrassment or expense of an actual churching, she thought to borrow the Sergeant's name of Snudden for herself and little Sary; and the next year enrolled the child as a pupil for the penny day-school in Alfriston. "To give 'er the benefit of some company of 'er own age," as Annie put it to her Fred. "Some other little maids who'll value the kiddy for what she is 'erself." An expectation which in the event proved optimistic.

"Brat of a harlot – all dressed in scarlet!" the village children had chanted at Sary Snudden's unexceptionable white scuffle-smock whenever the old dame who taught their class was out of earshot. And if its object understood the insult but imperfectly, the malicious sentiment behind it could hardly be more plain.

"These damn self-righteous countryfolk 'old it unsociable, 'twould seem, and even downright wicked to set up 'ouse with any fellow out of wedlock," her mother explained wearily when Sary ran home to her in tears. "Though for my life I vow 'tis a greater wickedness to go 'ungry and to see your child go 'ungry for want of an honest man's protection. And I don't care who hears me say it, neither. For, like it or not, Sary Ann, 'tis a man's world and always will be, as sure as you and me wear skirts." Ann Snudden had stretched down a large work-roughened hand on that occasion to dry her daughter's tears. "No call to look so tragical, my pet," she said. "They'll learn the lesson soon enough theirselves, as do we all. Meantime just you forget 'em, Sary Ann. Forget the girls, there's my advice to you. And recollect, their brothers are where your future lies, and ever will do. There's not a doubt in the world of that."

And so indeed it was to prove. At first the boys at school had followed on their sisters' lead, deriding poor Sary as a curious and a useless creature who had no place within their narrow village community. The chance-born offspring of local farm and trading families were commonplace enough in their experience – early proofs of fertility which formed the base for many a successful married partnership. But the brats of whores and soldiers were something still relatively new to rural Sussex. A new kind of gipsy brood that were seen as unemployable in field or stock-room, and were therefore naturally to be discounted and discountenanced.

Though Sary Snudden, as they soon discovered for themselves, was not so easily put down. "Sticks and stones may bruise my bones, but words cannot molest me," she scornfully proclaimed (and with sufficient force to lend conviction to that most fraudulent of proverbs). She didn't care an onion for their teasing, she informed them. It was obvious, moreover, after but a few weeks of schooling, that she was brighter, prettier, and better by far at skipping, tipcat and stool-ball than any other village maid – while, as the acknowledged favourite of the soldiers who ran the stores and gunroom and manned the battery at Cuckmere Haven, she held the key to military privileges that any village lad would give his new front teeth to share. In their gravelled parade-ground behind the square, forbidden to the other children, young Sarah Snudden was permitted to watch redcoat militia and green-jacket volunteers drilling with sticks in place of muskets, or making shot in the flint tower they'd constructed for that purpose there. And when the great cannon from the gunroom on the green was drawn up Long Barrow Hill for target practice across the Cuckmere valley, it was Sary who rode atop its carriage like a queen; while others, even older boys, must keep their distance at the rear.

With every month that passed, the village girls' hostility toward the daughter of the quartermaster's whore was thus increased, in inverse ratio to their brothers' admiration. Until, on the day of her ninth birthday when her mother presented Sary with her lovely Paris doll, the child might be alternatively viewed as the most – or as the least – envied pupil of Dame Chowne's penny day-school, dependent only on the viewer's sex.

Alfriston meanwhile, and all of downland Sussex, had become aware of changes in the nature of its military occupation. Events on the Continent proved that Master Emperor Bonaparty had postponed at least his dreams of invading England, to set about the conquest of the rest of Europe. And with broadscale militia ballots now abolished and many volunteers recruited to the line, the great sham battles on the Sussex downlands, the continuous summer training exercises and encampments (to which the Alfriston innkeepers and suppliers had so readily adapted) were succeeded by troop movements of a more sporadic and unprofitable nature; by weeks on end without tattoos and bugles; by empty fields and billets, and by idleness for the tiny local garrison of which Fred Snudden was a member. Dull times, dramatically enlivened by the arrivals and departures of great bodies of fighting troops *en route* to Deal or Portsmouth; with meadows reluctantly let go for hay to be flattened (a deal more lucratively for the farmers) by the tented quarters, kitchens, latrines and pickets of reinforcements bound for the Peninsular; or by Corunna veterans now earmarked for the Low Countries. Quiet lanes suddenly congested with waggons and canteen carts; and tavern taprooms, but recently deserted, now crowded with officers of the line in bright new regimentals. Light Dragoons and Buffs, brigades of Guards, and German legions with twirling canes and exotic waxed mustachios, now shortly two-a-penny in the village street.

At such times, had Annie Snudden really been the whore her neighbours branded her, she might perhaps have joined the farmers, brewers and tanners of the place in lining her own empty pockets at their paymaster's expense. But, as it was, she preferred to remain faithful for the present to the man whose name she had taken for her child.

"For he's a good 'un, Sary Ann, make no mistake about it," she assured her daughter when Freddie staggered home from the Star Inn taproom, to sprawl in a drunken stupor across the cottage table. "And good men are middling scarce, I'll tell ye," she added,

15

as together they struggled to relieve this one of his boots and breeches. "One way or another – Lor'amighty, I don't know, they never seem to last with me somehows for any kind of time."

And good women? Must the same harsh rule of life apply to them as well? A question Sary Ann had cause to ask herself in 1812, in the autumn when Buonaparte at last had overreached himself amid the snows of Russia – and at home her mother unexpectedly had entered a decline. At first Ann Snudden merely seemed a little weary, less hearty in her moods and appetites. "Lord save us – nothing in the world to get yourself in a pucker over, duckie," she reassured her girl with a smile that never could and never would entirely lose its sweetness. "Fit as fivepence in the space of a day or two, you'll see. Or you may call your Ma a Dutchman's aunt!"

But within that selfsame space, Annie's thick blonde hair had lost its shine instead, her eyes their brilliant periwinkle blue. In a month she'd shed a stone of weight, gaunt as a barren cow beneath her crapes and muslins as she huddled on a settle by the fire. And when Sary finally gave over education to nurse her mother in the tiny cottage that they shared with Freddie Snudden, it was clear to them, all three, that Ann would not see through the year.

Nor had she neither. Cold and set as stone, they'd watched her laid out that Christmastide – the sergeant and the harlot's bastard. A stranger in the end to both of them.

Sary Snudden, now approaching her fifteenth year, had long since lost all trace of modesty and innocence, if indeed she ever had possessed them. For years, and even before they came to Alfriston, she was accustomed to sleep within the same chamber as her mother. For years she'd been familiar with the bodies of her mother's military lovers – in uniform or naked, quiescent or aroused; for years inured to the rhythms of the blanket hornpipe the couples so regularly danced to, and to all its vocal accompaniments. In time, quite naturally, she had progressed to sampling its sensations too; experimenting first with her own body, and then with those of the series of young militiamen and agriculturalists who were so obviously attracted to it, in the barn beside the churchyard. To cast off without scruple or any sense of shame the shackles of her chastity – laughing at her lovers' guilty strategems.

16

For no one had taught Sary to place a value on her virtue. And the laws of God, as interpreted by His human agents, had little meaning for a girl of her bold inclinations.

So when in the flickering firelight of one dreary evening following on her mother's burial, an ale-sodden Freddie Snudden had looked across the cottage hearth at her with the eyes of a beaten bloodhound, she set aside her morbid thoughts to smile back at him as her mother would have done. She thought gratefully of the doll Jemima that he'd brought for her all those years before, and moved to stand above him in his chair. To let the man grope dumbly for the strong young legs, for the tender flesh beneath her skirts, while she reached down to stroke his thinning hair. To let him take comfort from her blossoming woman's body in the way that men have done since history first began.

* * *

And looking back across the years from her elegant drawing-room in St James's, while she recounted to the solicitor the story of her humble origins, Sarah could scarce recall her feelings then for Freddie Snudden. The clock on her mantelshelf still ticking loudly. *Tempus fugit*. So many, many men – and David – to come between that time and this.

Chapter Two

The village women knew of course. They'd known within a fortnight the way the wind was blowing in the Snudden household. When Sary crossed the street or ventured through the market square, she saw their sly and disapproving looks, in contrast to the soldiers' smart salutes and cheery greetings. They stood together silently to watch her pass, the tradesmen's wives and farmers' daughters, waiting only for her back to turn before they pierced it with their verbal shafts.

"Wrong from the start, that baggage – couldn't 'ardly 'ave been otherwise. And didn't I tell ye, Livvy Downer, the way things 'ud stand? Such goings on! Good sakes, 'tis the talk of all the parish. And with the mother barely cold in 'er grave, poor thing, for all 'er faults . . ."

Sary could guess what they were saying well enough. But Sary didn't care, or so she told herself. *Sticks and stones, sticks and stones* . . . She'd ever felt differently, God only knew, from these narrow close-bred village folk – and, please God, always would! Arrived now at an age which libertines and romantics agree to be amongst the most provocative of womanhood, she *was* different too without the shadow of a doubt. Her carriage and the swinging freedom of Sary's stride were distinctive in themselves, even without the voluptuous form and feature, the bright unfashionable colouring they displayed to such advantage.

"A female who's taken the trouble to learn 'er letters and gain a little conduct," old Dame Chowne made sure to inform the brightest pupil of her day-school, "a wench above the common run of village maids should do 'erself the justice to act ladylike as well.

18

Tain't nothing to it, Sarah Snudden, for one as sharp as you. Back straight, d'ye see? Feet together when you stand or sit. Eyes set to the pavement when ye walk, three good paces in advance. 'Ands folded neat and modest to keep your shawl in place. Never on your hips, gel, that ain't the thing! And dentical little steps. *Small* steps, Sarah Snudden, for gracious sake! It ain't a race you're running, is it?"

But Sary could never master such a mincing gait, however hard she strove. The straight back was not to prove a problem. (She had to keep that braced to show how well her breasts had grown.) But then the neck would follow on, to lift her chin and free her magnificent golden eyes to roam around at will. To outstare the village tibbys in their doorways, and wink first at the brave lads in scarlet and in green before they winked at her. The hands waved and gestured too, unstoppably. The shawl flapped free, however hard she tried to hold it in. And as to the feet – well, God made feet for walking and hips for swinging, surely? And legs as long and strong as Sary's were hardly to be constrained by narrow skirts and dentical little steps, however ladylike old Janey Chowne might like to think 'em!

Sary thus continued to prance along in the sensational fashion she preferred. A form of locomotion which no honest woman (and no man of any denomination) could deny suited her appearance to a marvel. Whether or not Ann Snudden's daughter could lay claim to any kind of beauty had for some time been a subject for debate in Alfriston; between officers in mess rooms and shepherds on hillsides, and women over garden wickets. And only the old men who daily met to discuss the progress of the war, and to consider life in general from the steps of the ancient market cross, could arrive at any kind of agreement on the matter.

"Unaccountable striking next to some, that Sary Snudden," the seers of Alfriston had cautiously declared. A qualified verdict which even the girl's most sincere detractors could hardly contradict. Her hair, the majority allowed, was of a middling handsome shade. (Though some still thought it red, and claimed they never could abide a raddle-poll.) In fact its hue had lightened somewhat over recent years, to something between her mother's blonde and her father's violent flame. "The colour of November beech-leaves," one old fellow ventured from beneath the market

19

stone. "October bracken, more like," averred another. "Or pinky polished copper," said a third poetically.

"But there again, to treat such hair the way she does," said Mildred Reed, whose own brown locks had never attracted any kind of comment. " 'Tis a gumptious gipsy's mode, and no mistake about it!" For Sary habitually went capless, with the coloured ribbons her Blatchington 'uncles' had brought her, red and blue and yellow, in her copper-bracken tresses. Ribbons looped and tied across her shining crown, and woven through the plait she'd coiled behind in the long outdated style of her little Paris doll.

As for the rest of Sary's person: the wench was too big, too broad in the back and shoulders, the village women held. She plainly was. "Breasts like a pair o' pumpkins, come to that – and not yet sixteen neither," affirmed Dorothy Pagden, the tallow-chandler's wife. "Where they'll end up, the good God only knows! And a rump on 'er like a Christmas bullock, I'll be sworn. The way she swags it when she walks! Good sakes, and 'aven't she got a nerve! You'd think she was cracking nuts in there, ye would really! And you can take that grin from off your face right now, 'Umphrey Pagden. Or you'll 'ave good cause to wish you 'ad, I'll give ye my word!"

And Sarah Snudden's face? What there? Fine eyes maybe, for them as liked a touch of ginger. A good clear skin, without the freckles or the whey-faced pallor that so often went with hair like hers. But a mouth impossibly too large to be well-looking, all the other women said so. Too full, too wide, too much inclined to laugh and show the world her teeth. A jaw a sight too definite as well. A chin too strong for any girl. And worse, a dimple in it – the Devil's fingerprint, the surest sign of a brimstone whore there was!

To maintain that Sary didn't mind being denigrated, or envied or disliked by others of her sex, would not be altogether true, whatever she might have told herself. In fact she needed approval as much as any youngster, and outside company to fill the gap her mother's death had left in her existence. And, were it not for a certain sense of loyalty to Freddie Snudden – had not the other younger males of Alfriston demonstrably admired her and competed to stand within her favour – why then she might perhaps have felt despondent. Yet, as things stood, she only had to wait.

"I'll tell ye what, Jemima – we only 'ave to wait until the war's over and Freddie has to go elsewhere," she confided to her little doll. "And then we'll go ourselves to mix in the great world. Would you like that, Jemima? For there's more to life than you an' me will ever see in this place, ye may be sure. And I'll not lie like a sheep on its back in Alfriston – not me! We'll go to Brighton, Jemima, that's what we'll do!"

Nor to be sure did Sary have to wait too long for her release from rustic vegetation. In the autumn of 1813 the Allies invaded France herself from the south and from the east. In March the following year they'd ridden into Paris. And in April the self-crowned Emperor was forced to bow to the inevitable and abdicate. The wars were over, and this time for good. Or so everyone imagined. The prefabricated barracks on the Cuckmere were dismantled and sold for lumber. The shopkeepers and traders of Alfriston (less inclined than most to celebrate a peace) were preparing to renew their ancient interest in contrabanding, and Fred Snudden to vacate his quartermaster's stores, when news came in from Brighton that the perfidious Buonaparte was once more on the loose!

'*We regret to state,*' the *Sussex Weekly Advertiser* informed its readers, '*that Bonaparte, the acknowledged scourge of mankind, has stolen from Elba and again invaded France, where he has hoisted his standard as the signal for another bloody rebellion . . .*'

This was the signal for more troop movements through the south of England than anyone had seen since the first serious invasion threats that followed the Peace of Amiens. With meadowlands at Alfriston too wet and stoachy still to bear them, men and horses must needs be housed in makeshift huts and canvas stablings on the parade-ground and the village tye; soldiers in byres and barns, in the church and clergy house and every village cottage with a bed to spare; officers of artillery and dragoons, light-infantry and grenadiers; with gold and silver in their pockets to pay for forage and provisions – to buy all the hay and oats, to eat all the victuals, drink all ale and smuggled spirit the taverns could provide. Alfriston's last hectic hour of commercial glory. All the excitements of that long anticipated invasion, without any of its more obvious disadvantages; before eventually the troops and baggage trains moved eastward to their embarkation ports of Dover and of Ramsgate, to sail from thence under convoy to Ostend and the old oft-trodden battleground of the Low Countries, where his Grace

21

the Duke of Wellington was mustering a force of twenty thousand, for a final confrontration with the bogeyman of every self-respecting English nursery.

Excitement was like a contagion in that spring of 1815. Half of London Society had already decamped to Brussels, complete with carriages and horses – to enjoy all the civilized facilities of that European capital, whilst watching Wellington campaigning for an action that all believed implicitly must end in victory. Alfriston youths of Sary's own age, boys she'd made standing room for in the old tithe barn behind the church, enlisted eagerly in the Duke of Norfolk's new band of Sussex Regular Militia, with Nelson's famous words of expectation ringing in their ears. In London the War Office called on the pensioners of the Chelsea Hospital to form a veteran battalion. Even Freddie Snudden, who'd spoken wistfully of changing the King's scarlet for the homespun of a rustic – even Freddie had lifted his head like the old warhorse he still was, to the sound of the fife and the drum; to rally to the call with men of half his age, when marching orders were sufficiently expanded to admit him to the line.

And Sary watched him limp away, knowing that he never would come back to rural Cuckmere. Not even if he lived. Sary stood in tears with all the rest of Alfriston to watch the final troop of militia volunteers march out, the first lovers of her youth amongst them; marching to enroll at Arundel, stepping bravely out to the strains of 'Brighton Camp' – the stirring Sussex march to which the great Rossini was later to refer as quite the finest melody he'd heard.

> Oh ne'er shall I forget the night
> The stars were bright above me,
> And gently lent their silv'ry light
> When first she vowed to love me.
>
> But now I'm bound for Brighton Camp,
> Kind heaven then pray guide me,
> And send me safely back again
> To the girl I left behind me!

Almost exactly two months later, the Brighton editor of the *Advertiser* had felt inspired for the first time in his newspaper's existence to venture a modest headline: GLORIOUS VICTORY. And, having gone thus far, cast all caution to the winds to exult:

> 'Wellington and Old England Forever!
> Huzza! Huzza! Huzza!'

Simultaneously, the bells of St Andrew's, Alfriston – and of Berwick, Alciston and Littlington and all the downland churches – pealed out the great and glorious news of Waterloo. And, two days following that, Sary Snudden set out for Brighton in the local carrier's cart.

It was an uncovered and entirely unsprung vehicle, with its driver's name, JOE FARREN – CARRIER, inscribed in large red letters on the side-boards. Sary, for better viewing and the better to be seen, had perched herself atop the straw hamper that held her pots and pans, her togs, her clogs, her curling-tongs; and the most treasured of all her memorials, her little Paris doll. Besides all that, she had in her reticule the five gold guineas and fourteen shillings in silver that Freddie had left her; on her head her very best bonnet, and in her mind a firm resolution to go her own ways henceforth; to take her own destiny by the horns and wrest from it all the colour and excitement that she craved. With Snudden and all the soldiers gone, and half the indigenous men of the place as well, there was nothing now to hold her to the Cuckmere valley. Her natural father, so they said, had long since died in New South Wales. And when his wife at last returned to him from shameful residence in that British penal colony, Sary's Corbyn uncle had sold up his manor and its farms at Chalkdean to move away (some said as far away as Bristol); to some new place where the family's past disgrace would not be known. Of her mother's kinsmen – Annie's father, old Farmer Ashby of Sellington, had also died long since. And though his elder son, Tom Ashby, still farmed the downland there, he clearly owed no obligation to his sister's bastard. Nor would Sary ever lay claim to such a thing from any unknown uncle; nor ever seek to change one narrow village prospect for another.

No, Brighton was the place for such as she! And the more Sary saw of the state of the farms and hamlets between Alfriston and Lewes, the more she was convinced of it. In twenty years of near continuous war, with blockades and labour shortages and a whole series of disastrous harvests, they were ploughing ever higher on the downland slopes: more land each year to feed a hungry nation. But land which had supported sheep from long before the Romans came had not the heart for wheat and oats. Ragged seams of flint and chalk showed through the cornstalks everywhere; so much of what remained already lodged and flattened by the downland winds. With fewer men to work them, the old farmyards at Winton Street and Bopeep Green were losing tiles and growing weeds. And it seemed to Sary, bumping backwards on her hamper through their rutted ways, that their days of rural plenitude had gone – and gone for good.

To avoid the Lewes turnpike and its tolls, the carrier had forced his laden conveyance and wheezing, undernourished horse up on to the old Saxon trackway that wound along the northern skirts of the downs from one ancient manor to another. A high chalk road that looked out over thirty miles of woodland, corn and dusty pasture to the far side of the great undulating valley of the Weald.

"You're like to meet some queer fish in Brighton town, maidy. And not all in the sea neither," the carrier observed to his passenger as they descended to the level once again between the flintstone walls of Firle. A hunched up backview with a round felt hat that seemed to sit directly on his shoulders; when Sary turned to look at him, the man appeared to her like nothing so much as a tenpenny cottage-loaf upon a baker's shelf.

"Aye, I daresay I will," she murmured through the creak and clatter, the whooping children and the barking dogs that sounded their entry to the village. "I daresay I will at that."

"Ah, and I'll good as bet a guinea you're on the lookout for some fellow with the pocket to pay your way for ye, and all," the carrier impertinently continued. "Brighton's no town for any wench to wander loose in, and that's a fact. You'll need a man, no doubt of it, to see ye safe."

"Well, that's as maybe," she provisionally replied. "Though like as not I'll manage well enough without, Sir."

The driver turned at that, to treat her to a solemn Sussex stare; to expose a broad and weatherbeaten visage, a clay pipe clamped between his teeth, a massive nose. And eyes beneath the hat brim which slowly stripped and then reclothed his buxom female

24

passenger, even as he turned away again to slap the reins along the horse's bony back. "Git up there, Phoebe," he enounced, without any very noticeable effect upon the creature's plodding pace. "We ain't got all day to waste, me and this 'ere almighty *indi-pennant* young 'ooman! Even if you 'ave yourself, ye old rattlebone!"

And Sary, so far from trying to defend her conduct to herself or to the man, sat back to review the possibility of selling her body on the streets of Brighton with a degree of calm that showed the idea to be a tolerably familiar one. Hers was by no means a temperament for intricate or subtle reasoning. Habitually she faced life's problems squarely – to examine them for just so long as it might take to come up with a practical solution, and then to put them from her mind.

'Well, if ye won't work in the heat, Sary Snudden, ye may as well go 'ungry when the frosts come,' she told herself with perfect truthfulness. 'And if this ol' rascal knows the right fellow to start ye in that way of business, you've nothing in the world to lose by seeing what 'e has to offer, that's pretty plain!'

Chapter Three

A little above the valley bottom of the Ouse, at a point where the Glynde Reach tributary wound down to its mother river between the high chalk headlands of Mount Caburn and Firle Beacon, a long wall of cobbled flints enclosed the deerpark of the famous Hadderton estate.

" 'Adderton Place," the carrier announced unnecessarily, clenching down on the stem of his pipe to jerk its bowl in the direction of a pair of towering gateposts, each crowned with the figure of a rampant dragon cast in lead (or more properly a *wyvern*, for neither beast had any nether limbs). Between the dragon-wyverns, the long ribbon of a metalled carriage-drive wound off into the park itself. Beyond them, and beneath the level of their outstretched wings, a lodgekeeper's cottage crouched in lowly deference. And beyond the cottage, the wall continued out of sight.

"Six mile around, that there wall," the carrier remarked, turning for a second time to study the effect of such a wonder on his passenger. "And every flint of 'er shipped up from New'aven Port to order of Lord Southbourne's granfer, so 'tis 'eld. Might just as well 'ave saved theirselves the trouble though, I say," he added, seeing that he'd caught her interest. " 'Tain't high enough at all. Not by yards it ain't! Deers jump out regular as night and day. And when they don't – well, hang me, 'tain't no kind of labour to fetch 'em over a little stumble-stone like that, now is it – 'owever many bleddy leagues it runs!"

And in truth the wall was not above six foot in height. A child on a man's shoulders might well see over it. As could Sary Snudden, perched upon her hamper. The carrier, crouched forward in his seat, saw only lines of russet coping-bricks and the branches of the trees that overhung them. But Sary, who overlooked the park itself, was already marvelling at the coolness of its emerald shadows after the dusty summer pallor of the downland they'd traversed. In a place where the trees fell back a little to disclose a wider view, she glimpsed a distant greystone tower standing all alone upon a grassy hill. And further on, a pair of riders beat the bounds of their estate. A gentleman and a lady, both young and arrow-slim, and both dressed dark and plain; he in a tailcoat and a narrow-brimmed top hat; she in a caped habit and a high-crowned bonnet of chocolate coloured velvet, with French kid-gloves to match.

Sary put up a reassuring yellow mitten to touch her own best gipsy-bonnet of chequered pink and white chip-straw. A head-piece trimmed but recently (though without reference to any recent fashion) with a back-kerchief of magenta silk, a red rosette and a splendid orange ostrich plume – the largest and most brilliant of its kind to be found at the Alfriston Spring Fair! An audacious display of colour was always Sary's first idea of style. And, by comparison, the headgear of the female in the park was austere to a fault. Yet the fabric was expensive. That was obvious at a glance. And, without consciously defining it, Sary recognised a caste and quality in both the riders that she knew to be beyond her own achievement. She'd heard of Lord Southbourne, had even seen him in the street at Alfriston with a troop of Pevensey Rape South volunteers. A wealthy landowner with estates extending far beyond the six-mile wall of Hadderton – a benevolent local despot with a reputation for the best horses and dogs in the eastern county: an old-school aristocrat, in other words. And these young riders in his park? His guests, or family? Perhaps his children even? Titled aristocrats at least, that much was all too obvious.

In the moment before the cart-track departed from the wall, both riders had glanced up; dark-eyed, fine-boned, both faces – creatures from another world. And in that same instant, looking down, Sary wished herself what she was never formed to be. She wished herself that slim young girl in brown, so straight and elegant upon her high-bred hunter! In a moment of uncharacteristic romanticism, the chance-born village girl imagined how it might be to ride at will in the great deerpark of Hadderton . . . to attend a ball within the mansion that stood there somewhere beyond the trees! To stand up with the smiling young man in the high silk hat, and without calling down the censure and disapproval of every watching eye!

Then, as the carrier's old horse leant into its collar to make the turn, her view had changed to that of a disgraceful hovel with a broken paling-fence and a pair of naked children scratching like chickens in the dust before its door. Joe Farren was heading westward now toward the river, to cross at Beddingham and thence to make his way to Lewes, where a fair proportion of his deliveries were directed. And, as he did so, the sound of someone's laughter floated back to Sary from behind the flintstone wall.

To David Blundel Stanville, sixteen-year-old Viscount Denton and heir to the Eighth Earl Southbourne of Hadderton Place, the sight of the girl with the chequered bonnet and clashing orange feather, jerking backward and without visible means of propulsion along the top of the boundary wall, was quite the funniest thing he'd seen in ages! To reveal his amusement to the face of even so obviously low-bred a creature, however, would be to deny his own distinguished breeding. And that he wouldn't dream of doing. But no sooner had the apparition disappeared from view, than he turned to Octavia and she to him – their dark brows raised, two pairs, in silent query. Two well shaped mouths, first twitching, then curving, and finally bursting forth into helpless laughter.

"The *belle sauvage* and her feathered head-dress!" His cousin Octavia was the first to speak, the first, as ever, to regain her self-possession. "Oh Davy, did you ever see a headpiece so utterly outlandish?"

"Not recently," he had to confess, his eyes returning to the wall in case the insouciant orange feather should see fit to reappear. "At least, not since the turban you had made up for my mother's little celebration of the Queen's birthday in January, Tavie. That ran it pretty close, I think."

"My *esprit* turban? Why, Cousin, what can you mean? I'm sure it was the very essence of good taste." Her dark brows pleated in a frown, but then abruptly shot up again. "You hateful thing, you're poking fun at me!" Amongst the foliage above and all around her the spiky burs of forming chestnuts hung suspended. And, as she spoke, Octavia reached out to wrench one from its stem and fling it at his handsome grinning head. Waiting, not to see it find its mark (her aim, intentionally, was faulty) but only to ensure the 'hateful thing' was ready to give chase – as she wheeled her horse around to gallop off across the park.

She rode well, with more strength in her slim arms and legs than she ever would acknowledge – reining in to let him catch her within the golden grassy prospect which that peerless landscape artist, Lancelot 'Capability' Brown, had enlarged before the house – Octavia's favourite place in all the world – to let him catch her there, and then to find himself perplexed by what to do with her. Three years before he might have snatched her hat or riding crop and raced away with them, or even hauled her from her horse and made her beg for mercy. But, for a sixteen-year-old Viscount of the Realm and a young gentlewoman eleven months his senior, such freedoms could no longer apply – not even between cousins. They stared at each other, their faces flushed, panting still from their exertions. And, while his young Lordship hesitated, it was again Octavia who took the initiative. She pulled in her horse alongside David's and, rising in the saddle, kissed him chastely on the cheek. This time her aim was faultless.

"*Voilà*," she said, "so now we must be friends again." And, in the silence that followed, both young people looked up instinctively across the park toward the house – like a pair of children making up a quarrel before a watching parent.

The north-west front of Hadderton Place – that aspect of it which invariably featured in collections of engravings of English country houses – was as handsome, it was often held, as any in the kingdom. A nobly extended composition of local flint and white Caen stone – 'Sailing like a great galleon against the Sussex downland shaws', as Horace Walpole once described it. Its geometric angles and even rows of windows were softened by climbing jasmine and magnolias, by the moss that clothed its gables and the trees that stood behind them.

"I know how much you love it, David," declared Octavia, speaking out her thought aloud. (And also thinking that she knew the surest way to Cousin David's heart.) "And I do too. I really don't think even you could love Hadderton more than I do. The happiest times of all my life, you see, have been here in this dear place, with you."

He smiled, undeceived by her sketch of dewy-eyed nostalgia. "Like the time when we dislodged the wasps' nest, d'ye mean, Tavie – and your nose blew up like something in a Punchinello show? Or the time when my pony threw you, remember? And in the biggest nettlebed that *this dear place* can offer!"

"No David, don't tease me any more, I'm serious." But in truth she liked nothing better than to hear him speak of the childhood they had shared; and was smiling herself a little at the memories. For, although with others she might enjoy all the usual assurances of a good-looking and a well-bred girl, with her cousin, Octavia knew it was herself that counted. " 'Tis all very well for you," she said, "you're spoiled for Hadderton. You never could conceive how 'tis to spend the greater part of your time away from it. To think of Hadderton each day, and yet to know you may not see it, or its occupants, for weeks or months together!"

'*But Tavie, if you feel like that, then why not stay? Why not settle here for good, and as my wife? To make Hadderton your home as well as mine!*'

A supplementary observation which David did not make, however. For the very good reason that it was Octavia, and not her cousin, who'd just thought of it. Nor could he be brought to say it yet. Nor for some time to come, she realized. 'More's the pity!' Octavia Stanville thought.

Octavia had been barely nine years old when she first settled on the prime objectives of her life: to marry her second cousin, David; to become a Viscountess, and in due course of time the Ninth Countess of Southbourne, the mistress of Hadderton Place. To Octavia the high-spot of each summer had always been the final passage of her hired post-chaise from Redford between the dragon gates of Hadderton. An exciting annual excursion for which she had to thank the present Countess, David's mother. Or rather that lady's obstinate refusal to permit her only son to be sent away to school, or later to the perils of a university. "Schools!" Lady Southbourne had exclaimed to her husband on one occasion. "Schools for *debauchery*, I say, to drive all natural innocence and decency from their students and make of them libertines!" (Her own well known aversion for such things accounting for Lord David's lack of siblings, and perhaps for something of his father's bluff and restless manner into the bargain.) No, a tutor for the boy and not a sordid school had been his mother's prescription for the proper education of the heir to Hadderton; with visits from his cousins, Charles and Octavia Stanville, whenever juvenile companionship was needed. (It being taken for granted, naturally, that the younger offspring of Lord Southbourne's untitled cousins of Redford must welcome any summons to such exalted company.)

And so indeed they did. In glorious contrast to their parents' modest manor-house estate in the extreme west of the county, their cousin David's home was a paradise of luxury and privilege. Hadderton had five times as many rooms, ten times the servants, twenty times the parkland that they left to visit it. Hadderton had its own church, a stable block as big as their father's house and stablings put together, a picture-gallery so long that a child could scarcely see the end of it, and a ha-ha with a door in it which led underground to the kitchens. Hadderton had a lake and a temple and a hermit's tower. Hadderton had absolutely *everything*!

Charles Stanville, a second son who could give his sister four years, nonetheless, and his cousin almost five, had always made a great parade of independence. Charles was the natural leader of their summer expeditions through the cellars and the attics of the mansion, and to every far-flung corner of its park. It was to Charles, and not to his own father, that his young Lordship owed his skill with a fowling-piece and his good seat on a horse. Cousin Charles to whom the Earl awarded the fox's mask and brush, the first time he'd returned in the winter season to ride with the Southbourne Hunt.

Octavia for her own part had rejoiced in her good fortune. She'd marvelled at the statuary, the pictures and the furnishings that Cousin David's great-grandfather had shipped over by the boatload from Italy and France. She'd compared Lady South-bourne's caps and gowns, her millinery and footwear with the best that her own poor mother could command, and decided early – as one accustomed to look out for herself and her own affairs – to occupy a permanent place some day amongst the comforts and consequences of Hadderton. David and his parents might not guess at it as yet, but he'd marry her in time. On that point Octavia Stanville was decided.

In defence of Miss Stanville and her inflexible conclusions, it should be mentioned perhaps that matrimony at this time was the only respectable profession open to a gentlewoman, while no girl of any rank would ever marry, if she had the choice, but to considerable advantage. It was also true of course that the affection Octavia bore her cousin was absolutely genuine. During those later summers when Charles Stanville deserted Hadderton for the estates of his friends at Harrow – or, later still, at Oxford – his sister had continued with her visits in hired transport and on her own, with only the post-boy to accompany her. And this despite Her Ladyship's repeated invitations to bring with her some schoolfellow from the Misses Wrights' Boarding Academy at Midhurst. Octavia's summers with Cousin David were too precious, she told herself, to share with any other. Why, if his income and expectations had been worth but the half of what they were, she would still have risked her happiness with David at Hadderton. She was almost sure of it.

"No, Tavie, it don't follow," the object of such near unselfish love was now indignantly declaring. "How could I be spoiled for Hadderton by spending too much time here? 'Tis my inheritance! I love the place, you said as much yourself. You know I never could be happy for any length of time in any other landscape. Damn it all, you know that I could not!"

" 'Oh happy he who in his country seat from storms of business finds a safe retreat,' " quoted Octavia softly in the act of turning her horse's head toward the stables, " 'where all around delightful landskips lie, and pleasing prospects entertain his eye.' And did you never want to hunt away, David? Or stay away at other people's places in preference to your father's? Or purchase a commission in the Prince's Own Hussars, like Charles, and help to vanquish Buonaparte at Waterloo?"

She had no need to look to know that he was frowning – struggling to reconcile his abiding love for Hadderton with his natural envy of her brother; of Charles's good fortune as a second son to be encouraged to enlist for the Peninsular. Poor Davy! His sheltered immaturity made his cousin more conscious still of her eleven months' seniority, her seminary education, and her experience of a wider world than his young Lordship had yet to meet with. The pair of them were so close still to their childhood (and in many ways to one another; as Sary Snudden had observed from her perch above the boundary wall). And yet in certain things, it must be said, they were already far divided.

Chapter Four

All her life Sary Snudden had heard tales of the wonders of Brighton town. More than thirty years had passed since the present Regent had taken his first tentative dip in its amazing healing waters – indiscriminately hailed as a cure for goitre, asthma, ruptures, deafness, madness and sexual lassitude. And thanks to His Royal Highness's continuing patronage, none but the most pedantic of residents ever now referred to the place by its rustic name of Brighthelmstone; nor treated its fishermen's attempts to repair their nets amongst its fashionable promenades with anything but loud contempt. The Brighton season had long since eclipsed those of Cheltenham and Bath. Each several minutes, coaches left the place for London, and for towns as far afield as Oxford and Bristol. Brighton had now become the second capital of England. And more, much more: it was, its partisans declared, the liveliest, most elegant and cosmopolitan resort in all of Europe (which naturally meant the world). A Naples free of *lazzaroni*! A Paris blissfully without the French!

But, for all she'd heard about it, Sary, who thought of little Seaford as a bustling town, found herself entirely unprepared for the reality of Prinny's marine metropolis. After a number of deliveries in the county town of Lewes, and several further halts and deviations since, the carrier's cart was something less than laden, and the day a great deal more advanced, when finally they wound down through the flowering elder trees of Moulsecombe and into Brighton. On either side, to front and rear of the conveyance, new sights confronted Sary's interested eye: rows of tall villas of wonderful appearance, with iron balconies and bowed

34

windows – windows all of glass! Glazed facing-tiles of black or indigo, and long projecting metal canopies painted in stripes like canvas awnings; flags on almost every building in celebration of Wellington's great victories, with looped and trailing garlands of wilted summer blossoms; shops in astonishing variety – in time of rural scarcity stocked to overflowing with eatables of every kind. And passing constantly before them, coaches and carriages, phaetons, curricles and tax-carts in greater numbers and varieties than Sary would ever have believed existed!

Yet, for everyone who came to Brighton, and certainly its newest visitor, the marvel of the place must be the great treeless corridor of grass enclosures that divided the old town from the new – extending for more than half a mile, from the downs behind it clear through the centre of the place to the salty waters of the English Channel. An open conduit for the healthy breezes that blew up from the shore to wave the victory flags and ruffle the curtains at the open windows of the villas – and to invigorate the strollers on the neat brick pavements that bounded and intersected it. Female *promenaders* in every shade of pastel, all complete with drooping Norwich shawls and useless little parasols, and here and the e with prancing Pomeranians on ribbons. The very rank of fashion! And gentlemen too elegant for words – stiff-necked in pillory collars, their tailcoats cut away to show their cross-striped westkits and the ballooning Cossack trowsers which the Czar of Russia's visit had recently made fashionable; their hats tipped jauntily to one side, or raised to passing ladies to display the most telling achievements of their valets' curling tongs.

"Not lawns or grass, but 'Steine' – that's what you 'ave to call it 'ere," the carrier corrected Sary when she remarked on such a superfluity of lawn. " 'The Steine', that's what they calls it. Race anything down 'ere, they will. 'Orses, jack-asses, bullocks – women even! Any tarnation thing for winning money.

"And there's our Prinny's latest notion for losing it and all," he added, jerking his pipe-bowl westward across the Steine, to where a confusion of roofs and pillars and wooden scaffolding hedged in a further building with a huge glass dome. "An 'eathen Chinee palace is what he's set 'is 'eart on now, so they do say. All panjandrums and pinarets and such. To make 'isself a bleddy emperor I shouldn't wonder, in imitation of old Boney 'cross the

35

Channel. 'The Emperor of Brighton'!"

And Sary – who'd once seen an aquatint of the Taj Mahal in a Seaford print-shop window, and now carried with her in her hamper her mother's last three surviving mock-willow-pattern saucers – entertained an exotic vision of the finished building. An image as fantastical and dreamlike as an eastern fairytale! (And one which, incidentally, tallied all too closely with the Regent's plan, as interpreted by his latest architect, Humphrey Repton.)

On the corner of Ship Street and the East Cliff sea frontage of the town stood the Old Ship tavern, their final destination, and the oldest most important hostelry in all the place – so the carrier maintained as he urged his weary horse toward its yard. It had been a coaching terminus for London long before the days of Castle Square. A place which, like so many English inns (and many English people too, perhaps), concealed an unexpected character behind a formal face. Outside in Ship Street, a classic Brighton bow-window overlooked a narrow thoroughfare. A closed door, opaquely glazed, disguised the taproom regulars. Another, suitably embellished with a fanlight and flanking Grecian columns, admitted residents. But, through the vaulted coaching entrance that ran clear underneath this oldest section of the inn, another Ship – more modern and more lively altogether – awaited them.

As their cart emerged from the darkness of the *porte* and Sary raised her head to elevate the orange feather once again, she found herself within a large courtyard cobbled with seaworn flints; bounded on three sides by the outside galleries of the hotel and its assembly rooms, and on the fourth by its coach-house, lofts and stables. In the centre of the yard, near an entrance to the hotel coffee room, a coach stood ready-loaded and tarpaulined, waiting for its horses. Alongside it, three brawny fellows were briskly throwing up an assortment of trunks and boxes for stowing in the back-boot of a second staging vehicle – advised and cautioned by the anxious owners of the luggage, who stood about the yard or occupied the galleries above it. At the rail of one upper balcony a woman, evidently a maid, was taking in a feather bed from airing. At another across the way, a pair of blue-coat military men leant gossiping with tankards in their hands. And, in a further corner of the yard below, a heaped-up dungcart stood gently steaming in the evening sun; to add the aromas of the stable to the heavy blend of coffee, roasting beef and rotting vegetables that already filled the crowded court.

At the sound of the cart and the plodding beast that drew it, coach-porters, travellers, maid and soldiers all turned heads to stare as one at Sary's opulent charms and chequered headpiece with its violent fair-booth plume.

"Well now, Joe Farren. Strike me if I ever thought you'd take to carrying such fancy fowl to Brighton!" An ostler, leading out a plump coach-horse in either hand, emerged from the stables to break the unaccustomed silence of the yard. A massive aproned figure of fifteen stone or more, with a broad rubicund face and brown hair bursting from his ears and nostrils as if his head was stuffed with it, he leered up at Sary on her hamper in a friendly, a more than friendly, fashion. "And does your mother know you're out, my dear?" he impudently enquired.

"Aye, Sir, she does. She even gave me a penny to buy a monkey with," said Sary, who had her own ideas of how to take down unappealing men. "Are you for sale, p'raps?"

But the ostler only laughed and leered at her the more. "Strike me," he said again. "I like your cheek, Judy, I do really. And tell ye what, I like your hat and all." He winked at his friend the carrier. "A tail with a feather on it, Joe! And just the thing I'll vow to tickle a prime young rooster's fancy." He swaggered forward with his horses. And, as he came abreast their cart, the carrier Farren leant out to whisper something in his hairy ear. "There now, and do ye say so? Is that a fact?" The ostler's eyes, as he raised them to the girl, were red-veined and bulging, the breath he gusted up to her as evil-smelling as a jakes. "Well Judy, if 'tis a bit of flesh-brokerage you're after," he suggested coarsely, "what say ye plant it 'ere on me, my pretty? A feather for a tail-pike, eh? And a tickle we'll both gain profit from I'll warrant!"

"If you don't leave me be, and sharpish, I can promise you a tickle right enough, Sir," retorted Sary boldly. "And with something a sight 'eavier than a feather at that!"

A ripple of merriment ran round the galleries of the old hotel. Though if Sary felt gratified at all by it, then she'd yet to learn from life how most unwise it was to laugh in the face of any man, leave alone an amorous one.

37

"Too good – too good for me! Is that what you think, ye bleddy little whore?" the ostler shouted angrily. "Show us then, and let's all see how good you are! Let's ave a sight of what you're made of underneath!" And, doubling the horses' bridles in one hand, he reached up to grab at the frilled hem of Sary's gown, just as she herself had stooped to whisk it from his reach.

She screamed aloud, not at the man himself or his unlooked for violence, but at the sound of tearing fabric – her best flounced muslin too! The horses lunged, alarmed. But still he kept his hold on her, and on her precious dress. And Sary was in the act of hauling down a crate of wheatears from the stack beside her, to wallop the monster with it fair and square, when another male voice cut through the babel of the yard.

"Release that young woman!" A military command.

"Release 'er? And who the 'ell says so?" the ostler blustered, all too conscious of his watching audience.

"I say it, you dog! And if you don't let go that lady's gown, *instanter*, I'll make a salad of you here and now. Damme if I don't!" And, following the direction of the ostler's protruding eyes, Sary now beheld one of the blue-coat soldiers, descending in a leisurely fashion by the outside staircase from the galleries – a half-empty pewter tankard still grasped in his hand. A swarthy, broad-shouldered officer, with magnificently looped mustachios and side-whiskers; and more tracing braid and gold point lace upon his regimentals than the Duke of Wellington himself, she wouldn't wonder.

"Is that a fact? I'd justabout like to see ye try it then, that's all!" With which the ostler loosed his hold on Sary's gown, to drag the horses round behind the cart to face his adversary, just now alighting from the outer stair. "Come on, lad, come on and try me, if you're game!" He balled his free fist and flourished it threateningly. "I've not earned myself a name for bare-knuckles for nothing, lad, I'll tell ye! Come on then – come on and try . . ."

"And, for my life, I've not escaped from Frenchy shot and shell to risk damage from a brainless English dobbin-man," the other replied with equal candour – raising the tankard in his right hand for a mock salute, whilst at the same time driving with the left beneath the scarlet-lined pelisse that depended from his shoulder. A punishing flush that found its mark deep within the ostler's large, and largely unsuspecting, belly.

38

"And now, my dear, I feel emboldened to suggest that another drink is called for," he continued, fastidiously wiping his moustaches and then extending his arm to Sary, while the winded ostler, gasping and gaping like a landed fish but still clinging gamely to their bridles, was ignominiously borne away backward by his plunging horses. " 'Tis so unconscionably noisy in the taproom – perhaps in my chamber, where we'll not be interrupted or disturbed?" The assessment of her attractions more subtle in his dark eyes than in the other's, the invitation equally apparent.

'And when all's said, 'tis only fair to show the fellow some profit for his gallantry, so to speak,' thought Sary a little later in the place he had prescribed. 'To be sure there's never any 'arm to that?' And she smiled with very proper gratitude – first at the white kerseymere regimental breeches hanging with his sword and sabretache upon the chamber door, and then, a little closer to her person, at the comically active pair of buttocks which had so recently emerged from them; and now kept bobbing up into her line of vision.

'Not that any patriotic wench in any case at all could deny a young hero from the battlefields of Flanders,' she further re-assured herself. As, with a reluctant twist of her own broad hips, she dislodged the young hero at the proper juncture, to expend himself against her thigh. The demands of patriotism and gratitude both answered, so far as Sary Snudden was concerned, without any undue risk.

Later still, sitting reposefully together on the bed – he in nothing but his shirt, she only in her best Birmingham ear-rings – the chivalrous young officer and the generously obliging village girl discussed each other's lives with the kind of frankness which springs only from shared adversity, long acquaintance or, as in their own case, from a physical transaction: 'Friendly-like together,' as Sary put it to herself. They were a pair agreeably without scruples or regrets. While Sary rummaged in her reticule to find her *housewife* and stitch up her ravaged flounces, the fellow had puffed upon his German pipe and regaled her with the story of 'the great Flemish steeplechase', as he modestly described it, through the green corn, and ultimately the French Imperial Guard, at the village of Mont St John near Waterloo. As a lieutenant in the 10th Prince Regent's Own Hussars, he'd had the honour to be one of the original detail sent over from Ostend with Major Percy to bear the Imperial eagles and the news of victory to the Prince himself at dinner in St James's Square. And, now that the excitement was all over, he had accompanied a brother officer to Brighton, arriving by the midday coach to attend an evening levée in the town. Thereafter, he was to collect his sister from the estate of a cousin who lived nearby, and to return with her for a well earned week or two of furlough at their parents' home near Midhurst; twin duties to his regiment and family which, it had to be remarked, the Lieutenant seemed in no great hurry to perform.

"When you've survived a cannonade and charge, and lived with death for a companion, then held within your own hand the laurels of a fallen Emperor," he explained, "I fear that the restricting society of an English country gentleman cannot but strike you as the dullest work, to say the least of it. No kind of sport to find with shootin' pheasants after Frenchy *mounseers*, don't ye know!"

She did know, or could imagine – and advanced her own opinion that the dullness of an English country village in time of lasting peace would be, in every likelihood, a vast deal duller than a dashing military gentleman like him could even begin to imagine.

"My poor Sarah. And where d'ye have it in mind then to seek in Brighton town for your excitement? Up in some servants' eyrie will it be? Or down in a subterranean basement at Richmond Place, where you'll scarce expect to see the light of day from one week to the next? Or out on the pavements of North Row, my dear? To waste away your youth and beauty on barrack soldiers who, alas, make no distinction between one cracked-pitcher and another?"

"You tell me, Sir," she cheerfully replied, to put the best face on the thing she could. A young man still, no more perhaps than one and twenty – he was in Sary's eyes the very model for a modern hero. And just her ill fortune that he had to leave again so soon! "You tell me where a country girl can turn an honest penny, and not end up a drab or dollymop. I hardly care what 'tis I do, Sir. And I've never been afeared of work – so long as I can see some pleasure in it and a little profit clear."

He considered carefully, his dark eyes sliding down from hers to rest in the valley between her swelling breasts; on down to the stitchwork lying limp across her thighs and then away, blank-faced, to focus somewhere far away within his thoughts.

'And what a pity,' Sary herself considered with regret, 'why, what a crying shame 'e has to go!'

"Why damme, I have it – Mother Perrin!" Lieutenant Stanville suddenly exclaimed. "Upon my honour, the very thing! I'll take you to wait on Ma Perrin, that's what I'll do. To put you in the way of joining her *corps d'amour*."

"Her 'cordamore'? Her bawdy-house, d'ye mean to say?" said Sary Snudden, who liked things best in English.

"Her 'Academy of Venus'," he corrected, with a nicety that rather ill became a man so far outside his breeches. "Quite another case, you know. And a girl with your looks and accomplishments would soon find a place in such a house, I guarantee it. I'll take you there, and you'll soon see – old Madge'll bust her stays to get you in!" His opportunist's eyes were on the move again, slipping, sliding downwards even as he spoke – down through that seductive, softly shadowed valley to her stitchwork and the warm red scut of hair it lay across. A whole speech written in those eyes, and more, the promise of an action yet to come! *Pro Gloria et Patria*, proclaimed the regimental device embroidered on the sabretache that still hung with his sabre and his breeches against the chamber door.

He coughed, and hastily removed the pipe from in amongst his bristling whiskers. "That is to say," he amended huskily, "I'll take you there in just a little while . . ."

Chapter Five

That 'little while', as it transpired, had occupied the entire space of the neglected evening levée, all the long night through that followed, and a portion of the morning after that. During which time the young soldier, with the willing assistance of the innkeeper and his pot-boys, had contrived to avoid ever becoming completely sober. A twelve-hour extension to their acquaintance – with interludes for imbibing only, for supper, breakfast, and a little necessary sleep. So that, one way and another (which certainly described the case, thought Sary), it was after eleven on the morning following before the pair of them had left the tavern.

"Hang on to my coat-skirts now, or you'll be lost for sure," the hero of Waterloo and other more recent engagements thoughtfully advised. And, bearing Sary's hamper on his shoulder, he led the way down past the hotel's stables in Black Lion Street, to the warren of lanes and alleyways that once comprised the old fishing town of Brighthelmstone. Here houses leaned so close that in places upper storeys almost touched. Figures bumped and jostled, calling out cheery greetings as they brushed each other in the narrow twittens – men in red caps and knitted jerseys, women in tucked-up skirts and crackling oilskin aprons – their smiles for the valiant officer spilling over to the buxom country girl who strode along behind him. At intervals, the lanes converged in open squares of shops and dwelling-houses. And it was in one of these, the most imposing they had come to, that Sary's escort called his halt.

"You bring your pretty arse to anchor here then, sweetheart, while I send in the scouts," he told her briefly, swinging down the hamper and kicking it back to make a seat for Sary against a shady wall. "Just give me five minutes in there alone, and I vow I'll have that old buzzard cooing like a turtle-dove. Back in a brace of shakes, my dear!" With which he marched across to rap six times upon the door of a house immediately opposite. And, before she could think to offer any objection, to remove his polished helm and disappear within it.

On the far side of the square a woman briskly swept the litter from the flag-way before her own door into the path of her neighbour's, staring hard at Sary all the while. 'Just like all the others back at home,' Sary thought, straightening her feathered bonnet, seating herself once more upon the hamper, and preparing once again to face reality. In as far as she had ever seriously considered tail-trading as employment, she'd naturally thought of the men – and of the various situations in which one most readily imagined them. She had also thought of the money, and of what it might signify in terms of lodgings, food and clothing. What had never seriously occurred to her, until this fellow thought to mention it, was the idea of enrolling in any kind of an organized establishment. In Seaford and in Alfriston the soldiers' women were all installed in lodgings. Or, as in her own mother's case, in the billets of the officers who kept them. And, should Sary ever decide to charge for what she'd been happy to give *gratis*, she vaguely imagined herself in some sunny little cottage on the Brighton seafront, dispensing favours with cheerful efficiency in exchange for honest coin: an independent living with nothing owed and no one to account to but herself.

But now, perforce, she must consider the house across the square and all it represented. A prosperous establishment evidently, with freshly whitewashed stucco in place of the cobbled flint or black tar-boarding of its neighbours; it was square-fronted, with triple lines of modern sashes and a row of dormers in the slates above, and a cluster of mud-built martins' nests against the eaves to lend the place an air of domesticity. A brothel, and a successful one – nothing there to shock a girl like Sary. In London, so she'd heard, there were thousands of such houses, employing between them one in ten of all that city's population. And if Charlie Stanville wanted her to take a peek at this brothel here – well then, why not? No harm in that. Lord, anyone would be curious to discover what a high-class nugging-house was like inside! But that

43

was all, she had decided. Because if he and the old bawd who ran the place imagined for one minute that Sary Snudden would ever join a stable of plodding saddle-jades for profit or for entertainment – well then, they'd have to think again!

At which point in her deliberations the door opened, and Charlie himself emerged with masculine self-satisfaction writ plainly all across his military whiskers. Sary jumped up at once to meet him, surprised by the pounding of her heart, surprised by the loudness of her own voice as she demanded what his precious Mother Perrin had to say. She could not tell why she felt so apprehensive, only that she did.

"She's interested all right," Charles Stanville told her with a grin. "She wants to see you now."

'Just like a mare, and all,' thought Sary in high indignation. 'There now, she wants to see me, does she? Paraded in the saddling paddock to show my points?' Unconsciously she tossed her plumed and handsome head in keeping with her own image. "And what if I don't choose to stable myself in livery?" she said aloud. "Now has she thought of that, Sir – 'er precious Ladyship?" But already hamper and soldier, both, had disappeared inside the house. And wherever the hamper went, there too must Sary Snudden go. That much was clear.

The first obvious thing that struck her as she approached the open door was the smell that she was ever afterwards to associate with Mrs Perrin and her house. A distinctive odour that she was to find would vary remarkably little from room to room. Or from day to day, or even from year to year, for the matter of that. Because the very fabric of the place was steeped in it. It smelt strongly of Italian orris-powder (which meant, of violets), of *patchouli* and herb-scented Hungary water, with a whiff of something coarser beneath the cloaks of these exotic continental perfumes – something that pulled Sary up to stand and flare her nostrils like a scenting animal – the faint rancid smell of human rut.

"Ontray! Walk in then, gel. Walk in where I can see you!" A woman's nasal London accents impatiently commanded her from somewhere close at hand. A harsh challenge in that voice that Sary was more than ready to take up.

"I do have a name, and that is Sarah Snudden." She made the statement emphatically, and before she could rightly tell to whom

44

she was addressing it. "And whatever this gentleman may have led you to suppose, Ma'am, I ain't one of your common whores to order as ye please. No Ma'am, not by long strides!"

Immediately inside the door, where she might have expected an empty vestibule, an ostentatious little drawing salon had been contrived – with Chinese screens and Persian carpets, and red plush curtains lavishly draping every door and window. On the wall a large oil-painting depicted Leda embracing her swan with all four limbs at once, and more besides. Over a gold and crimson striped settee, Sary's erstwhile lover was in the act of stooping to set down her hamper. And on the settee itself a woman's form lay *à la Récamier* with one arm upon a bolster. In full evening dress as it appeared, with a pair of weighty ledgers, a metal cash-box and a pot of steaming coffee on a round rent-table at her elbow. A young woman Sary might have thought her at first encounter, so slim did she appear, so smooth her cheek, so full her lips, so youthful the arrangement of her combs and blonde drop-curls. But by then of course she'd heard her voice. And, when she spoke again, the sinews of the woman's neck drew taut beneath the lacy Cobourg ruffle that she wore. Two faint lines appeared beside her scarlet mouth, the lips themselves now shown to be drawn up beyond their tight compressed reality. ('Ewe-mutton dressed up lamb-fashion', as Sary's own mother might reasonably have put it.)

"You are a bleeding 'ero, Charles, and no mistake," the woman unsmilingly declared, entirely ignoring Sary's own remarks. "First Bonaparty – and now, I swear, the Duchess of the Cuckmere! Small wonder you're so slim and trim yourself, you cracksman!" Her eyes were narrow, and dark in contrast to her hair, with heavy wrinkled lids that seemed to press down on her spiky lashes. Hard eyes that examined Sary steadily while she spoke. The same steady stare that calculated a client's potential for a second climax, and for doubling his partner's fee in consequence. "Well, she ain't no fairy Columbine, and that's a fact," she added rudely. "But ye could be right. She has the face for it, and could 'ave the makings of a gay-girl, I will allow. Well then, Sarah Snudden, if that's your name – 'ave you got your character?"

Sary drew in her own generous mouth as small and tight as possible. "No, Ma'am. But I've got yours right enough," she rejoined. "And I'll tell ye now, I shan't be working hereabouts!"

The other woman sighed. "Save your breath for when it's needed is my advice to you," she said, still poker-faced. "Now turn around gel, and let's see how you're arsed at least."

"I'll show ye my arse all right, Ma'am, that I will. I'll give you the sight for just so long as it takes to walk it through that door!" said Sary roundly, hands on hips and red with anger. "Mr Stanville, Sir, you fetch me out my 'amper this very minute. For my life I'll not stay to be insulted by a *slagger* such as this! Not for you, Sir, and not for anyone!"

Mrs Margery Perrin's body stiffened perceptibly beneath its splendid velvets, and her dark eyes began to glitter savagely. Then all at once the scarlet mouth split open wide. As Sary watched with fascinated horror, the smooth-painted cheeks crazed like an eggshell, and peals of raucous laughter filled the room.

Laughter which ceased as suddenly as it had begun, as Mrs Perrin's hand stole up to feel the damage to her face. "Strop me senseless! Now the silly highty-tighty wench has gone and made me crack my brandy-glaze," she cried with genuine mortification. "Well, you tell 'er straight then, Sir – you tell 'er where she'll find another flash-house to touch Madge Perrin's this side of Plymouth 'Oo. Or who else would think of offering a raw game-pullet such a chance!" She rose in a scented cloud of *patchouli* to sweep up her coffee cup in one hand and the cash-box in the other.

"The nooners will be 'ere soon," she added, "and I ain't fit to be seen like this, that's certain. Mary!" She lifted her golden head and shouted it at the top of her considerable lungs. "Mary! Where the 'ell are you now, ye lazy haddock?"

"I'm here – I'm here, Mrs Perrin." A pair of small feet sounded on the stairs, and through the arch came scurrying a little grey-haired rabbit of a woman in an apron and muslin bonnet. "Here I am, Mrs Perrin."

"And about precious time too. Are all the gels up and abroad?"

"All but Miss Rosine – and she won't be long I'm sure. I've given her her coffee."

"Idle bloody placket! Strike me, but I'd throw 'er out tomorrer, if Frenchy fashions weren't in such demand. *I'll* deal with Mam'selle Rose then. You watch the door and show the cullies through. It ain't yet noon, and I'll be down by then. Oh, and Mary, this here's Miss Sarah Snudden." She waved a casual hand in

Sary's direction. "She'll be joining our little convent as a novice for the present – though not got up like that of course. She'd give anyone the frights! When I come back she'll need a bath and all the rest. So look sharp, woman! Go and heat the water up, if you can't think of nothing else!

"And now then, Charlie, d'you know what I think?" she said sweetly to the only male as yet admitted to the house, and once again ignoring Sary's loud expressed objections.

"Madam, I have not the most distant idea."

"I think that you should stay to demonstrate Miss Snudden's form to us *à deux* with Barbara. I know you're partial to 'er. A little diversion, eh, to whet the nooners' appetites and save us all from getting dull? And at a discount, naturally. What d'ye say, Sir? For Barbara's tailing-fee alone? I can't say fairer, now can I?" She tweaked him playfully by the whiskers and awarded him a killing ogle as she passed.

"Well as to that, Ma'am – I think it must depend on Miss Snudden here herself. Although I daresay I could defer my visit to my relatives for an hour or two in such an interesting cause, if she can be persuaded to agree?"

"And that I won't, Sir – not on my mother's life!" Sary avowed as soon as Mrs Perrin departed for the upper floor. "And if you won't do me the kindness of fetching out that 'amper, then I'll shift it for myself. For I'm a-going, and I'm going now – on that you can depend!"

And only rabbity little Mary (who'd witnessed many such scenes before in her career as factotum to Madge Perrin) could possibly imagine then that the girl who made that confident pronouncement would still be resident within their house a twelvemonth later.

Sary had actually hauled her hamper as far as the street door, and was preparing to open it when Charles informed her of precisely how much one of Madge Perrin's *filles de maison* might hope to earn for herself in a good week of the Brighton summer season. And while she paused, her hand still on the handle, he'd gone on to describe the best she could expect elsewhere – as a servant working all the hours God gave, or as a common Cyprian. He told her of the diseases that the soldiers spread through wartime barrack-towns like Brighton, and of the care that houses like Mrs Perrin's took to avoid them. Madge's clients all officers or gentlemen, and all required to cleanse most scrupulously before performing, her girls all cared for by the house's own apothecary. He spoke of parties at which champagne flowed freely. He spoke of the time to be saved and the money to be earned by virtue of good management; of pleasures that harmed none and saved many from worse indulgences. A public service, nothing less! And, so long as he continued speaking, Sary remained standing by the door, neither turning back to face him, nor moving on to open it. Only standing to listen like some brightly plumaged bird, with her orange feathered bonnet cocked over a little to one side.

When it came to bathing, Sary had no personal objections to hot water. It was only that she'd never had an opportunity before to immerse herself in it. In Seaford her mother had sat her in a neighbour's copper washtub, regularly once a fortnight, in the grey and tepid suds that remained from two families' dirty laundry. Later, as a girl in Alfriston, she made do with a foot basin, a wet rag and some ingenuity brought to bear before the parlour fire. And until now she'd always thought of all-over hot-water baths as something for the unhealthy – for arthritis and skin ailments, or else for the very rich.

"Not in Brighton. Not 'ere they ain't, my gel," Madge Perrin remarked on her return, speaking carefully to maintain her fresh-enamelled mask. "Lord save us, I've known folk from common lodging-houses who'll bathe twice or three times in a day, at Wood's or William's 'ot seawater baths, and that not counting dipping in the sea. And, mark me, Sarah Snudden, any gentleman who'd take such pains to cleanse and polish up 'is trusty rapier will seek a sanitary place to sheath it in. Ain't that a fact now, Charlie?"

The soldier smiled at Sary. "As I'm a living swordsman," he agreed politely.

"Well then, Mary, what ye waiting for?" said Mrs Perrin impatiently to her subordinate. "The culls'll be along in 'arf a shake, and Lieutenant Stanville 'ere ain't got all day to stand and wait. You wash and shave the girl, and I'll be in directly for the rest. Go on then, move yourself!"

And Sary, when it came to it, had revelled in the heated bathing closet with its scented steam, the deep smooth-sided copper tub,

48

the novel feeling of the water closing in around her limbs. She could have wallowed there luxuriously until it cooled (though that of course was not to be allowed).

"Do use the soap, 'tis the finest Joppa, and the brush too if you will, Miss. And do mind your lovely hair. We don't want that wet now, do we? Leastways, not today . . ." Mrs Perrin's Mary fussed around her like a flustered little lady's maid preparing her mistress for some grand society occasion. "If you'll only hold still, Miss, I'll tie it up out of harm's way. There, that's better. Now, where's that little sponge to do your neck?

"Oh, but 'ere's our Barbara come to help ye shave!" Mary spun round with her hands all over suds to introduce another. A girl whose floating muslins concealed little of the very ample charms that lay beneath them; her great thighs and breasts and belly shivering delectably with every movement, she advanced toward them through the perfumed steam.

"Barbara, meet Sarah Snudden," cried Mary shrilly. "Only fancy, your Charlie brought 'er in for us not twenty minutes back!"

"I know – I've seen 'im, ain't I?" The girl smiled broadly. "Pleased to meet ye dear, I'm sure," she said with an appreciative glance. "And no need to ask what Charlie saw in you, I'd say!"

Like many of her type and build, the girl Barbara's hands were small and finely shaped, her touch exquisitely refined. And gentle too, gentle and caressing, as she soaped and shaved away the hair from Sary's legs and underarms and from her Mount of Venus. "Pity to lose these pretty little feathers," she remarked as her skilful razor swept the red-gold curls away. "But most gentlemen prefer depilation. They 'ave to be shown the way it seems, poor dears – or else they'd lose theirselves for sure!" She laughed a bitter laugh. "You left yer maidenhead like I did, with some clumsy young punch-clod in the country, I collect?"

"Yes, I did," admitted Sary frankly, distracted more than somewhat by the girl's immodest fingers.

"Well once they've 'ad it, the filthy strunts can't steal it from us a second time at least," said Barbara feelingly, "that's certain!"

"Most gels of this 'ere calling ain't so terrible wrapped up in men," remarked Mrs Perrin a little later, when she looked in once again to take a hand herself in the new girl's initiation. "But that ain't never made no obstacle to fitting ends with the rats. Nor yet to charging handsome for the service neither, I'm glad to tell." She was standing, looking critically at the shapely white stem of Sary's naked body, in a small carpeted chamber alongside the bathing-closet. A room crowded with mirrors of all dimensions – including, on a dressing shelf against one wall, a regular apothecary's store of bottles, gallipots and jars in every shape and size.

"Now, where's that jessamine?" she muttered to herself, interrupting her own lecture on the philosophy of whoredom to extract a wooden tub from beneath a pile of assorted containers. "*Jessamy butter*, we call this," she said aloud as she removed the lid, " 'the working girl's best friend'!" And scooping out a generous dollop of the creamy-coloured grease, she divided it in two – slapping half into Sary's own unsuspecting hand, and the rest flat against her naked belly. "Rub that in wherever you go out, gel. You'll like the smell and feel of that, and so will they! The rest is for the place where the sun don't shine, and that'll last you two or three culls if they ain't too slow. You'll find tubs in all the rooms. So do yourself a favour eh, and *use* 'em. There ain't no extra charge, and you'll know it soon enough if you put on too little, I promise you!" She paused for her noviciate to grasp the implication. "The thing wants method, d'ye see?"

"But if, as you say, 'tis better to mislike the fellows who plowter us," said Sary, who found that earlier disclosure a deal more interesting than any that had followed, "then what kind of a whore d'ye think a girl like me would make, who's always favoured men to women?"

Madge Perrin worked on efficiently, rubbing in the scented butter until Sary's body gleamed like satin. "I didn't say 'twas better," she declared. "Only that it makes no obstacle to fitting ends with 'em. For I'll fairly own that the best little workers of our trade, from Nelly Gwynn to Kitty Fisher, 'ave all liked the creatures more than tolerably!"

She smiled, a perfunctory little Giaconda smile to save her brandy-glaze. "No mortal harm in a partiality for the stiff-and-stout," she candidly remarked. "So long as ye never get to like the fellow on the other end of it too well, my gel, that's the great thing. A fool's job that'd be, no question of it. You've come to this business aright, Sarah Snudden. Not like some of these little trulls who've been broken to it by men – by fakers and buttock-brokers – and all against their inclination." Her eyes in the enamelled visor of her face were alert, intelligent and hard, the hardest eyes that Sary had ever seen. "Listen to Madge, for she'll tell you no lies," she added, developing her theme. "Approve 'em as culls if you will, but never you get to like them any other way. There's my advice to you. A standing strunt 'as no conscience. And so long as you recollect it you'll never be exploited by a Tom, not ever. And I'll tell ye straight, sweetheart, that's more than most of your fine ladies can boast, for all their pretty manners and fancy schooling!

"Now rouge," she appended on an instantly brighter note, pouncing on a parchment-covered pot, untying it and dipping in a soft wad of merino wool to save her fingers from the stain. "We always use the best Spanish cochineal (and you'll 'ave to buy this for yourself, gel, in the future, from your earnings). A touch 'ere, and 'ere on each pap you see? A little on the belly and in the button, and 'ere. That's it, gel, put your foot up on the bench – just 'ere along your grummet. Then heels, knees and arse – you rub it in, that's it. And on the other cheeks of course, and plenty there. The Toms all want a whore to *look* a whore, d'ye see? The wickedness all part of what they need. We charge them good prices for it, you may be sure. So no sense on earth in painting stingily."

Which brought her to the selection of a gown. "This one, I think," she said at once, holding up a flimsy shift of pink silk gauze from the three or four she'd brought along to try. "Slip into that dear, and let's see how it sits. 'Tis laced d'ye see, to push up your pretty bubbies and give the culls a fair sight of your teats. Slit 'arf way up the bum and all! Don't that look fine now? 'Ere, you take a look, dear, in the glass. Now all we 'ave to do is give the jessamy a chance to get a hold, to show through more of what ye got. There, that's lovely. And just you make sure you keep it that way, eh gel? Hang it up, don't throw it on the floor. And tell 'em anything they tear they pay for, that's the rule."

And in amongst a further course for dressing hair, for improving lips and eyes and brows, and sweetening breath, the indefatigable Mrs Perrin continued with instructions of a broader kind. "We could try henna on your hair, or saffron," said she, whose own hair was of an improbable guinea-golden brilliance that was never made by nature. "But there, I doubt we'd strike a better shade to please the culls at that."

"I doubt ye will. Not while I 'ave breath to stop you," said Sary with the strongest resolution. "My hair's my own – you leave it be!"

"Not that there's any time for that today in any case," said Madge, as if she hadn't spoken. "We'll just 'ave to dress it round a string of amber beads for now – and Mary can curl it for you later. Jewels in the hair is always good. But not round the neck. They can bruise you something dreadful there. And finger ringers can do the same for culls, if ye think about it. Now you'll pay for your own food, laundry, paint and powder out of tailing fees, understand? We all pay our way in this house, and no deception. I provide beds, clothing, towels and *butter*. The culls send down for drink as they require it. That clear?

"And now the face. You've got your rouge – and you don't need extra blanching, damn and blast you! (And when you do, gel, don't you never use *ceruse* for that, see? Not if ye want to keep your top skin! Use *Briançon* – that's safe at least.) Lip salve now – this one's carmine." She spat neatly into the small cake of crimson that she held out to Sary, to apply the resulting vivid fluid with a brush of camel hair. "Ten Toms a day, and only more if you can take 'em," she said in a tone that was clearly intended to reassure. "None of your fast-fucks or your thruppeny-uprights 'ere, gel. We leave them to the common sparrow-catchers in the lanes. This 'ere's an academy, as I said before. A decent house and all. No animals, no children or blooming virgin brides! We give fair service and we charge for it. Cash down – you earn a quarter. No unpaid favours, and no credit, sweetheart, without my say-so, see?"

"But how about the risks?" said Sary, mainly still concerned with practicalities. "Don't yer girls get scalded ever? Or napped with kids?"

"Never!" Madge Perrin snapped the word decisively. "Lead comb for the brows, d'ye see – like this. Yours need a deal of blacking. I can't answer for others, but Pox and Clap is words I don't like to hear of in *my* house, Sarah Snudden! Tuesdays and Fridays we 'ave our own apothecary come to tend the gels and keep their courses regular. And you may be sure I see to it 'e stays on, and all. To be attended *by* 'em, if ye take my meaning? That way he'll never make no error if 'e can help it!" She winked a black and white lined eyelid at her student in the mirror. Then showed her with some exactitude how to make its replica with Briançon talc, a pot of mastic blacking and another little brush. "You do what Madge tells you, and you'll 'ave no trouble, I'll be sworn," she said. "You'll be as snug as a duck in a ditch in this 'ere house of mine!

"Now look in the glass and tell me what ye think," she added, on a note of triumph. "Ain't that a sight to raise the cullies' drooping hopes then?" And Sary looked again into the mirror – at carmine mouth, at darkened brows and blackened lashes, extended and drawn upward at their outer edges; and at two bright triangles of crimson rouge. To see a whore's face, painted to the last stage of artifice, stare back at her.

Chapter Six

In the staircase hall at Hadderton, Charles Stanville stooped to kiss his sister – with Octavia standing up on tiptoe, even so, to reach the whiskery cheek. A ceremony which she most prettily performed – aware of David watching – before stepping down and back again to wrinkle up her nose in mock disgust. "Why Charles, you smell of *jasmine*," she exclaimed. "And tell me, have our British conquerors taken to the wearing of French perfumery now they have all Paris at their feet?"

Charles smiled, entirely unabashed. "Not our soldiers, Tavie, but all those multivarious English misses and matrons who make excuses to salute them." He winked outrageously at Cousin David over Octavia's neatly coiled coiffure. "You're not the first, I have to tell you, my dear sister, to demand this fearful tribute from the returning hero."

"And do these patriotic matrons all wear crimson lip-salve too?" enquired Octavia with demurely downcast eyes. "My poor Charles, how dreadfully you must have suffered at their hands."

Before Charles could frame an answer though, the door of the White Saloon burst open, and his Lordship the Eighth Earl of Southbourne, David's father, strode forth with open arms. "My boy – my dear, dear boy, what splendid news!" he bellowed, at once demanding the returning hero's complete attention. "Come in and see your Aunt, she's all agog! And after that we'll buzz a bottle or two between us in the library – and draw out the battle on the carpet, eh? As you remember it? Your sister will have you in the carriage home – hang me, she'll not begrudge your old relative a little of your time. Now will ye, Tavie girl?"

She shook her head. But David's father had already steered his prize back into the saloon, where Lady Southbourne waited. "Word is that infernal Bonaparty's skipped to America, blast and damn him!" he shouted. "Have you heard aught of that, Charles? They'll catch him though, I'll lay – you mark my words – and shoot the traitory little frog forthwith, I hope! He's fit for nothing else for sure. Alethea, my dear, here's Cousin Charles returned to us in glory from the battlefields of Flanders . . ."

Leaving David, as his parents had so very often left him in the past, smiling hopelessly into his cousin's eyes. With Octavia smiling back in quiet amusement, ready at an instant's notice to be fallen in love with.

The next morning early, David stood in the yard of Hadderton at his father's side to farewell his cousins on their journey home to Redford. A cross-country expedition of near sixty miles, to be completed in two days at this season, with the necessity of only one posting-house along the way – the Earl himself was confident of it – in Lord Southbourne's own capacious barouche landau.

"Don't let 'em overdrive the horses, Etheridge, that's all I ask," he shouted up to the coachman on the box. "I know what these youngsters are like for making up the time. D'ye hear me, Charles, you rogue? I'll see you in October – don't forget it, mind. 'Twill be a capital good shoot this year unless I'm much mistaken. And God speed to you, Tavie my dear." He kissed his hand in the direction of his youngest female cousin as she gathered up her skirt to ascend the carriage step.

"Gad's death! I'll swear that skimpy little piece grows prettier by the day," he observed a moment later, as the vehicle turned to rumble through the gate and Octavia's fluttering handkerchief replaced her bonnet at the window. "And eyes for none but you, eh Davy? Don't think your Dad ain't noticed it, ye sly young whipper-snapper!" And he'd already nudged him in the ribs a second time before the boy's face informed Lord Southbourne that he'd blundered yet again. To young Charles now, to Charles he might address such downright observations at any time without fear of an embarrassment. No harder swearing nor blunter of speech than any other country gentleman of his acquaintance – with his own son he somehow always seemed to miss the mark.

"But there again, 'tis early days for anything so forward, I'll allow," he added awkwardly, shifting his booted feet and straightening out his weatherbeaten features to correspond with David's own. "I daresay your mother has her own opinions on the matter. And mayhap the chit's too narrow in the girth to bear the sons you'll need for Hadderton," he added reflectively. "No sense in rushing fences, eh boy?"

"No, Sir, no sense at all. And now if you will excuse me, I promised Mamma that I would call in to tell her when Charles and Tavie were on the road, and in what order they departed. You know how she likes to hear the details of these things."

"Of course, of course – you run along." In Lord Southbourne's angular, high-coloured face the natural affection of a parent struggled briefly with a sense of relief at being thus released from a further difficult exchange. Struggled and lost. "And as for me," his Lordship declared, "I've a notion to step down to the stables to see how the new filly's shapin' up. Be there for a tidy while, I daresay. Generally am," he added unnecessarily, already halfway to the gate. "So come down and take a look yourself if you've a mind, boy – when your mother's pumped you dry. We'll stroll back together, maybe, and take a bite of breakfast?"

"Yes indeed, Sir, I'd like that fine. I doubt that Mamma will keep me very long."

Lord Southbourne gave a bark of disbelieving laughter. But all the same he waved a friendly hand before disappearing through the archway, where the dust of the carriage wheels still drifted hazily.

'And why ever is it,' thought David, 'that we're always closest, he and I, when our paths diverge? Why can't I treat him pleasantly and easily, as Charles does? Or even Tavie? Why can't I simply take Father as he is, and stop expecting something of him that patently he'll never be?' But David's misfortune, like that of so many other sons and daughters before and since, was that he wanted his father and mother as they grew older, to grow more like him. While Lord and Lady Southbourne, naturally enough, anticipated some kind of similar development within their only son.

If David's present ideals for his parents involved more insight and imagination, more sense of the uncommon variety, than either was capable of acquiring – then for his own part, Lord

Southbourne would have preferred his heir to show a deal more swagger in his bearing. To make a bit of noise around the place; and, if it so fell out, to get the odd girl pregnant in the village. *Spunk*, the masculine essential he himself possessed in such abundance, was what made great families. He'd always held it: a little wildness ever preferable to an excess of refinement – the thing that kept the country on its feet and showed the frogs what Englishmen were all about! Not that his David was any kind of a milksop. His Lordship would floor the man that said so without a moment's hesitation. Davy shot well and rode always in the first flight of the hunting field, his father thought with pleasure – living as he did himself for hounds and horses. The boy could already hold his liquor as he ought to, like a gentleman. Next year, had the war held out, he would have joined the Yeomanry Cavalry as an officer. And in due course he'd take his seat within the House of Lords. He was just too damn stuff-full of sensibility – too bookwormish, too difficult to swear at! Too jossing young and other-worldly, that was all!

This opinion of Lord Southbourne's was, in fact, one of the few with which his wife unquestionably concurred. For David's mother also considered their son a deal too quiet and introspective for anyone's lasting good, least of all his own. Nobody could deny David's looks, his charm, his natural breeding, his aptness to adorn the title he was born to. And yet the irritating boy refused to exploit the gifts that nature and circumstance had so showered upon him. He was willing enough to spend his time with the estate people, it seemed. Or below stairs with the old housekeeper, Mrs Graham, in her snuggery behind the stillroom. He'd speak familiarly enough to the maids and kitchen staff, and accord his cousin Octavia all the smiles that she demanded. To make sure to capture every unworthy female heart within his mother's household. But when it came to lighted drawing-rooms, in Sussex or in their London mansion of St James's – when it came to her own afternoon tea-boards, to card parties, to local balls and routs, to Vauxhall masquerades and Almack's assemblies – why then it was a very different matter! Then it was all that Lady Southbourne could do to induce David to exchange civilities with her friends, or to speak at all in company! For some reason she could not fix on, he would remain in moody silence, unpardonably negligent of his duty. Or else withdraw at the first opportunity from the circle of élite and well-provided females from which, she had resolved, his future wife and mother-in-law must be forthcoming. And then confess afterwards to his Mamma how tedious he found them all. As if it were they and not he who'd behaved so disagreeably!

Lady Southbourne had called her son 'David' less, as her husband believed, for his own father the Seventh Earl (whose mother had been Welsh), than for an accurate plaster reproduction – glimpsed at the Royal Academy in London – of Michelangelo's virile young statue of that name. An ideal of adolescent manhood; that was what her own dear David always represented to his mother. And undoubtedly she loved him as sincerely as she was capable of loving anything outside herself and her own immediate comforts. Which was why she had felt both pleased and irritated to discover the boy in her bedchamber so early in the morning. The night before, it was true, she'd begged him to come up and report to her the details of his cousins' departure, just as soon as they were safely on the road. But that had been primarily to excuse herself from having to rise to see them off. For she hardly thought enough of either Charles or Octavia to consider such an unwarrantable exertion on their behalf. And now that the reckoning had come, and David had arrived, the pleasure of seeing her precious only boy so fresh and young and handsome at her bedside, was marred for Lady Southbourne by an uneasy suspicion that her own appearance amid the duckdown and the rumpled silken sheets could well be something less.

"But Mamma, you asked me most particularly to come and inform you when they left, and of what kind of a day they'd chosen for their journey," David pointed out in response to his mother's bleary-eyed complaints. "Even you cannot have forgotten that, I think. And besides, 'tis such a glorious sunny morning – I insist this once you see it for yourself. Come let me draw the curtains for you this very minute!"

"No, no, David – you'll do no such thing!" squawked Lady Southbourne, who avoided the too-searching light of day at any time; and never looked out of a window or into a mirror if she could help it before the hour of noon. "My dearest boy, you're surely old enough to know that a lady may not always mean exactly what she says? You're no longer a child, David, to burst into my chamber at

58

this godless hour. And whatever I may or may not have said out of simple courtesy to your cousins, to be sure you should have known not to disturb your mother on such a trivial errand, at least until eleven."

From his position at the window, David regarded her by the pinkish half-light that the drawn curtains admitted to her chamber. According to her early portraits, Lady Alethea Blundel had once been very slim and pretty, with rich brown hair and the delicate, etioliated features of her paternal forbears. But whatever lights-of-life there might have been behind her eyes were long since extinguished. In recent years her hair had also faded, all but the false fringe of chestnut curls she wore inside her day-caps. And the pallid Blundel prettiness had sagged into a caricature of petulance and discontent from which she was now incapable of extricating it. As had her temperament, sapped by years of luxury and indolence. 'And yes, Mamma,' he thought, with all the contempt of youth for age, with all the disappointment of a son who yearned to admire his mother, but could no longer do so, 'oh yes, Mamma, I should have known to leave you to your beauty-sleep!'

"So, if you really want to make yourself of use," the Countess said, sensing David's criticism, "then you will kindly stop staring so unmannerly at a lady in her *déshabillé*, and ring the bell for Maynard to fetch me up my morning chocolate.

"Then run along with you, dear boy," she added, recalling to mind how very fond she was still of her only child. "And come back to tell me all about it at eleven – or perhaps half past."

'*Run along, run along, David.*' It was no coincidence, he realized, that both parents had employed that same trite phrase to dismiss him from their thoughts. It was a formula they'd always used, all through his childhood, for such a purpose. And, now that he was grown to manhood, they found it useful still it seemed, to deny him his maturity. Yes, that was it, he thought – to imply that it was nothing more than youth and inexperience that made him so completely different.

From his mother's darkened bedchamber, David crossed an upper hallway to the long picture-gallery that traversed the north-west frontage of the house. The curtains here at least were open, for it was only in late afternoon that any sunlight reached the windows of the gallery. And even on a sunny morning the place

59

was cool and filled with richly coloured shadows. It smelt of floor-polish, of turpentine and beeswax; and looked to David's eye like nothing so much as the warehouse or display room of some fashionable London furniture-dealer.

When the old Tudor manor of Hadderton was refurbished and enlarged some half a century earlier, the gallery had been specifically intended to house the art collection of David's great-grandfather, William Ainslie Stanville. An estimable gentleman whose Continental travels and selective purchases in France and Italy had earned for him the epithet of 'Collector Earl' (and the later admiration, incidentally, of the current heir). With its long windows and polished floor, its chaste white mouldings and pale pink-panelled walls, the new picture-gallery had made the perfect setting for Lord William Stanville's treasured Correggios and Canalettos – his Zuccarelli landscapes, and the fine melancholy portraits of himself and his second Countess, by Pompeo Batoni. But, since then, the Collector Earl's descendants had seen fit to remove the original pier-glasses from between the windows and displace the console tables from the walls – in order to make way for a number of inferior paintings and portraits of themselves; for a series of illuminated pedigrees, and for every outdated relic of gilt and ormolu, for every piece of Chinese lacquer-work that they could lay their hands to. Most of the gallery's splendid floor was covered now with busy modern Axminster carpeting and, on the carpet, jumbled sets of Parisian and Florentine chairs and sofas, with marquetry, painted screens à la Chinoise, and whole cabinets of Lady Southbourne's hideous Sèvres porcelain. The classical simplicity of the original obscured now by the wholesale ostentation of less discerning occupants.

David longed to sweep it away, so much of it, and start afresh! To refurnish this great chamber, and every other in the house, to his own ideas of grace and elegance. Drastically to reduce the ornament. To bring in English Chippendale and Hepplewhite in place of the rococo. To sell off the Sèvres and pack off the chinoiserie to the Regent and the infamous 'Chinese corridor' of his Pavilion down at Brighton. And then to select for himself, from the very best that Rome and Florence had to offer, those masterworks of classic and Renaissance art that such a splendid gallery undoubtedly deserved. Some day he'd do it too! Some day he'd have the funds. His tutor, Roger Dean, had taught him an appreciation of what was good and what was not. And if the Almighty would only spare him long enough – as Earl of Southbourne, ninth in direct succession since the creation of the title, and with an eventual income of ten thousand a year at his disposal – David's time would surely come for Hadderton. And Hadderton's for David Stanville!

Impulsively the frustrated connoisseur pushed through a drove of gilded cabrioles and scrolled acanthus leaves, to stare out through the nearest window across the park. And there at least, thank heaven, its architect's design remained as he intended it. A spacious prospect which allowed the eye the freedom to wander through noble stands of timber to the open meadows of the home farm out beyond. A landscape now divested of the Frenchly-formal gardens, the paddocks and the tangled woodland that it once comprised. "Where all around, delightful landskips lie, and pleasing prospects entertain his eye," David murmured softly, taking heart as always from the sense of order and continuity that the scene inspired.

Moving closer to the house, however, his eye just then alighted on the grizzled, faintly bandy figure of his father, arrested in his boisterous progress to the stables by the sight of an employee in need of some correction in his work. An all too frequent occurrence in the Eighth Lord Southbourne's day, and one that every groom and steward, every labourer, attorney and man of affairs in his Lordship's employ had long since learned to dread. As David watched, smiling in spite of himself, the parent he'd so recently killed off in his imagination reached out briskly to snatch the scythe from the unwilling hand of the gardener's boy he interrupted; to demonstrate the method he had himself perfected for shaving lawns more closely. "And God and the Devil confound it! – never mind the odd little scrape," his son could almost hear him cry as, wielding the implement like his Yeomanry Cavalry sword, his Lordship plunged the scythe-point deep into the turf. "Death alive, the man who fears a scratch or two will never make a soldier, boy – on that ye may depend!" And David left him there to plough a second fearless furrow through the smooth perfection of his own lawn, secure now in the knowledge that he and his father would not be breakfasting together within the hour.

61

At the distant end of the gallery a pedimented exit led through a further suite of chambers toward the main staircase of the house. But, postponing his original intention to descend, David now turned to fumble impatiently with the handle of another unobtrusive little doorway in the panelling beyond. To climb instead by another smaller, darker stairway to the upper regions of the gatehouse. His motive as simple as it was disgraceful. The attic rooms of this least favoured north easterly gable of the pile had been abandoned long since, as too cold and draughty even for servants' accommodation. Now they were used for lumber; the domain of rats and spiders – in the wintertime of hibernating bats – and, whenever he wanted to be undisturbed, of David himself. In the old days, he and Charles and Octavia had often climbed that little stair for games of hide-and-seek and thundering foot-races through the blanched and dusty rooms beneath the roof. But, since Charles had joined the military, and Tavie become too ladylike to spoil her gowns with cobwebs, David came alone. Alone too to the 'secret valley' in the roofs, where he and Charlie had sometimes gone to find the sun.

One after another, David shot back the bolts which secured the door onto the roof, and pushed it open. Beyond lay the 'secret valley' of his childhood – the steep-sided gulley between the old Tudor roofs that had withstood the elements since the days of Henry VIII, and the Georgian gatehouse the Sixth Earl had built the previous century. A valley of mossy Horsham slates that concealed its explorer completely from the garden and the park below; closed at one end by the pitched roof of the gallery, and opening at the other onto the shaggy foliage of the beech trees on the hill behind the house. A splendid lofty place of cooing pigeons and tall octagonal chimneys, and miles and miles of wide blue sky.

David leant back against the slates, his eyes on the further roofline – undid the buttons of his satin waistcoat, and thought of the summer when his cousin Charles had first coaxed him through the little door to climb upon the roofs of Hadderton. Leaving their shoes and stockings in the culvert that ran through the centre of their secret valley, the two boys had climbed to sit astride the old manor roof and stare down into its outer court. They'd scaled the higher gatehouse wing. And – while David perched beside a chimney – Charles, four years or more his senior, audaciously slipped down to ride the pediment that topped the armorial bearings of the Stanvilles above the *porte-cochère*. Afterwards, sliding helter-skelter down the slates into their hidden valley, they'd thrown off their dirty clothes and given up their hot little bodies to the summer air; laughing uproariously and sitting on their breeches to save their bottoms from the scorching leads. Jumping up again to urinate, side by side, against the great stone slates of the ascending roof. Then to dodge back with shrieks and whoops, to evade the streams of yellow liquid trickling down around their feet. Later that same year, his parents had sent Charles away to board at Harrow. The next summer he'd spent with school friends far away from Hadderton. And, when he returned with Octavia the summer after that, it was very clear to David that he'd changed. For, when they climbed the slates again, resolved again to sun themselves without their clothes, young Charlie laughed in quite a different way. The body he revealed was different too. So was the abominable schoolboy habit for its pleasure and its easement, which he'd not scrupled to demonstrate for his cousin there and then by way of an accomplishment. A 'cooler', as he called it.

David had been first astonished, and then repelled to see his unbreeched cousin spend his seed upon the roof. In his embarrassment and confusion he'd avoided him thereafter and sought out his sister's company instead. But the image of Charlie in that shameless act stalked still as an erotic spectre through the fringes of his consciousness. And in later years, when his own body had developed, it was to the selfsame 'secret valley' in the roofs that he had climbed. In answer to the same irrefutable command.

With the sound of the pigeons in his ears, and his eyes still on the roofs above him, David began abstractedly to fiddle with the tight fly-closure of his awkward modern trowsers. At the age of fourteen he had first consciously become aware of the distinctive way that women moved – short-stepped, knees inward, feet one before the other. Thighs closely brushing in a way that must be awkward for a male – the slow soft milling of their buttocks beneath the muslin, the heavy swinging pendency of breasts above . . . He set his own feet more firmly on the culvert and leaned foward from the tiles. He'd watched the housemaids and the scullions, laundrymaids, dairymaids, women in the village – saw them smiling, curtseying, moving self-consciously – liking him to watch. As if inviting something further. And Tavie too. Something of the same thing in her eyes too, the same little twitching movements. As pleased as any of them to have her own desirability confirmed.

But Octavia was his cousin, born a gentlewoman. And the others, all of them, were bound to the estate. The families he'd grown up with in a sense; the plebeian community who administered to Hadderton and depended on it for their livelihood. A responsibility which, as heir to the estate, his Lordship never would evade. How could he? How could he do what his tutor had done to the kitchenmaid, Amy Ryan? Roger Dean, so tall, respectable and earnest – the scholar who'd published his own translation of the *Odyssey*, the guide and mentor of all his youthful studies! David jerked savagely at himself in anger and frustration. Roger Dean – disgraced and then dismissed for misbehaving with a kitchenmaid! And poor Amy herself, turned away from Hadderton and all her future prospects, to bear his child elsewhere, alone in shame and poverty. The gross and smarting violence to which David was at that moment subjecting his own body, in keeping with his feelings of disgust.

'Better this way than that,' he thought grimly. 'And if the good Lord wanted us to leave the wretched thing alone, then he'd surely not have thought to place it where it is – so very much to hand?' (He put it to his conscience by way of an excuse.) A peacock called from somewhere in the gardens down below. A wild harsh cry that chimed with David's physical sensations to claim for Hadderton the predetermined tributes of its heir. Hadderton at his back and at his feet and all around him. Hadderton his cradle. Hadderton in his blood and in his, his . . . Ah, HADDERTON!

'And, ah Davy, are you not ashamed to have succumbed again to such a senseless and a base temptation? To have become again the vilest beast in nature? And on such a morning too!'

He looked up into the pale blue summer-scented sky. 'And You, God, for inflicting such demeaning urges on Your creatures,' he demanded angrily. 'Do You not feel shame as well?'

Chapter Seven

But why in the world feel shame for something that could not, would never be amended? Sary Snudden never had, and never would. Or so she frequently assured herself. So hard to understand, when all was said, what all the fuss could be about! The urges that so distracted and demeaned the incontinent young Hamlet on his rooftop battlements had ever been a commonplace in her experience of bawdy barrack-troops and barnstack tumblings. All so simple and straightforward. As natural to her and as ever present as the weather. A fact of life to Sary. And at Mrs Perrin's establishment in Brighton, now become a way of life as well – in the daily, hourly sale of a commodity that never would go out of fashion, so long as one man required it more often than one woman was prepared to let him have it. Or wives still tired more quickly of its pleasures and varieties than their husbands. So long as ladies declined to act as whores, in fact, and gentlemen observed the rule-of-three within their breeches, no honest whore should be ashamed to earn her fees. No cull to blame for paying to spare himself or his fine lady from frustration and embarrassment. No time for such hypocrisies and subterfuges in a house like Mrs Perrin's, where morals were concerned far more with honest-dealing in transactions, than with the nature of the acts themselves. The trade was fair, quite patently. An exercise so oft repeated as to become routine. Its intimacies seldom more than technical. The only mighty wonder to Sary being that others wasted such a deal of time and energy in advertising their predilection or distaste for it!

Indeed, of the set of seven whores employed by Mrs Perrin, only the new girl and one other could be said to find the work in any way agreeable. In the mornings after ten, when the sleepy creatures took their coffee to one another's rooms, to help to wash or paint, or to dress each other's hair – or to discuss techniques or variations that appeared to answer, like friendly housewives sharing recipes – men seldom featured in their conversation, except as genitals, as butts for humour or as causes for complaint.

"Big?" scoffed Barbara, the generously built girl to whom Mrs Perrin habitually consigned those clients who laid claim to immense or oversized dimensions. "Gawd a'mighty, the poor dribs don't even know the *meaning* of the word! The way they brag of it, you'd think a paltry inch or two down there was worth the same in ten-foot curtain rods anywhere else in God's creation! And, 'Ooh Sir,' I says, 'how mighty *big* you are! Oh Sir, I'm sure I can't tell how I'll fit that handsome monster in! I'm certain it will stab me through to daylight!' (And, 'Aye, big for a peascod,' is what I'm thinking whiles I take 'im in without 'ardly noticing a whit of difference to the last fellow. Or the one before that. Handsome for an artichoke, p'raps – and a proper little monster, I'll agree, alongside the doodle of a doormouse!')"

Others volunteered their own unflattering opinions. "If the culls have ever had a grain of sense, then I'm thinking that they like to leave it with their breeches on the floor," said Bridie Brennan, the tough little Irish moll who regularly worked through more Toms between the last and first hours of each morning than any other girl in the establishment. "They'd strike their ladies' flints no more'n once or twice a week at most, and without any thought of catchin' tinder there ye may be sure! But bring it to a gay-girl, who scores her strunts by dozens, and they'll find her mighty dull if she don't pant and groan and near split her seams for joy. They think that we're made different, d'ye see? Never dreaming, the simple creatures, that we'd give 'em the performance anyway, just to fetch 'em off the quicker!"

"No *finesse* they 'ave, your sottish Englishmen," on another day and in another room declared the French grisette, Rosine. A haughty, harshly-spoken girl with heavy brows and brightly dyed red hair. "Bim-bam, bam-bim, *et oof! C'est tout*! Jus' like the leetle birds, *les moineaux*, in the gutter. No *élégance*! Or else they lie like pigs, like lazy pigs – and we must, as you English 'ave it, 'work the pump' for them!"

"Better than to 'ave to ride them to the post with whip and spurs. Or to sting 'em off with nettles, come to that," said Kate, an older, wearier woman, whose stock in trade was pain and degradation. For not even Mrs Perrin, who had no taste herself for 'special tricks', could afford to keep a house so straight as to exclude such skills as Kate's. Not when as many as one cull in ten had need of them. "Goads and chains and manacles and whips, to keep 'em up like kiddies' tops!" Kate heaved a feeling sigh. "Strong wrists and the bleedin' patience of a saint is what *I* need! Lord a'mercy, Rose – a few of your bim-bams and oofs 'ud be like a blooming 'oliday for me!"

"If only they'd just do what they 'ave to, and stop telling us about it," complained Louise, a gentle lazy creature with great cow's eyes and other features to match. "When they're not boasting and bragging about theirselves, then they're confessing and begging sympathy. Or else they can't do nothing 'less they hear the words. I sometimes think they'd near as soon pay for a willing ear, as for the other thing. I do really!"

And only Peggy, the tall black girl Madge had imported from the London docklands, seemed willing to credit the wretched clients with any merits of their own. "Takes all sorts of Toms to keep a whore in shoe leather," she pointed out. "I should know, I reckon. I've sampled most kinds in my time, and in most every way and all! Men are like dogs, I say. They get their lessons pretty well fixed if ye only trains 'em right. And I'll tell you this, gels – I've never met a cully yet without 'e 'ad the *one* thing to recommend 'im at the least. Thanks be!" She laughed a loud and deeply belling laugh. "This 'ere thing!" said Peg, planting a fist on the appropriate part of her own anatomy – and slowly, lewdly erecting a large and coffee-coloured thumb. "Lor' bless 'em for it too, I say! And bless 'Isself for making us the way to suit it best! For if any of you young ladies know a better way to eat and drink and dress in fancy style without Sir Nimrod's favour, then let's hear about it, eh? For I don't, and under heaven that's the truth!"

A truth with which Sary, for one, could readily identify. And from her first few weeks at Mrs Perrin's house in Brighton, she and the black girl, Peggy, had become the best of friends. Not that the other whores within the ménage were in any way unwelcoming. Far from it. Indeed their attitudes to her and to each other had forced Sary to revise her opinion somewhat of the sex. In Alfriston her easy-going ways had set her quite apart from others. The stiff-rumped village maids and matrons saw her as abandoned, her mother's daughter; while she herself had grown to think of women generally as hypocrites. As ready to cheat all soldiers in their charges for supplies and laundry, as they were to condemn a girl who gave freely of her body to but a few of them. Mrs Perrin's girls, on the other hand, were obviously of quite another breed. Women who cared less for 'decency', as the hidebound country dowds perceived it, than for the more tangible benefits their clients' fees afforded them. Less for 'consequence' and 'reputation', than for the *esprit de corps* of their own sisterhood. Women whose existence without the narrow confines of convention and society had made them exclusive. Unrepentant whores, whose realistic view of men and male desires could only make them value female qualities the more.

That most, if not quite all of Mrs Perrin's girls, preferred each other in every way to the men they entertained, was soon made obvious to their latest recruit. And although it might never naturally have occurred to Sary to solicit a woman's caresses in preference to a man's, she found in them a pleasant enough substitute she had to confess. In the mornings, while they amused each other with descriptions of their clients of the night before, it was nothing unusual for one girl to climb into another's bed. Or to follow her by invitation to the cosy bathing-closet; and indulge in pleasures there which no man Sary had encountered could find the time or patience to dispense – however urgently he might require them for himself. Activities which, in their voluntary nature at the least, must prove more intimate than anything the girls could hope to meet with in the normal line of business.

Yet, notwithstanding, Sary invariably found herself looking forward to the first 'nooners' of the day. For however they might differ one from another, in age or manner or appearance, there was to all of them at base – to every man-Thomas who walked through Mrs Perrin's door, the same endearing defect. Strong men with a universal weakness of genital obsession. Like the carving of St Michael on the beam of the old Star Inn at Alfriston. A little man with legs astride and tunic lifted, to show off his shapes to all the world, as he so proudly thrust his sword into the gaping dragon's maw.

'*Hoddy-doddy, hoddy-doddy – all strunt and no body!*'
To Sary it was as if the jutting phallus, the fleshly monument to maleness which all culls shared, had become a kind of friendly ally against their other less sympathetic qualities. In her eyes, as in Peggy's, the clients' most useful, pleasant and familiar feature.

"Ye see it that way, Sary Snudden, on account of you're a *natural*," declared Black Peg. "Louise and Barbara now, and Mam'selle airs-and-graces Rose, they take it 'cos they're too damn lazy for any other kind of trade. Kate's never know'd nothing else since she were a kid in short-coats, and Bridie does it for the chink of golden sov'reigns. But you like it. You really like it don't you, same as I do – sticks out a mile. And that's the way we like it, eh – sticking out a mile! Born to it d'ye see? 'Strunt-smitten', that's the word! 'Twill take poor Peg to the gutter in the end, I shouldn't wonder – without 'er topknot or 'er teeth, all blind and rotted through with pox! But you now, with that skin and hair. Now you're a different matter! You play your cards aright, Milady, and like enough you'll end your life a duchess! Stranger things 'ave chanced in this 'ere business."

And for a fleeting moment Sarah saw herself the lady in the park at Hadderton. A girl who didn't have to work and never would, unless it be for recreation – pale-faced and modestly attired, as neat and nice as a nun's hen atop her breedy hunter. And then she'd burst out laughing at the sheer absurdity of the idea. A great lady she would never make, however circumstances might conspire to help her! As truthful with herself as any girl of seventeen could be, she saw that all too plainly. Such things were quite above her touch. One day she might perhaps set up her own establishment like Madge's, and fill it with merry *naturals* like herself. But that was for later, much later, when she'd lost her youth and energy. For the present, to be a successful and an honest whore was the height of her ambition. And a better life at that, she thought, than working as a skivvy in the town, or as the wife of some plodding punch-clod in the country!

Before noon each day at Mrs Perrin's, perfumed, painted and painstakingly underdressed, that trading-lady's hand-picked *corps d'amour* would drift downstairs in ones and twos to take their places in the salon. To play at whist or beggar-my-neighbour, to wield the billiards sticks and continue earlier conversations – while maids in dusting caps and aprons rushed around above to tidy rooms and make up beds that soon would be unmade again. While men in ones and twos converged upon the house at a casual strolling pace that deceived few who met with them in the lanes surrounding, as to their destination or their purpose there.

Sary welcomed each and every man who came her way – fat or thin, big or small, fair or dark, young or middle-aged – occasionally working *à deux*, or even *à trois* with Peg and Barbara. But far more often on her own. For the new girl's approach was one that few culls who came to know her were at all inclined to share, even with another whore. She owed them no kindness. That wasn't what they came for. Yet kindness was in her nature, and she always set herself to do her best for them, did Sary. She'd never look at a cull, as most whores did, with dead unseeing eyes. She smiled at each, contrived her utmost to make each poor fellow think she saw him as he really was. Allowed to each, as the occasion required, his own little fantasy of individuality and of conquest.

Hoddy-doddy, hoddy-doddy –

As if the man she welcomed in, the character he brought to her, was relevant in any way to the service she performed for him. Or to its familiar instrument.

Hoddy-doddy, hoddy-doddy –
All strunt and no body!

* * *

Because even now, looking back across all the years between – even now that's how she saw those men, God preserve them in their simplicity! She saw her clientele as legions of men with clammy hands and nervous smiles. An endless procession of friends, acquaintances and total strangers. Bodies writhing, thrashing, slippery with sweat. Faces with contracted brows and staring eyes. Voices degraded at the peak of their endeavours to the youps and grunts and groans of an animal more primitive than man. Fifty, sixty, seventy of them even, every week. And all so very much alike. Their individual characters and features almost unconnected to the helmeted warrior they all laid claim to – or to the urge that drove it as surely as St Michael's weapon toward the waiting gape.

*   *   *

Luncheon at Mrs Perrin's was carried up from the kitchens in the basement a little after five each afternoon. The hour at which, in the experience of all its servitors, the male libido was at its least demanding. The girls ate informally in their rooms whilst washing and douching and effecting necessary repairs to face and coiffure. Returning to the downstairs salon in curling papers for the period of quiet digestion that Madge herself prescribed, in preparation for the more hectic business of the evening. By then the young fishermen the house engaged to protect its inmates and man the outside door had been replaced by Madge's *apron-squire*, Bill Hodge. A onetime fisherman himself – now a daytime 'bather', who dipped gentlemen into the briny from his own machine on Brighton beach (and after five, a night-time 'bully' in his mistress's employ). A brawny giant of a man of two score years or more, with the white teeth and weatherbeaten countenance of all the fisher-folk. And Madge Perrin's confidence, besides.

"He's no great shakes, I'll grant you," she confessed to all her girls at some time or another. "Lazy, simple-minded and conceited as a lugger's parrot, that's 'Odge. But then, ain't they all? And I'll tell ye now, the first one of you to cast an eye within a mile of 'im, will find herself casting nets for sparrers in the street next thing, I guarantee. 'E may be just a man, poor fellow, but he's *mine*. And I don't share my men with nobody! I 'ope that's clear?"

It was. A rule that had long since acquired the status of a law. And for all the busy night-time hours at Madge's – while that lady welcomed in the clients, and consulted records to suit each one as far as possible for preference and physique – while little Mary hurried up and down the stairs with notebook and chronometer, keeping time – Bill Hodge would lounge on Madge's sofa in the hallway. Like Cerberus at the gates of Hades, with one eye on the cash-box and the other on the door. Occasionally a fractious or a drunken cull, or a bilk who wouldn't pay, must need a sample of his bare-knuckle skills. More often he was called on for an exchange of personalities with those hopeful Toms who sought admittance to the house without the proper introduction. And at those times when Madge resumed her place to free her *apron-squire* to drink and discourse with the whores and waiting clients in the salon, Bill

Hodge was quite as careful as the girls themselves to keep his eyes and hands from any undue straying. The rule was very clear. Even bawds and bullies observed their own proprieties.

At two or three each morning, when the last culls had departed, while Madge was entering up her ledgers and Hodge prepared to shoot the inside bolts, the girls hung up their working clothes and wiped away their paint. To wander down in wraps and mules to eat their suppers off their knees within the salon. And then to yawn their way to bed again. Another day completed. Another job well done, as Madge invariably observed. A demanding regimen maybe. But nowhere near as hard as scrubbing and laundering, or labouring in the fields for twelve or thirteen hours each day. And not without its recreations, neither. For, in addition to those occasions when whores would be dispatched around the town to call on certain favoured 'regulars' in their hotels and lodgings, the girls were encouraged to walk about at will – on Sunday afternoons, on the free half-day each week to which all were entitled, and on those three or four days each month when nature intervened to put them out of service. In many other houses, so Peg said, the whores were obliged to work right through their monthly courses – with the aid of grease and cervical sponges and Welch's pills or 'pothecary's laudanum. But not at Mrs Perrin's.

"Fresh air and exercise is what ye want, and whenever you can get it," Madge advised. "Never miss a chance, I say. Not in this game. Not when you 'ave to earn your keep within four walls and on your blooming back!"

And Sary, personally, was nothing loathe to do as she was bidden. Louise and Bridie and fat Barbara might be content enough to parade with other nymphs along the Steine and in the nearby Pavilion garden. Or to stroll across to the Donaldson's New Circulating Library. To take out a raffle ticket or examine the latest portfolios of cartoons. Or to consult the public visitors' books there for news of prospective clients. But Sary refused to squander leisure hours on anything so tame and tedious. She wanted to see and experience for herself everything that Brighton had to give. And whatever she did, wherever she went about the place with Peggy or with Kate, there were never enough hours in Sary Snudden's days for all the various amusements that gay and gaudy little town could offer her.

In fine weather it was the seafront and marine parade that drew her most consistently. To hear the cannon welcome in the packet-boats from French Dieppe, or see the coal-brigs blackening unwary bathers with their windblown dust. And then to watch the four-in-hand brigade spank past behind their matching teams, in carriages and high-perch phaetons of mustard yellow, emerald, mauve, or brilliant mail-coach scarlet. With all the latest modes displayed on either pavement, strutting beneath their high silk hats and parasols – in flapping pantaloons, in stripes and plumes and off-the-ankle gowns, and endlessly inventive new devices for concealing double chins and swelling corporations. At Sary's own shrill taste in colours and flamboyant style the *upper ten* might smile. They might look down their high-bridged noses at her all they liked. For under their assumption of disdain, she saw how fascinated such folk were with all the stock-in-trade of her profession. The hypocrites! Fine gentlemen who derided her in public to the ladies hanging on their arms, only to attend her later in a very different frame. Like children begging pennies for the sweetshop then, all round-eyed promise and apology! And the ladies they escorted, so far above the likes of Sary Snudden in refinement – who'd later beg for telescopes. To count the sails out in the roads, they claimed, whilst focussing instead on the number of naked gentlemen who waited for their bathers at the doors and on the steps of bathing caravans far closer in to shore!

One sultry summer afternoon at the height of the Brighton season, Sary and Black Peg paid their coins to be dipped in as well, demurely clad in oilskin caps and flannel drawers, and shrieking quite as loud as any lady when the bathing women seized their arms to plunge them once, twice, and thrice into the salty water. On another day they'd seen the Regent Prince himself out riding on parade, in a tall black hat and chestnut *Brutus* wig, his legs all swathed in bandaging. So gouty now, 'twas said, he had to be winched up onto his horse and rarely ventured out beyond the Steine. And yet he'd smiled to right and left and touched his hatbrim to the ladies as he passed. And Sary had been moved to call out "God bless you, Prinny!" at his bulging blue silk back. For whatever others chose to make of him, all of Brighton adored the royal eccentric who'd put them on the European map.

Meanwhile, that same eccentric's seaside palace continued to grow steadily in size and ostentation beneath its bristling hedge of scaffolding to the west side of the Steine. 'To bring the frontage into harmony with its Chinese-oriental wings.' Or so the Regent had declared in defence of his extravagance. With Indian domes and Indian columns recreating in a Sussex fishing town the unlikely splendours of a Moghul court. Day by day and month by month the noble work progressed, while all the time the Prince's German band drowned out the sound of saw and hammers with selections from Italian operas, from the lawns in front.

Behind the Regent's oriental pleasure domes, another kind of palace opened up for Sary a whole new world of spectacle and fantasy. The new Theatre Royal in Brighton was not a whit inferior, so its patrons claimed, to the Haymarket in London. And she was ready to believe them – sitting with the other whores and cullies on the tight-packed benches of the pit, with eyes only for the stage. When the orchestra struck up the national anthem and the curtain rose on brightly flaring lights, on the painted scenery and glittering costumes that the square proscenium framed, she felt like crying out aloud for sheer delight (and often did, to the amusement of those about her). Pantomime, comedy or tragedy, she adored it all – thrilled to the ringing words and brave dramatic gestures of the actors, laughing or weeping with them as the piece dictated, convinced for the time of their reality, and applauding loudly at the end of each performance.

At those times of the month when Sary's courses spared her the normal demands of commercial hospitality, she enthusiastically attended public teas and routs and balls instead, in the large hotel assembly rooms – well caulked and padded down below and decked above in gowns of brilliant coloured silk and satin. Or else she'd rise early with the dawn, as once she had in Alfriston. To see the herring boats come in and beach their cargo in amongst the nets and lobster pots and squabbling seagulls. And watch the London fish-carts loaded up for Billingsgate. While others worked or slept through those four precious days each month, she patronized the milliners and silk mercers of the town, and spent her earnings to the hilt on every kind of finery. She ventured everywhere abroad with the red-capped fishermen that Madge employed as 'bullies'. Or else with favoured clients like Lieutenant Charlie Stanville, who cared nothing for being seen in the company of whores, when he found himself in Brighton for a levée or a review. They went to the races up on Whitehawk Down, to cock-fighting at the Old Ship and Castle inns, to bull-baiting at Rottingdean and cricket matches in the meadows under Hollingbury Hill. Sometimes they hired a donkey-chaise, and a boy to lead it up the East Cliff to where whole terraces of pastel-shaded stucco villas were sprouting from the chalk. Or they'd take a private phaeton through the downland combes to Ovingdean or Preston Village, for *al fresco* picnics in secluded places where Sary herself might usually be prevailed upon to offer the dessert.

In autumn and on milder winter afternoons Sary took her exercise, when free to do so, along the seafront still – without her paint and in a warm pelisse, with gloves and muff, a woollen scarf tied firmly round her bonnet. She never tired of watching hats bowl down the promenade or ladies' skirts blow over heads. She loved to see the crimson waves reach up to catch a sinking sun, while roosting starlings wove their noisy patterns through a bruised and bloodstained sky. And then to hasten back to Madge's through the darkening streets to claim her share of luncheon, and to wallow in a steamy-scented bath in anticipation of exercise of quite another kind. For Brighton houses such as Madge's kept very near as busy in the winter as at any time but at the height of the Royal summer season.

"Long dark evenings I put it down to," said Madge herself with every evidence of satisfaction. "And if the sea's too cold for dipping – well then, poor dears, where else to come for it but 'ere? 'The Brighton Cure', eh gels?"

Sary certainly could find no reason for complaint. In her first summer in the town she'd seen a poor woman sold in Brighton Market for a sovereign, with a hempen halter round her neck. 'Sold as seen', by one man to another. Whereas in Madge's house, she and her little band of Cyprians were plainly the ones to do the selling – while at the same time miraculously contriving to retain their freedom! A much superior arrangement to Sary's way of thinking. She'd had her misfortunes to be sure. Twice in her first two years of whoring, the house's own apothecary must needs prescribe his 'patent female pills' to restore her monthly courses. A little indisposition and discomfort to be born with. At other times, in company with every girl of her profession, she'd had the itch –

75

'the scrubbado', the 'Pavilion-garden gout'. But cachets of iodine and mercury, and the apothecary's good counsel, had soon cleared those as well. And, undaunted, Sary had blithely gone on to earn Madge Perrin's special commendation by satisfying more gentlemen and wearing out more bedsteddle springs in the profitable course of duty than any other girl in her employ (with the exception, naturally, of Irish Bridie).

Chapter Eight

Now to Brighton all repair
To taste the pleasures that flow there.
Sure no place was e'er like this –
All is pleasure, joy and bliss!

"My dear young gudgeon," Captain Charles Stanville exclaimed, without attempting to disguise his amusement. "You will allow 'tis hardly an excursion to the underworld or life membership of the Hellfire Club that I'm proposing. I'm merely taking steps to complete your education. An exercise that is lamentably overdue, by all accounts."

"Yes, I realize that, Charles, and I am obliged to you. But I still say that to do it this way seems – well, confounded cold-blooded somehow." It was only with an effort that David could bring himself to relinquish his study of the rutted surface of the road ahead and look his elder cousin in the eye. "To ride out like this in the full light of day, I mean, and sober . . ."

Patiently, Charles transferred his reins to fish out from his pocket a *tabatière* and tap the painted lid. "Are you saying then that you'd rather we made the expedition after nightfall, and with a bumper or two of brandy in our bellies?" He extracted a pinch or so of dark brown rappee and enhaled it sharply from his glove. "Is that it, Denton?" he enquired.

"Well, yes, if you want to frame it that way, I suppose . . . At all events . . ."

"And that's the trouble with a private tutor's education, bigod!" his cousin interrupted. Charles flicked shut his snuff-box and exercised a silk bandanna beneath the sweep of his moustache. "Good heavens, man, I'm taking you to a *woman* – to an amatory adventure, not a surgical amputation! And let me assure you, David, that nine times out of ten a healthy young fellow of your address may be relied on to survive the professional removal of virginity without recourse to alcohol. My dear fellow, 'tis a medically established fact!"

"Don't be ridiculous, Charles. You know exactly what I meant." David Stanville flushed with vexation. Though in truth, as much with himself and his embarrassing lack of carnal experience, as with Captain Charlie's teasing manner. Innocence in a young lady like Octavia might be attractive, even vital. But in a nineteen-year-old young man of any persuasion, leave alone a titled viscount, it had to be absurd to say the least. "I just happen to think that one should be in the right mood for this kind of an adventure before ever undertaking it, that's all," he added, feeling quite as desperately foolish as he sounded.

His cousin laughed outright, and leant across to punch him on the arm. "Mood, d'ye say? And is *that* what it is you've been waiting for these four years past? Because if it is, I have to tell ye, Denton, that your mental state's the last thing on this earth you should be thinking of at times like this. Confess to yourself the nature of your ailment. Then find yourself a pretty Paphian, one of Mrs Perrin's lambs, to help you with the purge. I needn't refine upon it, surely? You don't require the cloak of darkness or libations to the gods, for pity's sake! You need a woman – a *merkin*, your Lordship! And that's really all ye need. And when you have one within your sprawl, the mood will come to you damn soon enough. You can take my word on that!"

The two young men had ridden out through the dragon gates of Hadderton that May morning of 1818, ostensibly to attend a spring race meeting on Whitehawk Down. But in reality to do their own jockeying, and on fillies that could be relied upon to run slower with every additional guinea that was placed on them. Charles this spring had succeeded in securing yet another furlough from his regiment. A leave of four whole months this time – requested and granted for the very practical object of a formal courtship. The second daughter of a wealthy Hampshire neighbour was become quite desperate to be married, his mother had thoughtfully written to inform him. An opportunity on no account to be wasted by a warranted Waterloo Man. His commanding officer saw the sense of it, certainly. (For in peacetime the British army were always willing to encourage such gentlemanly pursuits as fortune-hunting.) So, naturally, did Charles – despite his immediate intention of spending his initial weeks of freedom in a visit to his relatives of Hadderton, and in concentrated whoring down in Brighton. This last, a necessary preliminary to the duller work of matrimonial courtship; and one he had it in mind to share fully with his uninitiated cousin.

That Cousin Denton had succeeded in attaining the age of nineteen without more than a kiss and a promissory fumble from a laundrymaid, had in fact shocked Charlie almost more than anything he'd heard – when the poor boy solemnly confessed to him as much over their second celebratory decanter on the night of his arrival.

"My dear fellow, nothing simpler than the treatment for that ailment," he'd promised, with a dryness that was intended to conceal his real astonishment at such a thing. "You follow my prescription twice daily for a week – twice weekly for a further month, and I'll wager that you'll scarce remember what 'twas like to be a sufferer. To be sure we'll start the remedy at once. Tomorrow morning, Denton, I insist on it!"

And here they were embarked upon the cure together, riding down through Moulsecombe in a balmy scented atmosphere of may and flowering parsley; with the song of birds and the brilliant verdure of the springtime fairly shouting their approval. The kind of day when even celibates and aesthetes must feel the tug of natural instinct. Yet with poor David sitting tense and upright, holding back his horse, as if an executioner and not the soft and willing body of a woman awaited him in Brighton.

They left their mounts, and a silver coin or two, with an obliging groom in the Royal Horse Artillery barracks on the Lewes road; and proceeded down the Steine on foot. Charles of soldierly appearance still – complete to a shade in dark blue superfine and buckskins, with a military black silk stock and beaver hat. David rigged out in yellow nankeen breeches – a green silk swallowtail set admirably across his shoulders, close-fitted to an ornamented Marseilles weskit. Two proud young chins uplifted by shirt-points

79

of quite prodigious height. Two pairs of elbows squared, two pairs of elegant, well-muscled legs deliberately exposed. Patrician peacocks in ritual display – clinking their boot-spurs past the Regent's fantastic Hindoo-Chinese palace, now rearing up a vast new onion dome beneath its scaffolding – striding westward into Castle Square, where coaches stood in ranks awaiting passengers. And, on the stroke of noon, to bend their way down through the crowded lanes and twittens of the fishing-quarter. Two smart and proud young gentlemen demanding passage of the throng.

But, whereas Charles's pride was founded on the very solid conviction of his own superiority – David's, as they approached Madge Perrin's house, was still nine-tenths bravado. He felt unsexed, less amorous at that moment than he ever could remember. Few things that he'd less rather do just now than follow on his worldly cousin's heels into a Brighton whorehouse. But, as with the roofs of Hadderton when they'd first scaled them together all those years before, he knew he'd almost sooner die than show his fear to Charles. There was no turning back.

"You're privileged, Denton, d'ye know that?" his cousin said as he briskly rapped six times with his gold-headed cane upon the brothel door. "For you'd never be admitted here, ye may be certain, without presuming on my acquaintance with the house." He turned with provoking good humour to flash a grin at David.

Resisting the temptation to turn himself and run for his young life, his cousin swallowed convulsively and dragged up the corners of his own mouth into the expected response. At the same time rummaging beneath his coat-tails to blot his palms on his nankeen buttocks; in case he might be called upon to shake a hand – or something. Inside, they heard the sound of footsteps. A small Judas window in the door flicked open, and then shut again. To be followed by the sound of well-greased bolts and the rattle of a chain.

"First come, first served," said Charles with satisfaction as the door began to open. "This way you get to pick from all the merchandise on offer. Aye, and pick 'em fresh into the bargain. No ready-buttered buns for us, eh Denton?

"And a good afternoon to you, Mary," he added imperturbably, sweeping off his beaver and bowing to the figure in the doorway with the courtly air he used to mask his own excitement. "Your very obedient servant, Ma'am."

"Lieutenant Stanville, I declare!" cried out that functionary with very obvious pleasure. "Bless us, we 'adn't heard you was in town!" But even as she said it, her eyes were travelling past him to the young man at his shoulder. Cautiously assessing eyes in a pinched unpainted face. A brothel housekeeper no different, it would seem, to any other kind.

"It's 'Captain Stanville' now, Mary," Charles corrected with another little bow. "I'd show ye the French braid on my jacket and the extra band around my shako if I had my regimentals with me. And this young tulip of fashion I've brought you is my cousin, Lord Denton," he added with a wink. "David, meet Mrs Mary Price."

"Servant, Ma'am," said David gravely.

The woman acknowledged the salute with a coyness that was surprising in the circumstances; and a moment later had closed the door behind them. "Mrs Perrin won't be but a minute," she apologized, pulling back the curtains of the vestibule to admit a little sunlight through the blinds. "And shall I fetch you Sary Ann, Sir?" she said aside to Charles. "Or Barbara?" She gave David another swift assessing glance. "And little Louise, too, maybe?" she suggested.

"We want them all, confound it! His Lordship wants to take his pick," Charles Stanville declared grandly, while David made a detailed study of the mouldings on the ceiling.

Poor David, his mind a battleground of contradictions. Half of him accepting the practical necessity for this initiation; the other half appalled by the dispassionate way in which Charles and the female denizens of this place proposed to go about the business. A simple, basic and entirely loveless act – he knew that's how it had to be with whores. A compromise with nature; an adult man's solution to his adolescent fumblings on the roofs of Hadderton, and to the guilt that he attached to them. No need to be ashamed to choose between the girls they trotted out for his approbation in Mrs Perrin's salon. If harlots wished to sell themselves like nags or cattle at a fair, the buyer had no ought to feel degraded. No reason, surely? And yet he did of course – most comprehensively.

"And 'ere's our Sary Ann – just ye look at 'er shape and face! Now what a living beauty. Did you ever see such hair and eyes?" demanded Mrs Perrin in the rattling manner of a market auctioneer. "Or is it Barbara that takes your fancy? Now she'd be

81

an 'andsome handful for any young gentleman, your Lordship – as Captain Stanville 'ere will bear me out. Eh, Charlie? Or how about our Peg for something out of the common way? Show 'im, Peggy. There, Sir, smooth as silk and black as ebony – there's a prize! And this 'ere's our little firebrand, Bridie . . ."

He chose in panic, almost without thinking. Anything to escape the woman's leering painted face. To stop her strident commentary. To stop the girls exhibiting their undoubted charms in gowns that clung or parted so upsettingly as they walked by. Above all to escape the insufferable irony of Cousin Charlie's smile! David made his choice almost without thinking – almost, but perhaps not quite entirely. Because one girl's face had seemed to him less openly suggestive than the others. The expression in her eyes mayhap a shade more kindly. And she it was he chose.

The girl herself seemed genuinely pleased. Her smile deepened, and with an absurd naturalness she hooked her arm through his. From the head of the stairs she guided him through a second lavish salon. Its taste Parisian (or what in Brighton passed as such), faced all around with looking glasses purposely hung low. Smelling of fresh-applied perfume, with something else beneath it, staler and less appetizing. A corridor beyond exhibited an impressive collection of French engravings – folio prints, which derived their original appeal less from the artists' varying skills than from those of their enthusiastic, and even athletic, models. At intervals between the pictures were narrow panelled doors; from one of which a maid emerged to brush past David and his escort with eyes downcast demurely (and a little oddly, in view of her immediate surroundings). At another door a little further on, the girl Sary Ann disengaged herself from David's rigid arm.

" 'Ere we are then – 'ere's where your fondest dreams come true," she announced in the immemorial way of her profession, beckoning him to follow her inside. "You pay two guineas a time, or ten for the afternoon. All right? But bless you, dear – ye don't 'ave to find it *yet*," she appended on a warmer, more informal note, as David reached inside his coat. "Not until we know what suits."

He nodded dumbly while his eyes still travelled round the chamber with a helpless fascination. Like someone disassociated for the present with this ill-matched pair of strangers and the act they shortly would perform here. The room itself was scrupulously clean. Bright, not only with the sunlight that flooded through its open window, but with the astonishing array of colours and of textures it illumined. Curtains of deep red moreen with golden tassels. A blue and yellow carpet. A vase of curling ostrich plumes dyed orange, puce and purple. On chairs and ottomans and on hooks around the walls – gowns, sprigged, spangled, striped and tamboured in every rainbow hue; with bonnets, shawls and parasols to match or clash with them. A doll perched upon a cushion with a gleaming carnation ribbon tied around its waist. And on a table in the window, a fresh bowl of living crimson roses.

"I do like to see a bit of colour in a room," the girl explained unnecessarily, seeing David blink. "If the good God wanted us to be dull in our traps and togs, then 'E surely wouldn't 'ave coloured 'Is own flowers and butterflies and all so bright and fanciful. That's what I always say. Now would 'E though, your Lordship?

"But there," she added, her own warm golden eyes appraising, "wouldn't do no harm to shut out a bit of sun for the moment, I dare say." With which she strode over to slam down the sash and tug the tasselled curtains half across it. Leaving David with an image of painted features as loud and obvious as her taste in clothing. And yet the girl *was* something special, his first instinct had been right. A realization that did nothing in itself to lessen his embarrassment. In the corridor outside he could hear approaching footsteps. The sounds of Charlie's voice and female laughter. The opening and latching of a door. The crash of one boot falling, then the other. And then silence.

"I won't be but a minute. So don't run away now, will ye, duck?" the girl, Sary Ann, instructed, turning smartly on her heel to disappear behind a dressing-screen on which an additional collection of copulatory engravings had been pasted. "Take off your coat, why don't you, and make yourself at 'ome." She meant it kindly – but that somehow didn't help.

"Yes – ah, capital," he forced himself to answer – as sturdily as he might, and a good deal louder than he need. And then he did so, with all the gravity of a Barcelonian bishop. Now quite beyond redemption, he felt a little sick.

Sary left the young swell gazing at the blue and yellow carpet of her bedroom, arms crossed defensively – poor gawky! By the time

83

she'd changed into an open *robe de chambre*, applied more jessamy and checked her painting in the glass, he'd progressed as far as pulling off his boots; his coat and weskit already neatly folded on a chair. But that was all. She knew his case. A 'Johnny-raw', and green as a gooseberry, so Charlie had whispered in the downstairs salon. That rarest of all brothel visitors, a virgin male! In nigh three years of constant and conscientious work, Sary had encountered but half a score of them. Like others of her calling, she preferred the older greyhead culls for choice – as generally less wearing and more appreciative of the skills she had to offer. Young men were too much in a hurry as a rule; too barbarous in usage and far too anxious to impress themselves and her with their performances. But these 'Johnny-raws' were something altogether different. They needed reassurance and practical instruction. A duty and a pleasure for any self-respecting whore to set them on the right path for the future. Although you didn't let them know you knew their secret, naturally. She'd tried that once or twice, and succeeded only in making things harder for the wretched young fellows. (Or softer, to be more accurate.) The memory made her smile again, which tended to be helpful.

"That's it – now you look more easy, duck," she lied, pretending not to notice how he'd started at her sudden reappearance. A reflex which very near upset her own precarious gravity. For unlike her titled client, Sary had always found it hard to hide her feelings. "So come over then and sit by me, Sir. And let's see if we can't find a way to improve on our acquaintance?" She plumped down on the bed and patted the green and scarlet Paisley counterpane beside her. "You won't find a better bedsteddle than this in all of Brighton, I'll be sworn. And just me to exercise it too. It's hardly 'ad no kind of wear so far to speak of – just me and not above five dozen pairs of cullies' knees and elbows, all in all. Why, 'tis very near brand new!" She patted the Paisley by her thinly covered thigh again invitingly. "Come over 'ere along of me and give 'er a try then, why don't ye dear?"

"Yes – yes, thank you very much, I will." His voice preternaturally bass still, and as confident as he could make it – with the trace of a rural vowel or two, she noticed, in the style of the provincial aristocracy, beneath its clipped and educated accents.

Something familiar too about his bearing, Sary thought. So very slim and upright, as he moved with jerky nonchalance toward her very-near-brand-new working mattress. And brown eyes – brown eyes he had, this Johnny-raw of hers; brimful with tension and anxiety, despite all his efforts to appear relaxed. Brown eyes and blackly feathered brows, and dark brown hair that flopped in a forelock like a colt's against his polished forehead. A face by no means above the line of being pleasing. A long straight nose, a narrow jaw. A mouth as yet too undecided to stamp the whole as handsome. A boy's face still, not yet a man's.

'Not yet, but very soon to be,' thought Sary, 'or I'm no spigotmonger!'

He sat down, careful not to touch her, bolt upright in his shirt and high starched collar. His hands upon his knees to stop their trembling. Long hands, she noticed, with dark blue veins and jutting wrist bones. 'And stiff everywhere,' thought Sary, moving closer, 'but where the poor thing needs it most, Lor' bless 'is innocence!'

"Well now, I'd think 'tis time to raise Sir Nimrod's spirits and invite 'im to pay the pair of us 'is compliments," she said aloud by way of conversation while she went to work. "Wouldn't you, my dear?"

A question that in fact required no answer. For as David himself had come to be aware, she already had its solution very well in hand.

'*Procul, o procul est profani,*' he quoted to himself from the sixth book of Virgil's *Aeneid*. 'Begone all you who are uninitiated!' His brain absurdly unconnected with his body and the things that she was doing to it. His eyes still ranging round the shadowed room, recording images. The doll on the ottoman. The roses in the narrow bar of sunlight which still fell between the curtains. His own reflection in an angled mirror – his face brick-red, his mouth ajar – while all the time she calmly, expertly went about her business.

"Warm gin," the girl presently remarked, as a muscle in David's left buttock went into spasm of its own accord, and his legs began to splay. " 'Tis what most use before, to keep 'em safe. But I don't hold with that. You leave it to Sary, Sir – she'll show you after what

85

to do. And as for now, we'll see how a little drib of jessamy will answer." She reached behind a tangled heap of ribbons on a bedside table. "Next article," she said and smiled. "Never you play at billiards, Sir, without a well-chalked cue!" And David in a moment felt, not chalk, but something closer to a wet live octopus at exercise within his lap.

"That's it, that's the dandy!" The girl was laughing now, deliciously. "That nice then, dear? Oh yes, I see ye think it is! And I'd say you're ready justabout, young man, to play your jack against my ace. Aye, *justabout*, I'd say!"

And so for sure he was. No time to think the thing contrived, or to glimpse his own sudden, clumsy movements in the mirror. Scarce time enough to find the place she offered – and none to savour it. Time left only for the final raw convulsion of the act – bellowing like a charging bull . . .

. . . Only to find he'd charged a solid wall and stunned himself quite senseless. All faculties suspended.

In a little while she gently heaved him off – marvelling, as she had so many times before, at the ruthless core of violence that is the legacy of Man. This one's innocence a thing now of the past. A gift he'd made involuntarily, and with a mighty cry that Sary found strangely touching. Behind the dressing-screen again, she squatted down to douche herself with tepid alum-water and a glass syringe. "If you ask for my opinion, Sir, I'd say you're like enough as safe with Sary Snudden as is a guinea in a miser's purse," she called out to him encouragingly a minute later from her precarious seat upon the chamber-pot. "But there again, we can't always tell for sure, ye know. And better safe than sorry, eh?

"So come on then," she prompted when he failed to answer, emerging from behind the screen with a small towel in her hand. "Come back 'ere and let Sary show your Lordship what to do to guard yourself against Pavilion-garden gout."

For the second time (and with a Johnny-raw there always *was* a second time, in Sary's experience of the type), she decided, on an unexpected and generous impulse, to dispense with clothing altogether, inviting him to do the same.

Hoddy-doddy, hoddy-doddy . . .

But not this time – for this young man did have a body, as she very soon discovered, to complement those warm brown eyes of his. Eyes free from tension now as they regarded her. Faintly clouded now, and dark – as dark and warm and soft as velvet!

So why not break her rule? 'Why not this time?' she asked herself – already knowing the answer, as she watched his smooth young limbs slough off their nankeen coverings. Sixty culls or more a week – each week. If she wanted to, why should she not pretend that she could feel as much as *he* could at the least? To feel as much at least as a green gosling Johnny-raw, in all his blundering maladroitness? And curiously enough, it was in that first moment of beholding young David Stanville as she'd impulsively intended, mother-naked, that it came to Sary who he was and where she'd seen the boy before. Fully clothed on that occasion – and yes, on horseback in the great deerpark at Hadderton! But of course, Charlie's cousin; she'd known he was connected to the South-bournes. And why the devil had she not thought of it before?

David, on his side, was a deal too much absorbed with present matters to recall the appearance, or the wearer, of the famous bonnet above the deerpark wall. Or to connect it with Sary's vivid ostrich plumes in their vase across the room. In his first few minutes as a finished man, he'd lain unmoving while feelings of relief and gratitude, and faint astonishment, washed back across him in a slowly ebbing tide. And then she'd called him to the washing stand behind the screen to show him what to do; and afterwards to lead him back to bed again to learn some more.

And now, he found, he wanted to discover who she was and what she was about. No longer merely a facility to him, but a girl. A lovely girl to be explored, enjoyed, and if possible to be understood. He wanted to know everything about her; how old she was, and where she came from, and how long she'd been a whore. All the mysteries of her personality. His curiosity insatiable. He had to know if he might kiss the smile that lit her face, kiss it through her scarlet salve. And how it felt to touch her here, and here – and, oh yes, especially *here!* And already he'd forgotten all the rest in an abandonment of touching firm warm-waxy flesh, the smoothest thing in nature! Of touching and of being touched. Of seeing and of being seen. Until mere sight and touch inevitably led on, through every shade and gradation of delight, to a state of plunging ecstasy that could scarcely be defined. Hot shoots – or were they cold, and thrills? – that pierced through all the normal barriers of pain and pleasure, intolerably to die of surfeit in the very instant of their birth.

'Oh God!' he thought exultantly, 'oh God, I want to die like this – and now, and with this glorious girl!' His head and heart in heaven. The rest of him consumed by flames of quite another origin. He felt as if at very least he must erupt like a volcano. (Which to be sure he did, quite soon, most gratifyingly.)

And afterwards he merely smiled at Sary and fell gently into sleep. His dark hair damp and rumpled, his mouth now softened, slightly falling open. 'Like a kiddy,' Sary thought, with a rush of sudden tenderness that took her by surprise. Her own nerves more agitated than she ever would believe. Her heart more loudly beating than she ever could remember. She touched his hair, and then the finer hairs between his collar bones. With an exploratory finger she coursed up his throat to feel the strange hard outlines of his windpipe and his Adam's apple; rasped through the growing stubble of his upraised chin to slip between his parted lips – the dark lips of a dark-haired man – to find the soft red wetness of his tongue. The most intimate voluntary act she ever had committed with a man. And then she stooped to kiss his eyes, and then again. Until they opened and looked up at her, as hungry as before.

'And my word, 'tis amazing how quick they are to grasp what's what, these Johnny-raws,' thought Sary breathlessly. 'They never do need showing twice, that's certain!

'And take heed, girl,' she belatedly advised herself, as David Stanville's arms reached up around her. ''E's just a man, see – just another cull, when all is said and done. So 'ave a care now, Sary Ann!'

Chapter Nine

In the drawing-room of her mansion in St James's Square, the respectably crinolined lady favoured the representative of Eustace, Smithson and Brown with another little smile; rising to interrupt her own somewhat abbreviated version of events and replace the shabby doll beneath its dome of glass.

"Now where in heaven's name has Octavia got to?" she exclaimed, glancing at the mantel clock. "I declare it's almost dark already!" She crossed in her tilting hoops to release the curtains from their cord retainers. (Another pair of deep red velvet curtains, half a lifetime away from her little room in Mrs Perrin's house at Brighton.) Outside, the snow was falling steadily again. A hansom trotted past. A stooping figure in a long cloak with an upturned collar moved out of darkness, through a swirling golden pool of lamplight, and into shadows once again. A man? A woman? Sarah wasn't sure. She stood for a moment with her hand still on the curtains, listening to the barrel-organ grind out its vulgar fragment of Italian opera down the street.

Traviata – but naturally it would be! Performed again this year at Covent Garden with Rosina Penco in the title-role; and now more popular than ever. A satisfying clash and scrape of curtain rings drowned out the melody. But as she turned back into the gaslit room to continue her narration, Sarah distinctly heard its echo. Not in the mechanical repetition of that infectious barrel-organ waltz. But in the stronger, slower tempo of the opera's *leitmotiv*:

'*Di quell'amor, quell'amor ch'è palpito dell'universo, dell'universo intero . . .*'

A young man's soaring tenor was what she heard, carried on the night air; up through the window to his faithless Violetta:

'Love – our love is the impulse of creation, at the heart of all creation . . .'

"I never really believed in love between a man and woman, you see, before I met Lord Denton," she said aloud, as if he must have heard it too. "Like poor Violetta in the opera, Mr Brown. Or, if I'm honest, I suppose like every other hardened woman of the town. If I thought at all about it, I thought that kind of love a poetical invention to dignify men's lusts and women's vapourings; and to spice their marriage contracts with some hope of lasting entertainment. Love to me, Mr Brown, was something that our clients often thought of, occasionally put into words of sorts – and sometimes even shouted out aloud, poor things! In that last furlong of the race, you know, with all caution to the winds and the winning-post in sight, as it were. Then afterwards of course, they'd forget they even said it; as soon as we turned the fickle creatures loose again!"

Returning demurely to the sofa, the lady compressed her spreading skirts to sit as far as possible without engulfing her solicitor. "The fact is, Mr Brown, I was not in any way prepared for all this business of loving and of being loved, despite the way I chose at that time to make my living," she confessed with a degree of frankness that could only be disarming. "I should not otherwise, I'm sure, have contracted the contagion quite so badly."

* * *

At first she'd told herself it was his youth and touching eagerness that most affected her. So young and sapling-slim was he. And so very ardent in his attentions, now that he'd discovered in himself his natural powers. She had known so many men before him. (Only Madge, who kept the ledgers, knew how many.) Some of them as slim and fine of limb as David Stanville, and some as dark without a doubt. Quite a few as young, and many more as deedy and as eager. But none before him that Sary could recall, in whom all those charming qualities had been united. And none whose pleasure in her own attractions was a quarter so pronounced. It flattered her immensely to discover that for this young viscount, at this moment in his life, she embodied all the obvious attributes of femininity. And further, that he thought of them as hers and hers alone!

90

"Well I'll allow it does me good to hear you say so much, my dear. But come to that, I ain't so different to the other girls," she thought it only fair to tell him, when David marvelled for the hundredth time at her perfections. "I daresay we all like to see ourselves as special, don't we? But give or take a bit of colour and a pound or two of flesh, and the truth is we're put together much the same."

"Oh no, but you're not – not you. There's no one in the world like you!" he cried out with such conviction that she had to smile; and hide her smile and hold her tongue. And then to let him try to prove it to her by any means he could. Never dreaming – or not at least until too late – how much she really wanted to believe him. Eventually, she told herself, even this young man would weary of his passion and come to treat her as the others did. As a plaything to be toyed with, then forgotten. And if in the meantime it pleased her to encourage him in all his most immoderate demands, and see him work his backside off in her embrace – 'Well then, no harm done to anyone,' thought Sary hopefully.

No harm, that is, until she realized how far beyond all competition she favoured him. How much his admiration had added to her confidence and looks. And how afraid she was that he indeed *might* weary of her company! Quite hard enough for any girl of her profession to catch herself preferring one cull above the rest. But worse, much worse, to live in dread of losing his attention. For therein, if Madge Perrin was to be believed, lay the swiftest way to ruination. Love but another word for *subservience* in the hard real world that whores inhabited. To dangle from a man's fob-chain the usual means by which, in Madge's wide experience, a decent working trull would come to lose her hard-won independence.

For David the problem was simpler, at least to begin with. The problem simply of survival between his visits to Mrs Perrin's house in Brighton! Returning from his first trip thence, he'd accepted Charlie's sly congratulation, faced all his inquisitions, with the blend of polite enthusiasm and well-bred understatement he judged to be appropriate. Yes, perhaps he'd go again, he said, now that he had the direction. Tomorrow? Well yes, maybe. Concealing from his cousin, as he hoped, the hot empty feeling like a hunger in his belly, which urged him even then to turn his horse and ride straight back to Brighton – and to Sary Snudden. Three times on that first afternoon with her he'd entered by the port through which each man begins, affirms and replicates his life. Each time to come away with something different and more precious than before. Three times within two hours she'd willingly received him. And already he was obsessed with the need to discover further, more intense and longer-lasting pleasures with the girl he had chosen. *The impulse of creation*. The fruit of the Tree of Life once tasted in the company of Eve, as Genesis would have it, then never more to be ignored.

So David, naturally, returned to the stews of Brighton with his cousin at every opportunity. And when Charles eventually departed the eastern county in pursuance of his duty (and his Hampshire heiress), David declined absolutely to go with his parents up to London for their seasonal rituals of social and parliamentary observance – preferring to remain in Sussex through the early summer, within riding distance of the only thing in life just then that seemed to him in any way of consequence. A willing and a lovely girl, constantly available. The youthful dream of every natural man!

He needed her so badly, and so often. 'Horn colic', as Sary prosaically had termed it. Each day his first thoughts on waking were for her – his first intention every day to ride to Brighton; to be there first before the other nooners. To find her freshly bathed and scented, ready waiting . . . Needing desperately to go, yet forcing himself to delay the going for as long as he was able. Setting himself praiseworthy tasks that must postpone the visit for another day, and then another. Resolving instead to exercise his dogs and horses – to meet with workers, call on cottagers, see to necessary repairs. Inspecting woods and coverts with the keepers, in preparation for the wholesale slaughter of the pheasants that his father planned for autumn. Helping with the haying on several tenant farms. Visiting his neighbours on their estates of Glynde and Firle, which marched alongside those of Hadderton; and wasting hours away hob-nobbing with the bailiff or the fond old housekeeper, Mrs Graham. Perversely postponing the moment of fulfilment, to savour its anticipation and fuel his own desire. Sweating like a peasant in the dusty sunshine of the hayfields, or playing the young Lord at home. And yet performing all without attending very much to anything. His thoughts shot through with teasing images and partially recalled sensations. Until in the end his body threatened to betray him – erecting unexpectedly; damping breeches, and on more than one occasion inducing him to ride halfway to Brighton with a weather-cloak flung casually across what others would conceive, he hoped, to be his saddle pummel.

Only to discover when he reached her that he'd done his Sary, and himself, a grave injustice in imagining he loved her only for the circumstances Mary took account of, and Madge recorded in her ledger. For when the fevers of those waiting hours had been assuaged, he discovered that he valued her still more. He'd lie there smiling like a fool to see her cross the room to do the careful things she did behind the screen.

"For your sake and the sake of others, Davy Stanville," she assured him with mock sternness at such times. "Oh you can smile, boy, but this is for your sake as much as mine; and never you forget it!"

The strong rural vigour of her voice so much more pleasant to David's ear now than Octavia's refined pronunciations, or his mother's genteel St James's drawl; appealing to a streak of coarseness in his own male nature. A young girl still in her glowing skin, her supple movements and her glorious red-gold hair, in all else Sary had already ripened to maturity; in her figure and her attitudes – and in the splendid confidence with which she strode to her ablutions, rising on her toes to show her lover all the pagan splendours of her body. More graceful to his eye than anything he'd seen in drawing-room society. A big, rosy-painted Venus in the style of Titian or Correggio – that was Sary; blooming with health and strength and warmth of tone that was all of a piece with her affectionate and unsophisticated character. Her intense vitality, her frank acquaintance with the most basic facts of life, blew through him like a gust of fresh, invigorating air – to deny the stigma that attached to her profession. To sweep away the conventions of his own upbringing and set him free. Life with such a girl could never be anything but thrilling, David realized. And already the lurid décor of her bedroom at Mrs Perrin's seemed to him less tawdry than original and bold. The old bawd downstairs less predatory. The French prints in the corridor and on the dressing-screen more impudent than actually obscene.

With a nature more truly sensual than his cousin Charles's and with a greater capacity himself for affection, David's first experience of love engrossed him totally. The things his Sary lacked – breeding, taste and education – seemed unimportant to him now; the way she earned her living immaterial. He could not explain very satisfactorily to himself exactly what it was he felt. But like so many others in his situation, before and since, he was convinced that the emotions she released in him were stronger, deeper, more enduring than any man had felt since time began! He loved her. That was all that mattered now. And, when she told him where she'd seen him first, and how, David failed entirely to remember his amusement at the time. The audacious orange feather he recalled. But (curiously enough) not how he and Cousin Tavie had derided it.

"Fate," he told her adoringly; his hands repeating restless explorations they had made a score of times before. "It was fate, you may be sure, that carried you past Hadderton that day. And fate that brought me here and made me choose you out of all the others." As ready now as any other ardent lover to believe that his selection was ordained by destiny. Forgetting his own past rejections of such claims by others as foolish superstition. Life to David Stanville now become so simple. All he wanted, so he thought, the right to love and to be loved by Sary Snudden.

But nothing of course is ever quite so simple. Because universal life is constantly in motion – growing or decaying, expanding or contracting – but never static. Never standing still. Not for any one of the emotions that mankind persists in thinking of generically as 'love'. Especially not for those.

David, to illustrate this natural law, rode down to Brighton and to Sary one brilliant afternoon in June, as full of manly pride and inspiration as any questing knight in train for Camelot. The sun was high, the downs shimmering that day with a summer heat that smelt of sheep and dust and chalkland herbs. The sky a canopy of blue; the close-cropped turf beneath it swollen and seductive in its treeless nakedness – curved and creased and shadowed like a female body. Or so it seemed to young Lord Denton, riding to his Sussex Camelot. A man in love with the animating principle of love itself, he rode and strode and bounded up the steps to Mrs Perrin's door. To rap six times impatiently; the warm blood surging through his veins. His thoughts exclusively for Sary.

Only to be told the lady was engaged. The first time for David that another man had come before.

"I had you in the book, Sir, for today. But seeing as ye didn't come first thing, I 'ad to let another gentleman go up; for these days none of us can afford to turn away good trade. I'll lay she won't be many minutes though, your Lordship," Madge Perrin avowed, with a brisk complacency that conjured images in David's mind he'd rather not have entertained. "So come in and part your coat-tails over 'ere, Sir, why don't you? Come and sit along of Madge, and share my coffee 'til she's disengaged. I'll send the gel directly to fetch another cup."

Perforce to sit and listen to the woman ridicule the recent nuptials of two of the Regent's unmarried brothers, and the third that was to follow in July. 'Three right royal old *knights of the pit*,' Mrs Perrin called them, who recognized at last their duty to beget an English heir. And, while she spoke of it, the young man's own desire for like activity had succumbed to jealousy. He'd known of course that Sary dealt with other men. How could it be otherwise for one of her vocation? But always *afterwards*; that thought had been his consolation. In coming to her first each day, he'd always forced the other men to follow. First to her bed, he believed himself the first object too of her affections. The others clients only – of no more significance to Sary than she could be to them. Or so he'd liked to think. But on this hot June afternoon, forced now quite literally to await another's pleasure, David was unable any longer to pretend the things she had to do with all those others were not abhorrent to him. And when at last he heard his predecessor's loud proclaimed descent, and saw him in the downstairs hall conferring with his hostess over rates and payments, it was all that he could do to stop himself abusing the fellow to his face. (And never, David told himself, had he so loathed a face on sight – a big, florid, handsome visage with fleshy cheeks and heavy-lidded eyes – and self-contentment evident in every hateful feature!)

"Hang me, worth every penny too, dear lady, every one!" the client said to Mrs Perrin as the coins changed hands, turning slightly to include David in a comprehensive smile. 'And, ah yes, to be sure, young man,' that odious smile seemed to say, 'you and I, young fellow; I'd lay we know the value of a well-trained whore!'

And David had to turn away and lock his fists beneath his arms, to stop himself from using them to punch the man clean through the seventh circle of damnation!

Later, stamping up the stairs to Sary's room, savage with humiliation, he imagined all too vividly the tumbled sheets, the foreign and familiar smells that he must meet with there. And the faithless Sary Ann herself behind her dressing screen, expelling one man's leavings to accommodate the next! Unconsciously, he encountered all of it before in his imagination. And when Sary, smelling as she always smelt, of jessamine, flung wide her chamber door – to reveal a smooth bed and fresh linen, in appearance undisturbed, David reacted not to the reality but to his expectation of it.

"Now Davy, you've no ought to look at me like that," she said at once, without pretending to misunderstand the reason for his scowling countenance. "I sell my time and skills. I hire my body out to culls, to any cull who'll pay the proper price. You've known that from the first, Lord save ye – 'tis what you came yourself for, ain't it? So never think you've bought some special privilege that other men can't share, your Lordship." She crossed her own arms and faced his silence, glare for glare. "And never ever think you've purchased Sary Snudden for your private use," she added. "Because I'll tell ye now, you 'aven't. *I'm* not for sale!"

All of which was true enough. Sary never would sell duty or affection or any part of what she was herself, to any cull. But in her heart of course she knew already that she'd made a gift of her affection, and more besides, to this young man. To herself she owned that she was fairly caught, even if he had yet to realize it. For why else would she have relented so completely in the moment that she saw his anger melt into despair? A child he was, a jealous child. And was that what every male must needs become to win a woman's love? A child within the body of a man? The reason she must now relent and take his face into her hands? To kiss each crease of passion into smoothness. And then to kiss it back into its corrugations once again – and into passions of a more familiar nature.

Octavia Stanville was scarce fonder of summer heat than she was of winter frostiness. Because, for any young lady worthy of that epithet, either extreme must necessitate an inconvenient quality of clothing. In wintertime, bulky long-sleeved redingotes, pelisses, muffs and mufflers to swathe the figure and hamper natural *élégance*. And for summer, gloves, shawls and veils to cover every inch of skin and preserve my lady's pale complexion from the injurious sun. It was not thus for any idle pleasure that Octavia pinned her fichu, donned her gloves and bonnet and sought out her largest parasol to brave the tropic wastes of Hadderton one afternoon that August; whatever she herself maintained.

"Such a very warm day," she'd murmured to the Countess after luncheon. "I think presently I'll take a little stroll out in the park, if you can spare me, Ma'am. I vow it seems a shame to stay indoors all afternoon."

"My dear, how very energetic of you," replied the other with more civility than interest. Alethea Stanville, drowsing on a *chaise* within her dark and stuffy upstairs drawing-room, could hardly imagine why anyone should want to set foot to the carpet, leave alone the sunbaked turf outside. Since her own girlhood, she herself had suffered monthly from pains and *megrims* and an excessive loss of blood. And, being assured by others whilst confined to bed or couch, that such weakness was proof only of her femininity and genteel breeding, had conceived a preference for the supine posture over any other. In consequence, she never rode or hunted, and only ever walked outside on terraces and garden lawns.

Not that anything Octavia might do or think could greatly concern her hostess at the present time, in any case. She'd done her duty by the girl in London, and handsomely. No one could fault her as a relative for the time and energy she had expended on her husband's unprepossessing female cousin – the quietude she'd sacrificed to sponsor Octavia into the Polite World. And when the summer recess had finally permitted them to leave the *cits* to their stinking Thames, and to escape to the fresher air and slower pace of Sussex, she felt at once absolved of all responsibility for the girl. Unlike her husband, she had failed to note his little cousin's penchant for their son; and lacked the imagination to see her as any kind of threat to David's splendid future. So long as she did nothing to upset the slow and peaceful pace of Hadderton routine, therefore, as far as Lady Southbourne was concerned, it hardly signified what Octavia chose to do for afternoon amusement.

"And as for sparing you," she added unexpectedly (and following a lengthy pause in which she'd somehow lost the thread of what was said, in the effort of stirring the air around her with her fan of painted chicken skin – and then woken suddenly to rediscover it), "I beg you will do entirely as you please, my dear. I'm sure there's nothing I can think of that I need, until 'tis time to ring the bell for tea." She bestowed a nerveless smile. "Who knows but that I may even perhaps contrive to sleep a little while you're gone."

Octavia left her snoring lustily, her false fringe jerked awry, and hurried off herself to find her outdoor clothes. She had no means of knowing if David would return to the house before she must herself, to spare his mother all the obvious inconvenience of rising from her couch to ring the tea-bell. Nor could she tell for sure if he would engage to ride home by the main west gate. Or through the village and his father's stablings. Or even by the home farm track across the park. She could only act on likelihoods; and chose in consequence the long white ribbon of the carriage drive for her perambulation. A road that wound down through the trees to the keeper's cottage and the pair of gatepost wyverns which had always so attracted her. The sun was hot still, the sky a pale exhausted blue, with scarce a breath of wind to stir the South-bourne standard up above the roofs. The park stretched out before the house as bleached and brittle as a pampas. In pools of shade beneath the chestnuts, the dappled fallow deer flicked flies from tails and ears with minimal exertion. From plumes of fireweed and from seeding thistles in the grass, down drifted lazily. Soft-throated ring-doves soothed the shrilling crickets. And in all the sultry landscape, only Octavia in the roadway moved briskly or with any sense of purpose.

In the several days which now had passed since she'd accompanied the Southbournes down from London, their son and heir had yet to spend one uninterrupted hour with his cousin; had failed utterly to seek her company or to share with her a single private conversation. So restless and distracted was he now become, and so regularly absent. An awkwardness between them that Octavia had resolved to set to rights. (For she was not, and never had been, a person to abandon a project she'd decided on. This project least of all.) Through all the busy overcrowded weeks she had resided with the Southbournes at their mansion of St James's, Octavia constantly looked forward to the day when she and David might compare their views of town society and celebrate her belated entrée to its ranks. His absence from the London scene this year the main disappointment of her first official season. Because it was David, naturally, and the position she proposed to occupy one day at David's side at board and in bed that inspired Octavia to polish up her manners and complete her urban education. Still child enough to be intrigued, excited even, by the soirées, concerts, routs and assemblies to which his mother grudgingly exposed her; she found that she could also distinguish very well between true worth and hollow ostentation when she met with it. Her own taste was in no special need of reformation. Thus she'd disapproved of Corinthian gentlemen who rouged and corseted and gossiped through the sermons at the Chapel Royal, St James's. She had little opinion of young ladies who revealed financial and other portions (most commonly of their upper anatomy), only to secure attentive partners to stand up with them for the waltz; and even less of hostesses who measured worth in yards of satin or brocaded silk, and ranked their guests according to their incomes and investments. She saw them as they were, the *haut ton* of metropolitan society – as spoiled and unattractive. From May until July, she conversed and danced and sipped at iced champagne in London. She smiled at gentlemen until her face ached with the effort. But she submitted only for her own advancement and instruction; watching and noting, coolly taking out of every situation the things she needed as a countess-in-the-making.

Which was all very fine in itself. But where was David now to justify her bringing out? Where was David to approve the refinements of conduct and presentation that she'd borrowed from the rich, bare-bosomed darlings of fashionable St James's? Or to laugh at her indictment of them for their many follies? With but the inside of a week to go before she must return to Redford to pay her respects to Charles's new intended wife, where, oh where, was David?

Octavia had ridden down the carriage drive a day or two before, and knew precisely where she'd choose to intercept her cousin if he passed this way. In a place where the roadway dipped to bridge the sluggish stream that fed the ornamental lake, an old redundant beech tree had been felled and cleared. To leave its stump – or 'stub', as the Sussex yokels called it – shaded by the other trees, yet in clear view of the drive; to make a most convenient seat for weary promenaders. Octavia furled her parasol, brushed away some sawdust from the beech-stub, and removed her kashmere shawl to fold it as a makeshift cushion – disposing her skirts neatly round her ankles as she sat. She consulted the little watch that depended from her waistband. She'd give him the half of one whole hour, she decided. And half an hour tomorrow. And the same the next day, if needs must.

A dozen yards away beside the stream a new sapling had been planted, protected by an upright wooden cradle from the deer and browsing cattle. A cosseted young growth to carry forward life on the estate in all its elegant perfection. 'Like me in some way,' thought Octavia ruefully, resisting the impulse even then to peel off her gloves and push back her stuffy veil. For some twenty minutes she remained there seated on the stub, watching a russet squirrel searching vainly for some sustenance amongst the fallen beech leaves. A wispy, ratlike creature in its time of summer fast, the hungry rodent jerked and rustled through the litter in quest of last year's beech masts; sitting up to weigh their empty cases in its paws and to fix its watcher with a black and brilliant stare.

The squirrel heard him long before the girl, and was already whisked aloft to safety before the sound of hooves on flint was clearly audible. He rode hatless, in shirt and riding breeches only – with coat, cravat and waistcoat held carelessly across the horse's withers. A romantic hero from between the covers of the kind of library novel she abhorred; and of an appearance which any but Lord Byron must distain as rustic. Not but what it suited him withal, Octavia thought – stepping forward a pace, two paces. First to reveal her presence, and then with cool deliberation to place herself directly in the horseman's path.

Chapter Ten

David's initial reaction to his cousin's dramatic appearance in the roadway fell some way short of her intention. For to say the truth, his heart descended swiftly bootwards at the prospect of a confrontation. And sharply reining in his horse, he waved and forced a friendly smile of greeting, while cudgelling his brain for some half-convincing answer to the question she was bound, he knew, to put to him.

"*Io te saluto!*" She hailed him in the Latin that they used to fox the servants, when as children they had planned some devilment. "But, Cousin, what a pleasing chance. And where do you ride in from, Sir, in such romantic disrepair?" Her features shadowed, almost hidden by the fall of fine dark lace she'd draped across her bonnet. An easy, friendly greeting. Yet something in her voice and her uncompromising stance that sounded the alarm.

"Hello, Tavie." His own smile his best, his only weapon still against her dark-veiled stare. "I've just been down to watch the faggers work at Beddingham. Best wheat of any yet this year – which isn't saying much of course. And then they wanted help at Little Dene; the cows got in amongst the shocks this morning after milking, you never saw such . . ."

"It really isn't any use, *mon cher*," she interrupted pleasantly. "I'm too well acquainted with your character, David, to be so easily deceived, you know. I always have been."

So very proper and controlled. Always the young lady first these days, before the girl that he'd grown up with. "Well then, perhaps you'll tell me what I have been doing, if you know so much," he said abruptly, taking refuge in an angry scowl.

"My dear brother confided to a servant when last he was at Hadderton, that you are smitten with some common Cyprian down in Brighton, and cannot keep away from her. And I gather half the household, and your father too, seem all too eager to believe it of you."

"Oh, for God's sake, Tavie! Manage your own concerns, why don't you – and leave me to manage mine!" Anger again, to cover his embarrassment. He turned away, and would have left her then, had not his cousin put out a slim hand to possess herself of his bridle.

"Myself, I would not credit such a tale," she continued coolly, "knowing the delight my brother has always taken in making mischief. And even if it were the truth . . ." She hesitated briefly. "David, even if it were the truth, it would not weigh with me. The generality of men – unmarried men, I mean – must have adventures of that kind, it seems. 'Tis only to be allowed. And I have it in mind to mention that I said something of the sort to you once, right here in the park. Do you recall it? I said I was surprised you had so little inclination then to hunt away from Hadderton."

In fact David had no recollection of the conversation. And, ignorant of the effort such a speech had cost Octavia, merely stared at her and thought of how obliquely women of her class and type approached the topics that concerned them. How prosy, how inferior to his Sary's bold and honest mode of speaking.

"So don't misunderstand me, Cousin," said Octavia, as if she'd read his mind. " 'Tis not the company you choose to keep, in Brighton or elsewhere, that signifies. It is the way you've changed yourself this summer that concerns me." She raised her head a little, and the light caught her eyes beneath the veil – searching his own face, David divined, for something that he knew she would not find there. "We used to have so much to say to one another. We were such friends," she said. "But recently I've come to think you hardly even like me."

A silence fell between them. He knew of course what she was driving at. To be sure he'd known for years what Octavia was about; and had even thought he might agree to marry her some day – the thing she sought – if only to escape a less agreeable alliance with the daughter of some horse-faced crony of his mother's.

"What confounded moonshine, Tavie," he said at last,

ungraciously. "Why naturally I like you fine. We're cousins aren't we?" An observation hardly likely in itself to prove much consolation to the lady.

But oh, if only it could be his lovely Sarah Ann who'd stand him to deliverance here in the road at Hadderton, thought David. To hold his horse and demand from him a place within his life! "And now, if you will excuse me, Ma'am," he concluded gruffly.

But she would not. The slender hand detained him still. "No Sir, whatever your inclination, I'll not believe that as a gentleman you'd leave me here to walk back in this heat alone and unescorted," she said with a mildness that he knew to be deceptive. Within it the echo of a childhood dare that he could not in any wise ignore.

"No, damn you, Tavie. I don't suppose you could!" His Lordship spoke before he thought. And then, ashamed at his ill manners, became still more defiant. "So take the horse then, I don't care," he told her ungallantly; and springing down, strode off at once across the park. Leaving his rejected cousin to manage the beast as best she might, and without the facility of mounting-block or lady's saddle to assist her.

It was not an episode that David cared to call to mind in after years. And even at the time, the sight of his cousin trotting past him up the carriage drive in perfect order and control did little to improve his own opinion of his conduct in the matter. He'd behaved abominably. There was no escaping that. Yet, living on the edge of his emotions as he had that summer, with thoughts of Sary and her clients ever in his mind, he hardly could have acted otherwise.

Heav'n has no rage like love to hatred turn'd. So said the poet, *Nor Hell a fury like a woman scorn'd.* And the fact that Octavia declined to keep that vulgar rule, treating David with all her usual complaisance and civility through her remaining days at Hadderton, tended only to make things worse between then. So, when in October the Southbournes were invited to attend a ball at Sir Terence Wilkins' Hampshire country seat of Monkwood, to celebrate the betrothal of his second daughter Frances to their cousin Captain Charlie Stanville, David begged again to be excluded. The foregathering at Octavia's home near Midhurst, which such a journey must entail, was not by him to be considered.

His parents could offer whatever excuses they pleased on his behalf – invent a riding mishap or a bout of autumn influenza. He simply would not go, he told them bluntly, and that was that!

"Aye, and I smoke the reason, damned if I don't! You're fixing to reserve the best shooting for yourself, ye crafty rogue," declared his father, in high delight at this new evidence of manly independence in David's unfathomable character. "And like as not install that piece of fancy *muslin* in your bed whilst we're abroad, I'll warrant! I've got your measure now, Sir – as she has too I wouldn't doubt – you randy young buck-fitch!"

An idea, once embraced, which truth to tell had found more ready favour with the buck-fitch aforesaid than with the fancy muslin of his choice.

"Never think that I'm not honoured to be asked, my dear," said Sary when he broached it to her. "But for gracious sake, I can't just go jauntering off to leave my clientele for days together whenever the fancy takes me. Now can I? I'd 'ave to lose good custom – and what would Mother Perrin 'ave to say to such a random scheme, I'd like to know?"

David smiled triumphantly. "Well, as to that, I have already spoken to the lady so as not to discommode her," he said, "and we've settled it between us. I told Mrs Perrin that I'd be with you, at all events, for most of the time my parents are away. And she agrees with me that we may just as well be there as here in Brighton. In fact she thinks it better that we should be out of sight at Hadderton – for the sake of the other girls, you know, and for the gentlemen."

"Oh, does she now?"

"Provided, naturally, we could agree a rate that she thought fair for a sennight of your time."

"And did you do that, Davy?"

"Well yes, we did . . ." He faltered slightly at the look she was awarding him. "But only think, my dearest Sary – seven whole days and nights together to do exactly as we please!"

"And was the rate that you and that old pandar settled on a fair one? Did I come cheap then, Davy? Or did ye think me dear for seven days of concentrated plowtering?"

"Oh well, now look here, Sary, that's all beside the point . . ."

104

"No, *you* look!" she shouted, hot with indignation. "You look, and try if you can see for once beyond the end of your own selfish strunt! You've settled on a rate for me, 'ave you, for seven days and nights of Sary Snudden? And how about your Lordship's butler and 'is footmen, might I ask? Are they to be included in the service? Or 'ave you and Madge agreed a special rate for servants?"

He flushed deep red at that. But Sary had already gone too far to spare him the rest of it. "I've told you once, and now I'm telling you again," she said. "I'm not an object to be bought and sold for private use on someone else's say-so, however much you're offering. It ain't for you to fix on what I'll do, or if I'll wear the willow or I won't. And it ain't for Madge and 'er account books, neither! *I say*, do you understand? And what I'm saying is that I'll stop pissing before I'll let myself be auctioned like a painting or a statue to decorate your Lordship's stately home – or paraded before your father's high-nosed flunkies as your private little piece of teazle! No, Davy Stanville, I'll not drive out with you to see your precious 'Adderton, nohows. Got that, 'ave ye? No, not for all the money in the blessed Bank of England!"

"So, why exactly did you come?" he tentatively enquired of her the next afternoon following, nodding to the gate-boy, Fielder, as they swept between the heraldic pillars of the west entrance and proceeded up the carriage drive.

She laughed and blew a friendly backward kiss in the direction of the startled servant. "Why, Sir, I came to please myself – what else?" she said. Which was at least a version of the truth. For, in pleasing David, Sary had to please herself; that much she already understood. Pride, she now discovered, but such a paltry inconsiderable thing to sacrifice for love. And danger, if she was honest, the very salt and seasoning of their relationship. She'd faced the truth of his ascendancy as squarely as she faced all other truths, and knew if he insisted she would go. (Besides which, from the day of her first glimpse of the outer fringes of the park at Hadderton from her perch atop Joe Farren's cart, she'd simply itched to survey all that lay beyond them!)

Following the fashion set by the Regent for gentlemen to drive themselves, David handled the ribbons of his own curricle, with a pair of his father's match-bays harnessed in the bar and now spanking at a brisk sling trot along the metalled drive. On either side and all about them, the park rolled out its splendours for Sary's admiration. Long vistas in the pristine light through trees of every noble type and autumn hue. Great stands of bronzy beech. Golden chestnuts, already shedding leaves and fruit; and ash trees laden with the pale green bunches of their 'keys'.

"Just like a picture!" she exclaimed; and then took in a breath as through the trees she caught her first sight of the house ahead of them. "Geemeny, 'tis enormous. A palace, nothing less!" Then, as they gained the higher ground, and the parkside frontage of the building emerged in all its majesty, she turned to deal David a hearty buffet with her muff. "You rogue, you never told me 'twas anything like this! Oh Davy I justabout *adore* it!" And since she had no other means of embracing his park, or his trees, or the great façade of flint and stone that loomed before her, she flung her arms around the heir to it himself and hugged him to her more than ample bosom.

"The old house is entirely built of chalk blocks from the quarry at Bopeep," he informed her a little later, with a self-conscious glance behind him at the groom. "But the subsequent dressings and the lintels on these fronts were brought across from Caen in Normandy." Trying so very hard to sound casual, to cloak his swelling pride with the offhand manner of a guide; and, as far as Sary was concerned, failing so delightfully in both. In another minute they passed beneath a pedimented archway, clad in vivid scarlet creeper and surmounted by the armorial bearings of the Stanvilles – to wheel in pretty style around an inner court and come to rest beside an open doorway.

"So here we are then," said David, tossing the reins to the groom already at the horses' heads, and leaping out to let down the steps himself for Sary. "Welcome to Hadderton!" And without waiting for the man to unstrap the boxes, without a word or glance for the footman in powder and knee-breeches who stood within the portico, he very promptly handed her inside.

And something in the lackey's wooden, disapproving stare made Sary lift her chin and clack her heels across the cold stone entrance hall of his ancestral home. And tell herself how glad she was that she had worn her best, most cheerful rig-out for the visit.

Delighted that peacetime had now finally extinguished English pastels in a flood of brighter Continental shades – she'd had the dress made up of turquoise satin, cut to ankle-length and part-covered by a vandyked overslip in sea-green gauze; with an emerald spencer jacket frogged *à la Hussar* in gold, and braided lavishly upon the sleeves. For contrast there were half-boots of buttercup jean, and a huge feather muff of yellow marabou. And to complete the ensemble, the tallest chimney-bonnet she could find, covered with emerald velvet and topped with another riotous explosion of blue and yellow feathers.

'Smart as a new-scraped carrot, all in all! And look down their noses as they will, I fancy 'is servants won't forget *this* little start of 'is Lordship's for a week or two!' she predicted to herself with satisfaction, switching her gorgeous sea-green rump as she progressed, for the benefit of the staring footmen.

The entrance hallway was vast and gloomily impressive, with its high beamed roof, its escutcheons, tapestries and pole-arms on the walls. "It was the old Tudor hall," said David, raising his voice to carry through the void. "Built by Sir William Stanville in the last King Henry's reign. And quite impossible to warm effectively," he added, "even though we burn a fire here for eight months of the year. Is that not so, Tillotson?"

The august personage waiting for them by the double-doorway at the far end of the chamber, bowed with a dignity that not even the shock of Sary's entrance through the hallowed portals could ruffle. "Indeed, Lord David; and I venture to say there'd be damp as well without the braziers." And as he raised his head, Tillotson's eyes alighted for a moment of frosty scrutiny on his distasteful guest. Of thoroughly ignoble parentage himself, the Hadderton butler despised that defect in others above all else.

"This is my friend, Miss Snudden, as you may have gathered, Tillotson," said David firmly. "Perhaps you would arrange for Mrs Graham to take her upstairs before we go in to luncheon?"

"She is already awaiting the young lady in the staircase hall, Lord David." The butler bowed again, excluding Sary so pointedly from the civility, that she immediately felt bound to take a hand herself in the exchange.

"Good afternoon, Tillotson," she sang out loudly for the benefit of the footman and the second footman with her band-boxes and cloak-bag in the portico. "I declare I'm very pleased to meet with you as well!" Then, pushing past him in the grandest manner through the double-doors, she bore down determinedly upon the waiting housekeeper with outstretched hand and ready smile. "Mrs Graham, I collect? And a good afternoon to you too, Ma'am!" And, although that stoutly aproned individual was no more willing than the snobbish butler to encourage Lord David in his plan to entertain at Hadderton a young woman who at best must be a milliner or opera dancer (and in likelihood was something worse than either); so disconcerted was she by the frankness of the girl's approach, that before she knew it, Mrs Graham had taken the proffered hand and smiled back at the good-natured carmine smile. A lapse that made it impossible to lead her upstairs then in the way of censorious silence that she'd first intended.

Sary in the meantime was greatly taken by the old oak stair itself, with its broad and easy flights and twisted 'barley-sugar' balusters. "And whatever is the purpose," she demanded as it closed behind her, "of this funny little gateway 'arfway up?"

"Heavens save you – why, to prevent his Lordship's dogs from reaching to the upper floors," disclosed the housekeeper, with a reproachful look for young Lord David in the hall below. Quite shocked that he'd associate with anyone so ignorant of what was usual. "Lord only knows what havoc those creatures would wreck amongst my Lady's porcelain if they were able!

"And if you ask for my opinion," ventured Mrs Graham, who clearly felt the house to be her own, "we'd be better suited with a nice white marble flight and a painted ironwork balustrade. Like Lord Gage has up at Firle. The devil's own work it is, I can tell you, to dust and polish all this Jacobean nonsense." She indicated the elaborate finials of snarling lions and smirking cherubs which crowned the newel posts. "As you'd soon enough discover for yourself, Miss," she added severely, "if you had the charge of it." (A remark, as Sary realized all too well, the housekeeper would never have thought it proper to deliver to a lady.)

Downstairs again, divested of her spencer, gloves and bonnet, she met up with David in the lofty dining saloon. To share a cold collation with him beneath the even colder eyes of the butler, a brace of footmen, and half a dozen Stanville portraits round the walls. A banquet of a meal such as two people could hardly be expected to consume within a week; and laid out on a table of such impressive length, that Sary at one end had to shout continually across twelve feet of linen cloth to David at the other, only to feel sure of being heard. Afterwards he'd promised a post-prandial tour around the house. A programme which, in the event, nicely filled out the five hours or so that they must wait before another gargantuan meal was set before them.

Directly across the staircase hall from the dining-room were the doors of the White Saloon. "Built on by Robert Adam fifty years ago," said David conscientiously, opening up the room for his visitor's inspection. "And once sat in by the Regent when he was Prince of Wales for the best part of *one whole hour*," he added from behind her turquoise shoulder. "As my mother, Lady Southbourne, would doubtless wish to impress on you if she were in my shoes. And, what's more, His Royal Highness is in possession of a standing invitation to take Hadderton in his way whenever he is passing by. (She tells that to all our guests and visitors at their first glimpse of this sacred chamber.) Although of course he never will. I'faith, he only came here in the first place to see a match-pair of my father's that he had a mind to buy."

"Oh, but Davy, 'tis *tremenjous*!" she cried out in rapture. "Just like the Castle Inn Assembly Rooms!" And innocent of the silent apology which David offered to the great Adam's affronted Scottish shade, as in she ran to see it all the better. 'White' the saloon might once have been in its Palladian heyday. But long since then it had been embellished with as much gilt and brilliant decoration as even Sary could desire. Gold on the Ionic capitals of its pillars, gold leaf by the ream on its door-cases and window reveals, and on every arm and leg of furniture within. Festoon curtains of blue and gold brocade. Red and green-streaked commodes of porphyry and marble. Sofas and chair-seats of bright Italian silk. And a carpet which repeated the flower-baskets and twining garlands of the design upon the plaster ceiling, with the addition only of chromatic colour.

"My parents are most anxious to be smart, yet have no idea of simple modern elegance. All show and very little style or harmony, I fear. They think the more you have of everything, the better it must be," declared the young Lord Denton (who could afford to scorn such excesses).

But Sary, who entirely shared the Southbourne's ostentatious tendencies, was just then rapt in admiration for a marvellously showy Continental timepiece, set into a little gilded alcove of its own above the mantelshelf. "T-e-m-p-u-s f-u-g-i-t", she laboriously spelled out across his commentary. "Now stop that flummery will ye, Davy, and tell me what this means in plain King's English."

It was the same elsewhere – in every other passage, vestibule and chamber of the house. With David apologizing constantly for a sumptuous style of ornament which Sary, who'd refined her own taste amidst the bold theatrical furnishings of a brothel, could not but think magnificent beyond compare. From room to silent room they passed, with gold leaf gleaming everywhere – with enormous crystal chandeliers reflecting fractured sunlight onto painted walls and polished marble statues and the glass casings of more precious treasures still. And however hard he strove to diminish or to qualify the splendour and profusion that was Hadderton – it was clear to Sary, watching him, that David took huge pride in it; that he was himself a part of what it stood for, whether he confessed to it or no. In the great picture-gallery he insisted on releasing blinds already drawn against a westering sun, to illuminate an endless row of brass wall-studs and crimson cords, and the portraits they supported in their gilt-encrusted frames. To recount for her the histories of his forbears – of the handsome Sir Richard Stanville, whose neat-trimmed beard and tight white hose had caught the roving eye of Good Queen Bess and earned for him, eventually, an Earldom. Of the Fourth Earl, Lord Robert – one of an exclusive score or so of noblemen who'd dared to bed King Charles's mistress, Barbara Palmer. And of the Sixth, Lord William Ainslie Stanville, who'd adorned his house with art treasures from the *marchand-merciers* of Paris and of Italy.

"I think I may say that I know more about the pictures in this house than Tillotson does, or even Mrs Graham," he boasted proudly. "And certainly a great deal more than my father, or my poor Mamma, who can't name above half between the pair of them!"

No longer to Sary the greenly nervous gosling that devil, Charlie Stanville, had brought to Mrs Perrin's for instruction, David was a different person here – so confident and proprietorial did he appear. The Young Lord, every inch! And so keen, moreover, to

110

introduce her to his home and ancestors and all the rich possessions they'd amassed, that he actually endured the entire five hours of their internal tour, from luncheon through to dinnertime, without one solitary attempt to reintroduce to her that part of his anatomy with which, perforce, she'd lately become so familiar. In her experience of Viscount Denton, a record in itself!

If Sary was so much impressed by this new view of David in the splendid setting of his country home, he in his turn was equally enchanted by her response to it. From the first moment that he'd seen her swagger through the entrance hall in her yellow boots and shimmering kingfisher-coloured gown, he knew how right he was to bring her here to Hadderton. How right to fling together the two parts of his life which seemed most disparate, and to fashion for himself a brand new future from their unlikely meeting. That his father's servants were affronted by the appearance of a woman of the town at Hadderton, there was no room to doubt. But that, decided David, was because they'd grown so old and stuffy – like the house itself. They reacted only to her paint and fancy mode of dressing, entirely failing to appreciate, as he did, what fresh new energies and inspirations a character like hers must bring into their trammelled world. They saw her swinging country gait, her brilliant colours flash from room to room. They heard her comments and her laughter, her cries of unaristocratic admiration and surprise. How could they not? Yet somehow they had failed to see, as David did, how much this great house of theirs and Sary Snudden could have to gain from one another.

To Hadderton she brought her fresh outspoken attitudes. To reveal it to them all in new and unexpected lights. The house itself, its state-rooms, its gardens and its park, she proclaimed more wonderful than anything she'd ever seen – including Prinny's still unfinished Royal Pavilion on the Steine. The marble, gildings, crystal, silk and damask, that David found oppressive, were in Sary's eyes the verriest apogée of decorative art! The pictures, on the other hand, failed entirely to engage her. (Except in the likeness of the Second Earl to David. Or in the certainty that Lady Susannah's eyebrows in the Lely portrait were made of mouseskin and stuck on with glue.) She thought the priceless Zuccarelli landscapes a deal too dark and gloomy. She opened up a case to try on a riding-glove that no one else had dared to touch, except to dust, for perhaps a century or more. Queen Henrietta's hands, she pointed out, were quite amazing small and thin. The famous lock of Barbara Palmer's famous dark red hair was hennaed for a fact, she said – as anyone with half an eye could see. And when in the library David reverentially displayed for her the original wax *maquette* for the Pantheon Hercules; a masterpiece, he told her, which the sculptor Rysbrack had presented to the Seventh Earl while working for him on a marble chimneypiece, she threw back her tawny head to roar with hearty laughter.

"I wouldn't know how far it may be like this 'Erculis of yours when he's at 'ome, duck. But 'tis very like a man, I'll give you that," she granted, pointing to the corrugated belly, crossed thighs and bulging femoris muscles of the naked statuette. "Sucked in 'ere and pushed out there to show 'is tackle up to best advantage. A goat-house cully to the very life! I see 'is like by dozens every week, you take my word for it."

But then again, if Sary had repainted Hadderton before the eyes of all its household in the raw colours of her own uneducated reactions, the old house had something of its own to convey to her, when she at last had done with touring it. While David sat with her at supper in the dining saloon, she watched through the tall window at his back as the moon rose up to shed its yellow tarnish in the trees, and to flood the park with silver.

"We take our guests out driving sometimes after supper at this time of year, when the moon's this full and bright," he told her. "Even Mamma's been known to recommend the expedition."

She turned her stare on him. "You never? Go away! Out driving in the moonlight, just for the idle pleasure of it?" To a girl used to reckoning the cost of working hours, the idea of calling out the horses, grooms and coachmen on such a whim had seemed amazingly extravagant.

He laughed at her surprise. "But of course. Why else but for the pleasure of the thing? We drive across the stubble of the harvest fields – or high up onto the downs at Firle to see the landscape all lit up below. And for the matter of that, my love, we could have the curricle sent round right now if you would like it. Why not, Sary? You only have to say the word."

But Sary for the while had had enough of new experience. And she besought him only to pinch out the candles when the meal was cleared, and join her at the window that gave onto the terrace walk, and the deerpark out beyond it. She really hadn't understood at all what David meant by *elegance* and *harmony* when he applied such terms to indoor furnishings. But the perfection of this moonlight shone through the gay disorder of her own ideas on life, to reveal a rich man's concept of existence she dimly grasped to be beyond her own horizons. A world in which a man could order grown trees moved and lakes dug out without ever having to reckon up the cost. To act the god and have an artificial landscape made only to improve the prospect from his window! A strange and very perfect place where her David was master, or some day would be. But where she could never be the mistress. Her function here scarce different to his curricle's, when all was said. She was a means of transport, that was all; to help to bear his Lordship on his flights of fancy in the silvery moonlit landscape – or in his four-post bed. And then to be sent back to the coach-house, to the stable or the brothel where she naturally belonged. To be used again, and by another man, for his convenience.

David, standing by her in the window, had never known her so quiescent or abstracted. Nor to look so lovely. Her painted features, blanched in the moonlight and softened by the sadness of her mood, appeared to him more delicate and sensitive than in reality they were. He thought he knew what she was thinking. Her melancholy gaze he mistook for a new perception of the things he saw when he looked out across the shining stillness of the park. She understood his love for Hadderton, that much was clear. For had she not declared as much a hundred times that afternoon? He fancied that she felt about the place as he did, rejoiced with him in all it represented. And surely that appreciation, and her own obvious strength of character, were all his Sary needed – he more than half believed it – to become in time a more than worthy mistress of both man and house?

Because, from that first evening of her visit to his Hadderton estate, David Stanville was determined that Ma Perrin's youngest and most charming whore would one day join her fate to his within the marriage bond. He arranged it neatly in his own mind to suit his

113

own most earnest wish. No future plan of life he could envisage now that did not include his Sary at his side. No compromise now possible. No hope of felicity without her. So simple and so natural an arrival at the decision and inspiration that would determine all his future life that David at the time had barely felt its magnitude.

Chapter Eleven

For more than a twelvemonth Sary gallantly stood out against every argument and exhortation David Stanville could advance for his preposterous plan of marriage. Although not against his person, naturally. For that she continued to receive in Brighton, and with such enthusiastic regularity that Mrs Perrin – for all her cautions against personal attachments – was moved to solemnize the union within her ledgers by the opening in Lord Denton's name of a fortnightly account.

The first inkling Sary had of David's ultimate intention had come one day towards the end of her illicit week at Hadderton, in that October of '18. As on every other day that week, they'd risen late. And, inspired by a mild and sunny autumn morning, decided to take their breakfast *al fresco* on the sloping lawn behind the house – spreading a carriage rug upon the grass, and inducing a footman and a serving maid to labour up to them with trays of hot chocolate and buttered eggs and sliced York ham. A piece of spoilt-child wickedness that well deserved the scowl the overladen maid bestowed on Sary when she thought his Lordship wasn't looking. (And Sary, in little doubt of it herself, had scowled back cheerfully without a touch of rancour.)

"Nancy!" Both girls had started at the sudden loudness of his Lordship's voice. "How dare you show such impudence towards Miss Snudden. Apologize at once!"

"Oh, Lord David – I'm sorry your Lordship, I'm sure I didn't mean . . ." The little maid flushed crimson in her embarrassment. But David, uncharitably, refused to spare her.

"God above, not to *me*, you imbecile!" he shouted in a passion.

115

"Apologize this minute to the young lady, and hope to heaven she'll be good enough to let you stay in my employ. For I warn you, girl – and you can tell the other servants this from me – one word, one look of disrespect toward Miss Snudden, and you can pack your bags and leave, that's all! I hope I'm understood?"

A side of David, as employer, that Sary had never seen before. And when the girl blushed deeper still, and shed a tear, and stuttered her atonement, he too it seemed had felt the need to offer an apology.

"Oh Davy, leave it be for lumley's sake," she begged him; anxious only to enjoy her day of stolen luxury, and careless of the price. "You know you'll never make 'em treat a bang-tail like a lady, however you may wish it. And come to that, I wouldn't think that your Mamma would be best pleased to lose a serving maid in such a cause. Now would she, dear? So let's us just forget it, eh – and do the proper justice to this breakfast 'ere."

"No, Sary, 'tis not to be allowed. I simply will not have it." David became decisive and a little pompous. "Depend upon it, one way or another I intend to make them treat you with the respect that you deserve."

"Oh, do ye now? And why is that then? What, Sir, and will I be calling in so often then at 'Adderton, to take tea, Sir, with my Lord and Ladyship when they come home to roost?" She poured out his chocolate for him from the silver jug the maid had brought, and handed it across, her black-drawn brows raised up in query. "Is that 'ow you plan to bring us all together then, my Lord? Across the tea-board in the White Saloon?"

But he'd refused to catch the twinkle in her eye, staring out across the park instead. And building for her there, she already guessed at it, a future which he had no right to offer nor means to accomplish for her. "They will respect you as their superior," he obstinately repeated, " 'tis all I'll say for now. They *will*, I am convinced, for my sake and for Hadderton." It was all he had said too on that occasion. But later, when Sary resumed her duties in the salons and steddles of Mother Perrin's nugging-house in Brighton – and the green-eyed monster of his jealousies inevitably emerged once more to plague their hours together – David left her in little further doubt as to the magnitude and folly of his intention. "You have no need to so demean yourself – to torture me like

116

this," he cried out to her one day in his frustration. "No, Sary, not when you could be my wife!"

"Your wife? Don't make me laugh," she'd told him then without the flicker of a smile. "Well, you can get shut of that notion for a start, Sir."

The thing, now said, must needs be faced with all the strength and honesty her mother had bequeathed her. "Oh, Davy, this is fool's work," she added in a somewhat gentler tone of voice. "You might as soon put a poultice on a wooden leg, I'll tell you, as consider such a thing."

"Sarah, Sary, I said my *wife*; and that is exactly what I meant. For you to marry me and come to Hadderton – one day to be its mistress!"

And bless the boy, so privileged by life that he still thought wanting was three-quarter way to getting. So mortal clever and well educated that he couldn't see the obvious! "The heir to all the 'Adderton estate, and that great palace of a house? A Viscount and a Lord – to choose 'is Lady from amongst the Brighton stews? A painted lady?" she enquired. "A fine thing that'd be! Why, Lord Southbourne would rather die than see you coupled with a painted whore, Davy, you know 'e would!"

"On the contrary, I am persuaded my father knows as well as I that gentlewomen may just as well be trained to their estate as born to it. My Ladies Barrymore and Berkeley, for example, were both of humble stock. And some think them greater ladies altogether for the necessity of rising to their rank."

"And others think that swallows spend their winters under water in the mud," retorted Sary.

"Then the Earl of Derby wed an actress, and Lord Devon chose a pump girl – Fanny Clack from the Angel Tavern at Henley, as I recall it – to preside with him at Powderham," persisted David, warming to his theme. "And the late Lady Exeter, the mother of the present Earl, was once upon a time a milkmaid known as Sally Hoggins, that's very common knowledge."

"Pump girls, milkmaids and actresses – that's as maybe," conceded Sary. "But what of us doxies, Davy? How many practised *whores* is that who go to court and answer to 'Milady'?"

He caught her eye and had the grace to colour. "Well, Lady Lade for one," he said defiantly. "Sir John first came upon her in a house of no extraordinary fame on Broad Street, St Giles, in London. I have that as a certain fact."

"Aye, and I 'ave it as a fact that Lettie Lade was mistress of the foulest tongue and lightest reputation of any titled skirt, since My Lady 'Amilton set the fashion for such ways in ton society," she countered. "And is that really what your Lordship seeks for 'Adderton? A mistress whose visitors and lackeys laugh at 'er bad manners behind their hands and strive to cap each other's stories of the scandals in 'er past?"

But he wouldn't see it. Not if it came up and hit him on his noble head! It would seem that nothing she could say or do would deflect David from his object, now he'd stated it. "No, of course not," he'd impatiently exclaimed. "But don't you see, my dear – the fact that you already do perceive so much is only proof that you yourself are made of something finer?"

"Oh yes, I'm very fine, that's true. Fine and dandy as a whore! But how much butter d'ye think I'd cut in London, in the Season, when you went to take your seat in the 'Ouse of Lords? How fine d'ye think I'd seem in amongst the duchesses and princesses at Almack's? A pelican in a blooming wilderness – that's how I'd look!"

"I've already told you, not all are gently born. Why, you'd soon pick up their manners, a girl as bright as you. And act with a great deal more discretion too, I'll answer for it, than the Lettie Lades and Emma Hamiltons of this world."

"*Discretion*, Davy? And is that what it is you think I 'ave such store of?" she innocently rejoined. "Is that why you love me, dearie? For my discretion, is it?"

Everything about her in flagrant contradiction of any such idea – the mischievous inflexion of her voice, her laughing golden eyes and brightly painted face. Not least the way she sprawled back on the tumbled bed – one long leg raised, the other provocatively swinging to display the main avenue of her trade and most obvious aspect of her femininity to frank and open view. Discretion scarce an attribute that anyone in his rightful senses would attach to Sary Snudden! But then David Stanville was not a young man remotely in possession of his senses. He knew that she was right to mock his inconsistency. Not even his love could blind him to the likelihood of her disgracing him at Hadderton. Or elsewhere in society. Yet already he'd progressed beyond the point of no return. He'd take her home and introduce her to his parents within the sight of all, he was determined, in preparation for the day when they'd be wed!

"And, by Christ, I'd like to see ye try it, boy!" cried Charlie Stanville, on a timely visit to the Eastern County with his wife and sister, Tavie. (And a party to the first stage of his cousin's daring plan; if not, as yet, to its final resolution.) "Hang it, weren't I the fellow who smuggled stolen beef into his tent in Belgium? And on the hoof – and wearing jack-boots to disguise the creature's foot prints in the mud? And now our Sary, eh – and posing as a tight-arsed virgin at your mother's tea-board? I'faith, I'd give a fortnight's pay to see her carry that one off!"

Sary herself, meantime, continued vainly to oppose him. "You people really think that rank and property and all the power that goes in hand with 'em must serve to fetch you anything ye need," she told her lover with some justice the next time he sought to raise the subject with her. "But I'm 'ere to tell your Lordship that real life ain't so simple. All very well in 'ere, my dear, with nothing so much as a shift to come between our characters. But outside this room, outside this house, I 'ave to tell you 'tis your very wealth and rank that most keeps us apart." His parents, she told him bluntly, would very like deny him his inheritance before they'd see him wedded to a whore.

"In which event, we'd be advised I think to contrive for you a different character for your first meeting with them," he'd put in quickly, seizing on the chance she gave him for enforcing his proposal. "Something obscure, don't you see – yet undeniably respectable. Perhaps the daughter of a country parson, now deceased? Or of a noble émigré who chose to stay and breed up a family this side of the Channel?"

"Oh no, my Lord, you don't catch me like that again! I've told you twice, for gracious sake – and now it seems that I must say it all again. I'll sell my time to you, or to any other cull who'll pay the going rate. But not my honesty, that doesn't 'ave a price. I've not been educated at Mrs Anybody's Seminary, nor taught in French and German by some Friday-faced Swiss governess. Nor even learned to play the pianoforte. I don't know what to say that's proper – and first thing I tried, they'd find me out for sure." Sary proudly raised her chin. "I'm nobody for lying, Davy, and I never was," she said. "So let that be an end to it, my dear."

The end though, when Sary finally talked herself out of arguments, had been secured in the teeth of all her better judgements. Her own transparency of character had long since shown to David that she cared for him far above her common run of clients. He knew that in the end, for the sake of that affection, she'd capitulate to all his love demanded of her – if only he held firm. And so indeed it was to be. For on a sunless day in the following November of 1819, Sary Snudden had reluctantly consented to sit beside him for a second time, to ride in through the dragon gates of Hadderton.

A formal tea in the White Saloon, and with Her Ladyship the Countess in attendance! Perhaps even with the Earl himself? The absurd and terrifying picture she'd drawn for David in her attempts to bring him to his senses – the thing she had herself considered beyond all possible imagination – was for Sary, that afternoon, come hideously to life! The gate-boy, Billy Fielder, gawped at Lord David's younger female passenger exactly as he'd gawped at her the year before. But this time Sary neither smiled nor waved at him. So differently she felt this time – so disadvantaged, so conscious now of how she must appear. Stiffly she raised a grey kid glove to tuck a vivid curl inside her plain black bonnet, reacting unnaturally without her paint and brilliant colours; more uncertain and sincerely frightened than she'd felt for years – since the day when as a girl in Alfriston she'd realized that her poor dear Ma was not to live.

David had insisted, not only on providing the new outfit for this crazy social visit to his parents, but also on accompanying Sary to the draper's and the mantua-maker's, and to the milliner's, to oversee its manufacture. Her own first choice of Imperial purple velvet, to cover a striped silk walking dress in lavender and silver, he'd rejected out of hand in favour of a caped pelisse of blue-grey kerseymere, with Russian lambskin cuffs. All very plain and sober, and lined throughout in black.

"But I can't wear *that*!" she'd exclaimed when he held the fabric up against the mantua-maker's fashion plate. "Lord, I'd look no different to the trulls who dress themselves as nuns and quakeresses and the like, only to make the culls feel wickeder when they unfrock 'em! Davy, I need a bit of show, you know I do. I'd never keep the line in such a dismal mode!"

His Lordship earnestly begged pardon, but he thought she would. She'd look most elegant he assured her (with an apologetic glance for the flustered little dressmaker behind). "You don't require the paint or colour, my darling, take my word for it. You already have the looks and style – Sary, you have everything you need without it. Believe me, only trust in me and you will see. In plain and well cut clothes like this, you'll look a very princess!" And how could she deny him, when the cards were down? With those dark eyes of his so full of adoration – and faith in her ability to change the rules of life to suit his dearest wish? To make black white for him! And how to tell him now, as his great house rose into view across the park, how wrong he had been then? How wrong she looked and felt – how ill-equipped to brave the den of noble beasts, waiting inside to tear her limb from limb!

Standing before her dressing glass in Brighton that morning, in a modest blue and white sprigged-muslin gown, she looked – not elegant and simple, but merely *large* and simple. Used to taking reassurance from her own appearance in a mirror, she'd then felt positively betrayed by it. An awkward country girl, she looked, got up in Sunday best! The addition of a fashionably tight spencer-top in navy watered silk served only to emphasize the width of her shoulders, the voluptuous dimensions of her breasts and upper arms. Her pinky-copper hair, dressed high against a comb in antique Roman fashion, was as beautiful as ever. Nothing could detract from that. But bereft of its flying filaments and softly framing curls, the countenance beneath had looked too wide and strong and altogether open of expression to be anything but lowlybred.

'You play your cards aright, Milady, and like enough you'll end your life a duchess.' That's what Black Peg predicted for her once. But how in heaven's name could she achieve it, looking as she did? In desperation, Sary experimented in the glass with elevated brows and lowered lashes, pursing up her mouth in imitation of the distainful heiresses in the gallery at Hadderton. But succeeding only, she must eventually acknowledge it, in appearing like some

121

wretched abigail practising to ape her mistress. Without the comfort of her eyebrow-blacking or coloured salves, without even Spanish cochineal to aid her (for David had unkindly outlawed every form of paint) – without her usual finery, she felt that she had lost her personality. As naked as a fresh-shorn sheep.

Plain as they were, the addition of the pelisse and bonnet at least afforded her some sense of vague protection. But only in the safety of her room. For halfway down the stairs she'd perforce to witness Madge Perrin's first sight of her in such a garb, and hear from her the worst.

"You'll never do it, my lovely," the other woman told her baldly as she descended to the hall, while at the same time reaching up to tease her bonnet ribbons into better shape and pat her on her pale and paintless cheek. "A sow's ear never did go to make a silken purse. Ye know that as well as I do, Sary Snudden. But there – your life's your own and always 'as been. I'll wish ye well and 'ope to Gawd I'm wrong."

But it was David, plainly, and not Madge, who had been wrong in this. As wrong as any man could be, to dress his Sary up as she herself had sometimes dressed her little doll, Jemima – for the entertainment of her culls, in their cast-off cravats and handkerchiefs. To make them laugh at her absurdity. Madge was right. She felt and looked no better than Jemima in her borrowed clothes. And no amount of subterfuge on David's part could make it otherwise.

Having in due form rejected his first idea of presenting Sary to his parents as the orphaned offspring of a parson (a type undoubtedly too commonplace to satisfy their minimum requirements of birth and rank); and then dismissing the 'noble *émigré*' invention (on recalling his father's notorious aversion to France and all things froggish) – David, by process of a logic that Sary herself had found it difficult to follow, arrived in time at a still more outlandish proposal. "Listen to this, my love – I have settled everything!" he'd told her eagerly. "Now, this is what we'll do; we'll introduce you to them as the only daughter of a *Nabob* – a gentleman who made, but sadly lost, a fortune in the service of his country out in India. 'Sir Nathan Smythe' I have it in mind to christen him. What d'ye say to that? A name with a certain ring to it, wouldn't you agree?"

"And me 'is only daughter, Sary Smythe?"

122

"Well, just 'Miss Smythe', I think, since we've spared you any sisters," he corrected her. "And 'Sarah', never Sary. You're meant to be a lady, recollect."

"Or how about 'Miss Cock-Smythe'?" she helpfully suggested. "That 'as a certain truthful ring to it and all, wouldn't your Lordship say?"

"No, Sary, listen damme! This is important and we have to get it right. I'll tell them that Sir Nathan was married to a lady, an English gentlewoman of his own rank, who most tragically sacrificed her young life in giving birth to yours. Later, in his inconsolable distress, your poor father neglected his own business interests and the proper instruction of his child (entrusting your education to a rustic English nurse). To die last year in India, a ruined and a broken man. How does that strike you for a romantic history?"

"*India*! But what on earth do you think I know of India?" she'd demanded, in a tone that sounded nearer laughter than the outrage which she actually felt. "Why, I'd only 'ave to open my mouth to give the game away."

"No, but you wouldn't, that is the entire point. Because I can assure you that neither of my parents know much more about the place than you do. The Polite World is all that ever has, or ever will, concern Mamma. As for my father, he's convinced that savages begin at Calais, and will only pity you the more for being forced to live amongst them. So we'll tell them you've but recently returned from Calcutta, all right?" he went on rapidly, to forestall her next objection. "To take up residence with an aunt – a widow, shall we say, a 'Mrs Pauncefoote' living by the Steine in Brighton? Which would be where I first met with you of course, at a Ship or Castle Inn Assembly!" He smiled in triumph at his own undoubted ingenuity.

"An *aunt* now is it! First India, Davy – and now a blessed aunt! And where, pray, do we hope to come by one of those at second-hand, when My Lady requests a sight of 'er? Madge Perrin, shall we 'ave? – a painted bawd, to let My Lady see what kind of house it is we keep in Brighton Town?"

"We have to have an aunt or female relative of some kind to chaperon you," he patiently explained. "And for your information, Sary, I have already found her. There is an actress with the

123

Jonas and Penley company – a Mrs Ariadne Sefton, who enjoyed some popular success as Lady Sneerwell in the last Sheridan productions at East Bourne and Hastings. She resides in Brighton, as I've discovered; and, now that the season for theatricals is over, is more than willing to oblige us in the role of your 'Aunt Pauncefoote'."

"Well, don't say Madge and I 'aven't warned you then, that's all I ask," she told him at the time, and later – when she and the actress, Mrs Sefton, had come to mount to his mother's landaulet in actual train for Hadderton. "I tell you, they'll never swallow such a story, not in a month of Wednesdays. And even if we could convince 'em of the half of it, they'd need a darn sight more from me, ye may believe, than pretty words and manners. A marriage portion and a proper stud-book pedigree – and the Lord knows what else besides!"

"I agree," he said, with a degree of calm complaisance that made Sary want to shake her youthful lover 'til he rattled. "But that's all for the future. We'll simply introduce you to them now and make them think you charming. And then next year, when I attain majority, we may be wed by licence whilst they're up in town – to announce it only when the Season ends and they return to Sussex. By which time," he added with a modest smile, "you're bound to be with child, my dearest Sary. And then you may be sure that it will be your health and fitness to produce an heir for Hadderton that weighs with them, not your pedigree and fortune. And if it ain't, well – hang them! It will be too late for argument in any case."

'Meantime, all me and Mrs Sefton 'ave to do,' thought Sary apprehensively as the pedimented entrance *porte* of Hadderton loomed up ahead, 'is *charm* 'is Lordship and Milady – the good God help us!'

Not that the woman on the seat behind her in the landaulet seemed in the slightest daunted by the prospect. A small loquacious person, who made up in projection and enunciation all she lacked in presence and physique, Ariadne Sefton had enlivened the dozen miles that separated her Brighton lodging house from Hadderton Park with alternate declamations on the subjects of the passing landscape, and on the child's play that the role of Mrs Pauncefoot represented to an artiste of her standing.

"Now don't you fret about a thing, Lord Denton, not a *thing*," she said emphatically. "And look now will you both at the sky up there! It calls to mind a painted cloth we used for Mr Shakespeare's *Tempest* at the King's. Such clouds! Such grand effects! '*The sky, it seems, would pour down stinking pitch!*' (That was my line, as Miranda, to cue the thunder-sheet.) '*But that the sea, mounting to the welkin's cheek, dashes the fire out!*' And the boy would throw saltpetre on the gas jets to make the flash. Oh yes indeed, my Lord, you may believe I've played enough of Shakespeare and of Sheridan for Mr Penley to have brought the speech and manners of the quality to the status of an art. 'Miss Smythe' may safely leave the main part of the talking to her aunt; and they'll be none the wiser for the subterfuge. To be sure I'd stake my reputation on it. And bless me, what a *park* you have, your Lordship! Such vistas and such noble trees! I vow I've seen nothing finer since the Duke of Marlborough engaged our touring company to perform for him at Blenheim."

But already they were through the arch and in the court. The great doors to the entrance hall already open to them. Two footmen waiting on the step.

"And, by the by," said David, hauling on the ribbons. "my cousins, Charles and Octavia, and Charlie's new wife, Frances, are staying with us at the present. Did I tell you?"

"What – Charlie Stanville?" All hope of anonymity shattered at a blow. "*Tell us*? Ye know damn well you didn't tell us! And I don't wonder, neither," said Sary feelingly. "Davy, that rogue'll give the game away as soon as look at us!"

"Not he. I've told my cousin what we plan this afternoon, and he's all for it. Says he'd give a fortnight's pay to see you carry it off." David smiled again to reassure her. But too late. If the nearest footman's eyes had not been fixed unwinkingly upon her, Sary would have leapt from the carriage and bolted like a rabbit. Charlie Stanville, for gracious sake! And Charlie's wife! And the girl Octavia as well – the rider in the park who represented all that she herself was not in the way of elegance and breeding!

"I have also tipped the servants not to peach, in case you wondered," David whispered as the man stepped forward to release them. "So nothing to concern you there." And too late now to argue even – with Ariadne Sefton already preparing to alight in the character of Aunt Pauncefoote.

125

"Why, what a *splendid* and *imposing* entrance-way, your Lordship!" cried the actress, throwing up a hand and pitching heroically to the gods. "And entrances I always hold to be important. I'm certain you agree?"

Sary, who all too readily agreed, looked desperately about the chilly hallway – trying to draw courage from the escutcheons, arms and armour on its walls – recalling her schoolteacher, old Janey Chowne's, long unheeded lessons on deportment, and striving now to put them into practice. *Back straight, Sary Snudden – eyes down, hands folded neat and modest, there's the way. And dentical little steps. Small steps, Sary, if you want to act the lady.*

In the staircase hall, a brazier filled with burning charcoal gave off a faintly comforting domestic odour; and, as they passed it, David reached across to squeeze the hand she'd thrust in beneath his arm. "Just look to me if you're at any loss for what to say," he told her, "and I'll supply whatever's needed, never fear."

"Or else *I* will," Mrs Sefton's well-trained voice sang out in high excitement from somewhere down on a level with Sary's elbow. "Just give us the cue, my dear, that's all I need – and leave the rest to Auntie! 'Act 1, Scene 1 – My Lady's Boudoir,' " she added conspiratorially, and in a ringing stage-whisper that surely must have carried through the closed doors of the chamber, and clear across to the ears of its waiting occupants.

'And 'ere's where the pudding's proven then,' thought Sary through the heavy thumping of her own strong heart. As fearful, she supposed, of her official entry into David's world as he'd been as a Johnny-raw on coming into hers. Her throat tightened, and she increased her grip on his supporting arm as the footman's voice announced Lord Denton and his party – and the three of them advanced in close formation into the White Saloon.

Chapter Twelve

The woman who rose to greet them was too young by a decade or more to be the lady of the house. Set down at once by Sary as a dullish kind of creature; and one, moreover, whose pretty fluffy little day-cap could do nothing but accentuate her likeness to a ewe-sheep of the long-nosed Romney Marsh variety.

"Fanny – hello!" cried David heartily, as if the merest sight of her was all that he needed to make his afternoon complete. "Miss Smythe – Mrs Pauncefoot, permit me to present to you the newest member of our family, Mrs Frances Stanville, my cousin Charles's wife."

'And my word,' thought Sary, greatly relieved to discover that neither the lady's husband nor his sister were visible within the room. 'Pity poor Charlie – 'aving to wake alongside of that each morning, only to cover 'is gaming expenses!' At the moment that she least expected it, she felt inclined to laugh.

"And here is my mother, Lady Southbourne," David self-consciously announced, propelling her forward to encounter a second figure, swathed in shawls and reclining languidly upon a fireside *chaise*. "Mamma, this is Miss Smythe then come to see you. And her aunt, Mrs Deborah Pauncefoote. Two ladies whose acquaintance you know that I esteem most highly."

"And 'pon my soul, I'm sure we feel the same ourselves about his Lordship," interposed the actress, passing over the usual civilities in her anxiety to take up the proffered cue. " 'Now *there's* a proper English gentleman for you,' is what I said the first time we beheld him. Is that not so, Sarah my love?" Her voice expanding to auditorium volume in her eagerness to do justice to the role she had been given. "At the Castle Inn Assembly Rooms it was, as I recall it. Bless me, *what* a crush that night! But then I dare say that your Ladyship avoids such tedious presses? To be sure I would myself, had I not this charming niece of mine to introduce into Society."

"Miss Smythe, I hope that you are well?" said Lady Southbourne, according the little aunt no more attention than such an essentially forward outburst was deserving of. Her heavy eyelids lifting slightly to observe the large, quietly dressed young woman her son had introduced into her drawing-room.

"Ah bravely, thanking ye," said Sary, caught somewhat off her guard by this direct address. Yet contriving very well, she fancied, to imitate these people's tip-tongued mode of speaking. "And all the better for your asking Ma'am, I'm sure," she appended quickly, seeing the other's brows flight up. "Lord save us, as fit as fivepence I should think!"

The Countess of Southbourne's eyebrows hovered somewhere up about the fringes of her unconvincing chestnut sausage curls. 'And as badly corked a pair as I 'ave seen!' thought Sary, attempting and failing to find any likeness in the woman's pale and doughy countenance to that of her only son; whilst at the same time rummaging through her inadequate stock of pleasantries for something more to add. "And yourself, Milady?" she finally vouchsafed. "We find you sound in wind and limb still, I should hope?"

The eyebrows rose a fraction higher, to all but disappear beneath the lady's ornamental turban.

"Well now, Mamma . . ."

"Your Ladyship, I do declare . . ."

In their anxiety to spare the Countess any further kind enquiries as to the state of her water or digestion, David and the counterfeit Aunt Pauncefoot both hurried into speech together. Then paused, and then rushed on to clash a second time.

"So sorry, Ma'am!"

"I do apologise, your Lordship!"

Each gave a hollow little laugh, then paused again advisedly.

"I was about to declare," the actress hazarded at last, "how greatly I admire the proportions of your salon, My Lady. How truly elegant I find its furnishings."

"You are by no means the first to do so, Madam, as you may suppose. The Regent himself said much the same, as I recall it, on his last visit," complacently recited Lady Southbourne. "For the best part of *one whole hour* he sat here in this very room and paid it many compliments. Most gratifying. His taste is excellent you know."

And amid the satisfactory outburst of exclamations and enquiries which had followed these not wholly unexpected observations, the tea was rung for, the visitors bidden to be seated, and the Countess's ill-corked eyebrows perceived to have returned to something near their normal altitude.

"Miss Smythe, you know, Mamma, has recently arrived in England." David waited only for the ladies to be settled in their chairs before proceeding boldly to the main topic. "Her home, until her father's death, has been in India."

"India – oh yes," repeated Lady Southbourne vaguely, toying with the fringes of her shawls. "But how very singular, Miss Smythe. And your father? I believe he was some kind of a . . . ?"

"Magog," Sary, diverted of a sudden from the grand procession of urn and cake and sandwich bearers which was just then commanding so much of her attention, supplied the word without a thought. "And as good an Indiaman I'll lay as I have ever known," she added for good measure. "Or ever hope to, come to that."

"A *Magog*?" His mother, slightly puzzled, turned to David for enlightenment. "But I confess I'm quite astray. I was under the persuasion that the term was 'Nabob'. Or have I heard you wrongly, David?"

"Well, yes. I mean, no, you may have heard aright. I may very like have called him 'Nabob'. Because to be sure the thing means much the same," suggested David, gleaming rosily. "Sir Nathan held both titles, as I understand it, within different collection districts of Bengal, d'ye see? Is that not so, Miss Smythe?"

Sary nodded dumbly, inwardly mortified to have made so elementary a blunder. 'And if you'll swallow all of that, Milady, then I dare say you'll swallow anything,' she thought, catching Mrs Charles Stanville's interested gaze around the large loop-handled silver urn they'd set before her, and forcing an unwilling smile.

"Really, do you say so? But how extremely fascinating," drawled Lady Southbourne, yet sounding something less than totally enthralled. "A dish of tea, Miss Smythe?" She waved a languid hand. Mrs Stanville filled to order from the tap and a footman stepped in to hand the fragile porcelain cup across to Sary. "And what kind of an establishment did your father run, one wonders, as an – er, Magog? A large household I suppose?"

"Oh, yes – quite oversized, Milady."

And having got thus far without discovery, Sary decided she might as well be hung for a bullock as a lamb. "More like a palace than a house, to tell ye truly. Domes near twice as big as Prinny's – I mean to say, as large as your Prince Regent's – down in Brighton. To say nothing of the minaretties," she added, quaffing her tea at a single draft to assist with the invention. "Twenty-six of 'em as I remember, not counting those above the gates and stables."

"Twenty-six?" In her astonishment the Countess so far abandoned her fashionable languor to raise her voice and sit near upright on her *chaise*. "Did she say twenty-six?" she appealed to Frances Stanville. (And somewhat impolitely, Sary thought, considering who it was who'd thought up the number in the first place.) "Twenty-six domes *excluding* those on gates and stables? She surely means to rally us?"

"Not a bit of it Milady, twenty-six at least, and maybe more for aught I can tell," said Sary firmly, gratified to have at last secured so great a part of Lady Southbourne's wandering attention. " 'Twas so mortal hard to count the devils from the park, you may believe. Unless you might chance to be up on one of our old elephants, that is," she concluded as a finally authentic touch, and feeling more confident by the minute.

"Elephants! And did Sir Nathan actually *own* such beasts, Miss Smythe? And did you really ride upon them?"

"Bless me, yes! We had 'em grazing in the park as you have deer. I dare swear four hundred at the least. And all white or spotted every one – none of your common greys for my poor dear Papa. And all as tame and slow as Sussex oxen in the bargain!"

"White elephants? And did you infer that some were *spotted*, Miss Smythe?" enquired her hostess, this time with the liveliest of interest. Her tea now slopping in its saucer, her shawls cascading quite unheeded to the floor.

Mrs Ariadne Sefton, in the character of Aunt Pauncefoot, opened her own small mouth preparatory to a long overdue *ad libatum* interruption. But somehow the cue of 'spotted elephants' suggested to the actress absolutely nothing, not even from *Antony and Cleopatra*. And when she looked across to Viscount Denton for support or inspiration, it was to find the heir to Hadderton similarly transfixed. Despite his earlier undertaking to the girl, he too sat speechless, while 'Miss Sarah Smythe' plunged recklessly onward to disaster.

"Well Ma'am, I'd say more packled than spotted. Nay, I tell a lie – less packled than patchy-parti-coloured, as you might say. Like great big old gipsy ponies, if ye take my meaning . . ."

Her careful diction slipping somewhat, her speech now losing impetus – with the realization maybe that already she had gone too far. And David, listening, experienced a pang of shame at having so exposed her. Yet in amongst the shame, and the efforts he was making to find something apposite to say himself, he also felt a wild – and wildly inappropriate – urge to laugh at her outrageous claims. And underneath it all, the panic and the laughter, the small firm core of knowledge that two worlds which in theory never should or could come into contact, were here meeting together without a major cataclysm. Sary Snudden, here at Hadderton by invitation, and talking with his mother! And however unlikely their meeting, or bizarre their conversation, they *were* speaking, demonstrably. Already they'd broken through the Polite World's most rigid laws. The rest consisted only of refinement and adjustment. The thing indeed was possible!

David might have thought so. But did the wretched Sary, still floundering in amongst the tangled webs of the deceptions he'd prescribed?

". . . and so unaccountable tame, my Pa's old elephants. Tell ye what, we even used 'em for the ploughing if you'll believe me, Ma'am . . ."

The Countess's eyebrows were once more invisible beneath her turban, the belief in Mrs Charlie Stanville's sheeplike countenance also evidencing signs of strain. And despite David's warnings to speak only when she had to, here was she already hopelessly entangled in her own overcoloured descriptions, gabbling like a fool of things that she knew nothing, less than nothing of! Sary felt the cold sweat trickling down her spine.

". . . Glory yes, so tame and gentle they were – Lord save us, I'd swear that you could lay yourself right down beneath their feet, and they'd never so much as think of squelching ye. And as for riding. Most every day we'd take 'em for a canter . . . a *slow* canter, that is to say. For everlasting a-riding on the elephants we were, as I'm a living soul . . ."

Her voice trailed into silence – unable somehow to end the sentence that she'd started. A '*dry*' – one cue to which any actress worth her salt must automatically respond. "Bless me, such a very *useful* training for a girl!" Ariadne Sefton at once observed, setting down her teacup on the little piecrust table at her elbow to free her hands for visual emphasis. "A young lady *fortunate* enough to grow up in India will be equal to the very greatest challenges that life can offer, I always have upheld it. While any little refinements that may be wanting in her are very soon acquired, in my experience, within the right society. I'm sure you must agree, My Lady?"

"On the contrary, a true refinement in *my* experience is invariably inborn and seldom, if ever, successfully acquired." Not Lady Southbourne's, but another lighter, cooler voice to answer from the doorway. The new entrant's face betrayed no more emotion than her voice, as gravely she inclined her head to David and the seated ladies. "Which in no way excuses my own interruption," she added, glancing at the clock. "I have been to watch my brother and Lord Southbourne coursing up at Furlongs and I fear mistook the hour. Do please forgive my lateness to the tea-board."

"Tavie, but of course! Come in and meet our guests!" David, on his feet again to effect the introductions – all too obvious in his anxiety to hear Octavia approve his choice of mistress, and see Sary act politely in the presence of his cousin. To have the two girls friends.

Preparatory to coming down to tea, Octavia Stanville had exchanged her outdoor clothes for a gown of damson silk, with a little ruff of stiffened muslin and a heart-shaped Marie Stuart cap to set off the darkness of her hair. A young gentlewoman to her fingertips, the female counterpart to David. A genuine *dame de qualité* who moved with sickening assurance to meet the base-born Sary Snudden.

"How do you do, Miss Smythe," she said, turning smoothly from the elder to the younger lady-visitor. Her nod to Sary one of the faintest specimens of politeness. "How very nice to meet with you at last."

Her eyes, meantime, denying every syllable. Octavia Stanville's eyes said, 'Swords or pistols? Looks, education, style or breeding – I'll fight you for him, fair or foul, with every weapon I can lay my hand to! Madam, do you understand me?' And Sary, who normally admired straight backs and steady eyes, had smiled her best and brightest smile. "How d'ye do, Miss Stanville. The pleasure's mine I'm sure," she said with a courtesy too perfect to be mistaken for a moment as sincere, her own fine golden eyes meanwhile acknowledging the challenge without a blink or flicker. No hostility on earth like that between two rival women.

*   *   *

And here she was in London, forty years or more advanced. Another place, another time. Another reason altogether *to await Octavia*.

Yet, looking back from 1861, from these first dark days of widowhood for the poor dear Queen; looking back to the very year of Georgian Regency in which Victoria had been born, Sarah found to her surprise that the memories of that first meeting with Octavia, face to face, still had the power to stir her. Not just the echo of that first unspoken battle-cry – something faintly heard and in the distance, as she described the encounter to poor embarrassed Mr Brown. But something real and vivid that thrilled her still beneath her tightly buttoned black silk bodice. How often she'd recalled it! The reflection in another woman's eyes of her own newborn intention in the White Saloon at Hadderton to fight for David – for David's body and his soul. To fight the elegant Octavia Stanville for him, and by all and any means on earth to win!

*   *   *

"Octavia my dear, Miss Smythe has been instructing us on life in India. So interesting and singular," murmured Lady Southbourne in the act of recovering her shawls from where they'd fallen. "Her father was a Magog, did you know?"

"Indeed, Ma'am? In that you *do* surprise me."

And Sary could willingly have struck her for the easy grace with which Octavia disposed her slim back-end upon the chair which David had vacated.

"And how long precisely have you been in England, Miss Smythe?" she enquired with icy cold civility.

"A sixmonth, Ma'am. And too short a time, I dare swear, to have learned quite all the tricks and manners of an English lady."

"Though your father, Sir Nathan, did employ an English governess for your education, as I believe," inserted David hastily, eager it would seem now to repair his earlier omissions. "A Sussex woman, I apprehend?"

"Oh glory yes – Jane Chowne." Sary confirmed it with a grateful smile for him, surreptitiously straightening up her back a little as she did so, and edging her slippered feet together on the carpet. "For my life I'm sure I can't think how I ever would have managed without our Janey Chowne!"

"Really now? How very enlightening," said David's cousin.

His complete obsession with the creature as clear to Octavia from the first moment she'd seen them together, as was the girl's own lack of breeding. It was obvious from his face, even from the movements of his body, when she spoke or looked toward him. Each glance between them charged with sexual passion. And the way he rushed to her defence when she was like to give herself away! The poor young imbecile!

"I'm certain then that your governess will not have failed to secure for you all the expected accomplishments of an English lady," she said aloud with honeyed sweetness. "A proficiency in drawing and at the pianoforte, and in the classics? And naturally a thoroughgoing knowledge of the modern languages? To be sure you must speak French, Miss Smythe. *Dites-moi, ma chère Mademoiselle, manquez-vous d'instruction et de savoir-vivre autant que vous le paraissez?*"

134

"Octavia! That's unforgivable!"

Though Sary was quite capable of course of recognizing the deliberate insult, even without the benefit of David's outraged exclamation, or of any understanding of the foreign language. And more than capable of answering it. She heard herself laugh shortly. "French, Ma'am? Well I do wonder you should think so. With all your own education I felt sure you must have known that teachers favour local dialects out there. French is now outmoded altogether in Indian Society."

"Now this *is* fascinating hearing to be sure." Octavia perceived her opening and mercilessly took it. "But shall we not ask Miss Smythe for more *éclairissement*? May we not hear a sample of some or other of the dialects that you have learned so cleverly, Ma'am? I am sure that Lady Southbourne here, and Mrs Stanville, are quite as eager as I am myself to hear you speak as Indian natives do."

Sary looked across at David, to find him once again immobile, sitting like a waxwork, staring glassily. She tossed her unsatis-factorily feathered bonnet. Well then, she'd simply have to face it out herself, that's all!

"*Ai jai struntabelly panjandrum*," she proceeded to pronounce with slow and loud deliberation, "*eenie mynie maharajum nimruddi agapanthus calipash*. Which is to say in plain King's English, 'A sow in satin petticoats is still a sow, for all her fancy airs.' So quaint the ways these Indians speak," she added sweetly. "Don't you agree Miss Stanville?"

'And a proper valiant sport and all, she thought, to see the snooty baggage for the while as speechless as the rest of them. And you might not 'ave the education, Sary Snudden,' she told herself with pride, 'but you can hit as quick and hard as anyone who 'as. That's certain sure!'

Octavia Stanville, meantime, had turned a tolerably satisfactory shade of poppy-red, and begun to reduce the angel cake that she'd been offered with her tea into a small, neat heap of granulated crumbs. "Fine spoken, Madam," she at last vouchsafed in a low flat voice as yet but faintly tinged with anger, still working busily all the while to annihilate her cake. "I declare she is miraculously polite and engaging. Is she not, Lady Southbourne?"

"Why, yes indeed, most interesting. So singularly expressed," had willingly agreed the inattentive Countess. Only to be startled from her apathy a moment later by the appalling spectacle of an ostensibly well-bred female (and worse, a relative by marriage) in the grip of uncontrolled emotion! And the little mouse Octavia too – of all unlikely people – who'd never before been heard to raise her voice above a murmur!

"Aye, singularly *stupidly* expressed! As if anyone could possibly be taken in by that nonsensical recital," Octavia now cried, her flushed face working, her customary self-containment nowhere now in evidence. "*India*? I'd be very much astonished if our 'Miss Smythe' has ever even strayed as far as London in her travels! And as for you, Lord Denton." She turned upon her cousin savagely. "You ought to be ashamed at such outrageous imposture. To try to foist this creature on your mother as a lady. A nobody, and worse! An actress is she? Or a singer from the entertainments you attend so regularly in Brighton, in preference to more civilized society here where you belong?"

'And now the fox is well amongst the fowls!' thought Sary with an overwhelming feeling of relief. One game lost, the next as surely won! No longer herself at any kind of disadvantage, with plain speaking now become the order of the day. And no need now to deny herself the satisfaction of beheading that prim and proper little *Marie Stuart* at a single hefty blow!

"Saving your pardon, Ma'am, but you're a fair bit wide still of the mark there," she interrupted, gratefully slipping back into the lazy accent of her rustic origins. "*There's* the actress for ye," She pointed to the redundant and still speechless Ariadne Sefton. "For truth to tell I've never trod the boards, nor sung a note of music neither, excepting maybe in the bath. I earn my living spigot-mongering. Or, as ye might say, in common whoring. Aye, you 'eard aright, a WHORE, that's what I am! And, to my way of thinking, a far more honest and more truly useful kind of entertainer altogether."

From the reaction of the other ladies in the room, she might as well have cast an entire cabinet of *Sèvres* into the marble fireplace and trampled through the fragments, Sary thought. And in the very total silence that followed her remarkable announcement; while the warm colour drained from Octavia Stanville's face and Lady Southbourne fumbled through her shawls to find her vinaigrette, the sound of voices, and of footsteps on the flagging of the hall without, had slowly penetrated. Then all at once the double doors were flung back on their hinges to reveal the Earl of Southbourne, mud-bespattered and in great good humour, with his handsome military cousin, Charles Stanville, close behind him.

"God bless my eyesight, Charlie! Look ye here and see what we've been missing," his Lordship most amiably exclaimed. "Your cousin Denton as cosy amongst the ladies on the sofas as a mouse is in a churn, bigod! And female charm and affability all about him, the sly young pup!"

Chapter Thirteen

The first meet of December for the Southbourne Hunt was as ever well attended, with some hundred local riders assembled on the lawn at Hadderton; to fortify themselves with the stirrup-cup of port and sherry wine that Tillotson and his minions were dispensing.

"Morning! Good morning to you there!" Breath steaming as their greetings were exchanged. Hats raised, whips flourished in the frosty air. "Milady, good to see you! Good morning to ye, John . . . Consult your toes, Ma'am, there's my method – and if they're cooler than your nose, why then we shall have a scent! . . . Hey there, young Fuller, how's your father's gout?" Ruddy squires and weathered ladies. Stout tenant farmers, sporting clerics and rod-backed military men – holding in excited horses the better to unleash their own excited tongues. "Stand still, will you! Stand! . . . 'Two thousand guineas is what I'll give you for that piece of flesh,' I put it to him there and then . . . Stand, Sultan – stand sir, damn ye!" Loud-voiced and scarlet-coated, they surged and eddied round the mounted figure of Lord Southbourne, as their host and Master. With young Viscount Denton, quite as keen as any other for the sport, threading through their ranks to find a place to move off as close as possible to his father's well bred and high-fed grey.

In the three weeks since the fiasco of his mother's tea-board in the White Saloon, and poor Sary's aborted début into Hadderton society, David and his parents had exhausted all their views on the subject of his infatuation with her. As had his cousins, Octavia and Charles, and Sary Ann herself. There was nothing more to say that was not already said. And nothing more for David now to do this

side of Christmas than to go about the daily business of his life –
while he wrestled with the unresolved decisions of his future.

"You fine ladies like to think that girls who go a-whoring ain't
worth the bounce of a cracker to anyone. Though I daresay your
'usbands and brothers could tell ye differently, if you cared to hear
a cully's version of the story. That right then, Charlie?" Sary,
cornered in the White Saloon, had instinctively enlisted masculine
support against her female adversaries. "But I'll tell you this for
nothing," she'd progressed to offering the ladies on that most
unforgettable occasion, "I love young Davy 'ere. Yes, *love*, Miss
Stanville, that is the word! For even draggle-tail whores know how
to love, you may believe. And 'e loves me and all. A young Lord
who's dwelt with women of refinement all 'is life, set firm on
wedding with a trull – so what d'ye make of that? And where would
such a thing place ladies with fortunes of their own to offer, then?
And proficiencies in French and drawing and the pianoforte?
Think about it, Miss, and come and tell me when you 'ave."

On which unanswerable recommendation, and with all the
majesty of the greatest princess born, she'd risen to her feet and
swept out past Lord Southbourne. Ignoring Charles's ironic salute,
to await David and Ariadne Sefton in the carriage which had
brought her to the door, and which shortly would return her,
undefeated, to the stews of Brighton.

But now the Huntsman and his hounds were trotting into view.

"Hold up! Hold up then, Pincher! Towzer! Roly! Up together!"
Sixteen and a half couple of as level and as useful hounds as any in
the country. As Lord Southbourne had but recently observed for
the benefit of anyone in earshot. Black-and-tans and lemons, with
blood in them from all the best foxhound breeding-lines. Sterns
erect and heads alert, urine neatly rationed out between the trees
and fencing-posts along their route up from the kennels behind the
Hadderton coach-house and stables.

It was at the coach-house gate that Octavia once more had
intercepted him, as David returned the landaulet from taking
Sary and the actress back to Brighton.

"Now then, Tavie, before you start away," he'd said defensively, "I have just now come from Sary – or from 'Miss Smythe', as

you would know her. And I can tell you now that she has finally agreed to marry me when I attain majority. Is that plain enough – do you understand? We *will* be married; and nothing now that you or anyone can say will have the power to stop us!"

His cousin's face as pale as his, her mouth as firm. Her dark eyes steady, mirrors of his own. "I see too well how *she* must leap at such a prospect. But you, David? How could you even meditate it," Octavia had demanded. "Have you forgotten, and will you cast aside so easily all this place has meant to us? And all it could mean still? To expose Hadderton and the name of Stanville as a laughing stock in every salon and assembly room through all the length and breadth of England? Are you conceivably so lost to shame that you could see that happen?"

And Charles's attitude within the house that evening, as disappointingly conventional as his sister's in its way. "Denton, my dear young idiot – why be so *extreme*? All things in moderation, don't ye know," advised the Captain who'd never himself committed the solecism of involving his own heart in the *affaires* with which that organ was traditionally associated. "One day you're an innocent, a very monk where muslin is concerned. Next thing we know, you're so confounded taken with the sex that you're all for up and wedding with a Cyprian! A frolic's one thing, Cousin – and was I not the first to see the joke in passing off a harlot as a lady? But to think seriously of marriage with a common trull like Sary Snudden – there's no laughing room in such a cross-grained random scheme as that, believe me. Not with your patrimony and the future of the Earldom in the balance. *Noblesse oblige*, dear fellow – *noblesse oblige!*"

The entire meet that December morning responded as one to the sounding of the horn, as the Huntsman led on the hounds and summoned all the rest to follow them across the park toward the home farm coverts; young David as thrilled as any horse or hound or rider of the hunt, his heart absurdly active. All his nerves, it seemed, clenched tight and hard beneath his ribs. It was a sharp clear day that promised famous sport, with a pinkish winter sun already searching out the bronze and russet tints of fallen leaves and naked quickthorn twigs. A peacock, bereft since autumn of his gorgeous train and hundred Argus eyes, battered upward from their pathway like a great bejewelled pigeon. To peer down at them from the safety of an overhanging branch while the cavalcade passed underneath. And David's father, trotting at their head, levelled a jaunty shot at it along the barrel of his hunting whip. In best of harness himself, as always when riding out as Master of the Southbourne.

Downwind of the initial covert, ranged in a vivid line of scarlet all along the headland of Farmer Swaine's best and biggest thirty-acre field, they sat their mounts and waited while the Huntsman put in the hounds to draw. Next moment their combined activity released a flock of whirring ring-doves and a harsh-voiced crow from the far side of the coppice. Then all at once the pack gave tongue. And David saw a lithe brown form streak out across the rising land beyond, and down into the ditch that bounded it, already half a field to the good. *Charlie*, 'gone away'.

A whipper-in hallooed the fox's exit. '*Hike, hike!*' the Huntsman sounded; and Lord Southbourne's grey leapt forward, with David close behind – across the ploughed expanse of Swaine's best field, sparking through the cobbles that the flintpickers had missed.

"Hey, boy! And ain't this better then than chasin' laced-mutton through the lanes of Brighton?" his father shouted happily, leaning forward and applying spurs, to make up his horse's mind for him on the subject of the five-barred gate that loomed ahead. And, contracting his own hunter's stride to collect him for the take-off, David must perforce acknowledge the kinship that he shared; that he felt indeed within him, for the courageous, and in essence very simple, soul who'd sired him.

Perhaps surprisingly, of all David's critics within the family – and despite his own dynastic interest in the matter – Lord Southbourne had revealed himself to be rather the least severe in his opposition to his son's most untoward and wrong-headed choice of marriage-partner.

"Well, boy, you know a looker when ye see one, I'll grant you that," he'd told him in the private fastness of his library, whence Lady Southbourne's wailing execrations had driven both of them at last to earth. "A gal worth looking at, damned if she ain't. And with mettle too, by Jove – the way she faced Miss Tavie down!" He winked lewdly, as he turned to rummage in a cupboard for the decanter and the glasses that he kept there in amongst a litter of old

141

spurs and knots of whipcord. "You're a spunky fellow, Davy. And I'm hardly the man to blame a son of mine for playin' at top-sawer with a pretty whore," avowed Lord Southbourne, flicking a fa from pristine handkerchief across the glasses and pouring each of them a bumper-full of port. "But look here, *marriage* with her, boy? I ask you, is it reasonable?"

"I think so." (Knowing in his heart that it was not, by any standard that his father recognized.) David took the proffered glass and made the best of things he could. "Papa, I know how it must seem to you," he'd said. "You think me a young fool who's simply lost his head over the first girl that he's made love to. An 'infatuation', as Mamma is pleased to call it. And one from which in time I will recover."

His father finished off his port and poured himself another glass. "My dear fellow, damn it all . . ." He left the sentence unconcluded.

"But there's where you're wrong, you see! You clearly do not understand. I *never* will recover from what I feel for Sary. Not in a month, or in a year, or in a lifetime of separation from her! And I never want to, either. That's why I have to marry her!"

"And if you did tire of her, after all – shall we say within a year? To find yourself tied for that same lifetime to a woman who's unworthy of your title. Have you thought what then? Well have ye, boy?" A faintly astonished expression in Lord Southbourne's eyes, as always when exercising his mental faculties.

"I tell you it will never happen."

"Ha!" the Earl exclaimed, with all the sudden triumph of a clumsy intellect who knows he's outmanoeuvred a refined one. "Well now, if you're so sure of that, Sir – then I think I have the very answer to the problem that you've posed us. My dear boy, you shall *have* that year that you're so sure you would survive apart from your little ladybird. And spend it doing what you've always wanted to – I say in touring, Sir, and on the Continent!"

"In *touring*, Sir?" His father's support for such a civilized adventure entirely unexpected.

"God's teeth, why not? What's to lose, if you're so certain that you'll feel the same about her when you return? Go and enjoy yourself, I say! Go and see the damn antiquities in Rome and Florence – and even, if ye must, that dug up *Pompey-i*. And all the palaces and galleries and broken statues they can find you. Gad

142

knows, these days half of young Society's set up as foreign *tourists* and explorers. 'Tis all the crack again since Wellington's made Europe safe again, and fat Louis is back upon the Frenchy throne. So why not you, boy? When you're of age in March you'll have the shot in your locker for it, that's certain. 'A very tolerable independence', as they say – and more besides, to play whatever ducks and drakes you will in France and Italy."

At which point in their conversation, seeing the interest kindle in his young listener's face, his Lordship advisedly adopted a more reasonable tone of voice, to improve on his advantage. "You notice I don't speak, as your mother has, of disinheritance – or any thunderin' nonsense of that kind," he'd remarked as he returned the port decanter to its shelf. "And run me through the liver if I would! No, Sir, I ask only that you give yourself some time and breathing-space to think things over, and to make a trial of your affection if you will. Well, what d'ye say to it? A twelvemonth from your birthday, Davy – that's all I'm asking you to wait for. I'm an honest man, I hope," he added with some justification. "And if at the finish you're still as set on marrying the wench – well then, we'll see what can be done. I can't say fairer, boy, and nor I think can you expect me to."

And having burdened the pair of them for plenty long enough, in his opinion, with such an excess of abstract meditation, Lord Southbourne patted David encouragingly upon the shoulder, advised him again to think it over, and took himself off forthwith for some recuperative riding exercise about his own estate.

Leaving his incalculable son, who'd always had less trouble altogether with the abstract, to tantalizing images of Continental wonders, natural and man-made. To Alpine peaks and sun-bleached Tuscan plains. To the priceless treasures of the Louvre, the Pitti and Borghese. (And to those lesser Italian masterworks to which a realistic price might possibly be affixed.)

They came up with the Huntsman and his hounds again in the wooded shaw that ran beside the Lewes turnpike at Lower Tilton. And while Lord Southbourne exercised his Master's privilege of roundly abusing all and any of the field who dared to press too close, David took advantage of the check to turn his winded horse into the breeze and make his own selection of the hound he

143

thought would be the first to open on the line. Not that he or any other rider could tell just now in what direction their quarry lay. The scent of a fox and the sense of a woman two things, as everyone agreed, that men could never hope to understand. David for one had revealed his own too total ignorance of the female character, in imagining that attitudes like Sary Snudden's and his cousin Octavia's could possibly be reconciled, even for a single afternoon. Worse, in forcing a false character upon her, he'd publicly denied his own appreciation of everything that Sary represented. He saw that all too clearly now; and knew that somehow he must make amends.

Another 'halloo' rang out. *Charlie* broke from cover once again, and the hounds laid on in hot pursuit.

"Heaven and the Devil confound ye, boy! Hold back! Hold back, I say, and give the damn hounds space to work," Lord Southbourne thundered, to conceal his secret satisfaction at being over-ridden by his son.

And as he passed him, David made his father's day complete by uttering the words his Lordship had been waiting patiently all week to hear. "All right, Papa – I'll go!" he shouted with a kind of desperate triumph. "I've decided that I'll go and take that year in Europe after all!"

But not alone. (And no earthly need just now, he thought, to spoil Lord Southbourne's victory or his enjoyment of the hunt by appending those three illuminating little words.)

"Listen Sary, my love, and tell me if I've got the right of it – you're aiming to strike out for France, and Gawd only knows where else besides, in the company of 'is Lordship? That it? To wed 'im in a twelvemonth if ye can, and take up the title of *Vicountess*, no less," Madge Perrin repeated while the pair of them relaxed together in the upstairs salon of her house in Brighton. The old bawd in her cut velvets and her stays and her high concealing ruffles; Sary in nothing but the flimsy *robe de chambre* that she worked in. To share an early morning pot of chocolate together while they cozed, and Bill Hodge locked up below.

"That all you want then, dearie?" Madge added drily. "Or would ye like, maybe, to go on and try for 'Princess of Wales', now that our Prinny's talking so freely of divorcing Caroline?"

Sary smiled, unconsciously rubbing at the angry bruising which some recently immoderate client had left upon her neck. "I know it sounds fantastical," she said. "And to tell you truly, Madge, I can't 'ardly believe 'tis happening myself. Reckon I'd be a chuckle-head to turn 'im down though, wouldn't you?" She paused and raised her sleepy painted eyes to meet the other's. "Even if I 'adn't taken to Davy Stanville as never was."

For a long silent moment Mrs Perrin held her gaze. "Well Sary Snudden, I can only tell you what I've told to others as 'ave trod that path before you, even if they didn't get to tread it quite so far as France," she said at last. "I'll tell ye straight, you're a fool to love 'im – seeing as no woman, whore or lady, ever loved a man without 'e brought 'er grief. But you're right and all, you'd be a greater fool to let a chance like that pass by your door without so much as calling out good day to it. Go with 'im gel, and see the sights of Europe. And wed 'is Lordship in the bargain, if he'll 'ave ye after. For ten to one he'll never guess until too late that you can't stock 'is nurseries for 'im, or be the mother of 'is son and heir."

"But that's not true – it never is! I'm not barren! Why, I've twice 'ad cause to call for 'pothecary's pills to bring my courses back, you know I 'ave! I'm not yet two and twenty. I'm strong, I'm hearty, ain't I? You said yourself you've never 'ad a working girl who's stouter. Why, I daresay I could bear the man a score or more of kiddies if I chose to!" (The notion of bearing even a single living child – never before considered by Sary, except as an occupational hazard at all costs to be avoided – now of a sudden become a vital object of importance.)

Madge Perrin sipped her chocolate reflectively, her thick black mastic lashes lowered. "And how long is it now, my love, that you've been with us?" she enquired.

"Four years last summer. I came to Brighton in the first week after Waterloo, if ye recall it?"

"Four full years then, plus a sixmonth." Sary's employer set her decorative golden head a little on one side, and then proceeded to demonstrate its practical utility for mental calculation. "That's fifty-two times four – two 'undred and eight weeks, plus twenty-six for the 'arf year. Two 'undred and thirty-four then – minus one week a month for courses, which is fifty-four. One 'undred and eighty working weeks then altogether, if you agree?" She paused for corroboration. But Sary, already way behind, could only nod in silence.

"Good gels, and you know you're one, my love, must manage sixty culls a week on average," continued Madge complacently. "Add fifteen for double-helpings. That's seventy-five (and I'm counting 'is hot-cockled Lordship in as several, ye may be sure) – seventy-five times one 'undred and eighty. That's, let's see – thirteen thousand, five 'undred shots in the tail, give or take a few. And enough to last a very willing married lady a good 'undred years of faithful service, I should say!"

"So what of that?" said Sary stoutly, refusing to be daunted by mere arithmetic. "It sounds a deal, I'll grant you. But 'ard work never did hurt nobody, so I've 'eard tell. And if it ain't hurt me, I don't see how it signifies."

"Well if we're onto maxims, dearie – another that you might 'ave 'eard, tells how the often-trodden pathway grows no grass! And another 'as it that the tree too early robbed may never bear no fruit. You said yourself you've 'ad to call for 'pothecary's pills, and more than once – and like as not, while taking in a poxy Tom or two. Or am I wrong?"

"Well, maybe not." Sary's heart quite suddenly as cold and heavy as a stone. (No children – no heirs for Hadderton? If that was true, how would he bear it? How could she ever ask him to?) "But I still say it'd take a good sight more than that to make an hearty young woman barren," she maintained, with a confidence that sounded hollow even to her own ears.

"P'raps so. I'm only 'ere to tell you that whores who've served a three or four years' term of hackneyship don't generally need to fret no more about mislaying courses." For all the harshness of her accent, the older woman's voice was not unkind. "I can't say for sure," Madge admitted. "Maybe it ain't impossible for gels like you to still make feet for kiddies' slippers. I'm sure I 'ope it ain't. And if you're asking my advice, I'd say try like hell for 'em, before 'is young Lordship's inspiration and 'is year runs out."

Madge laid a veined and clawlike hand on Sary's arm. "But if it don't work out, my lovely, and 'e won't take you for 'is Lady after all – then tell ye what, just you come back to old Ma Perrin, see? I'll still be 'ere, Gawd only knows. And paying culls'll never be in short supply in Brighton this side of Judgement Day. That I *can* answer for!"

BOOK 2
(1820–1861)

Chapter Fourteen

The dawn sky was cloudless, faintly flushed in evidence of a sun as yet concealed behind the tall sea-houses of French Dieppe. The air on deck as sharp, as cold and clean as was the sea, which swelled but gently now around the anchored sailing-packet. A little weak still from its earlier effects mid-Channel, David leant upon the rail and strained his eyes for details of the foreign shore. Chalk cliffs and grey slate roofs. Sails of pale or russet canvas in the harbour, and double rows of shady lime trees hard against the quay. A town well nigh as close to Brighton as were Dover or Southampton, with less than thirty leagues of water to separate it from the Sussex coast. And yet a world away from all the confines and obligations which the deerpark wall of Hadderton, the cliffs of Albion itself fenced in.

France, *la belle France!* Home of England's greatest adversary, and of those stirring principles which Buonaparte had so distorted for his own aggrandizement. *Liberté, fraternité* – but above all as far as this young tourist was concerned, *égalité*. For here David dared at last to hope that he and Sary could be truly equals. Nothing in France to stand between him and his *amante de coeur!* Or so he felt on deck that morning.

For one reason or another the European tour which David finally agreed to undertake the previous December, had been postponed from month to month, to August of the following year of 1820. In January the old mad King George III, who'd sat the throne of England for almost sixty years, decided unaccountably to give up eating. And no Englishman, proclaimed Lord South-bourne, looking sternly at his son, could even think of travelling

149

until their Good King George was laid to rest at Windsor. In February, the succeeding monarch hastened to his favourite town of Brighton, to spend a month inhaling healthy coastal air and recovering from pleurisy. And with his marine pavilion now become a Regal Palace, and all his court and courtiers descending on the place, Madge Perrin had declined to spare her favourite working girl until a suitable replacement could be found for her. Meanwhile, David's father was called away to London – and with vital decisions still to make on what carriage, which team of horses and which manservant he'd have transported across the Channel for his son. In the spring, Her ignoble Majesty Queen Caroline had returned from self-imposed exile on the Continent to claim a consort's title. Only to be countered by a new Bill to relieve her of it, and divorce proceedings in the House of Lords to which near every senior peer and bishop in the realm was summoned. Lord Southbourne not excepted.

"Government business," he importantly declared, riding off to hear the details of how the fat Queen had cohabited with her Italian secretary at her villa on Lake Como, or else on tours through Germany and the Levant. "We'll settle the arrangements for your own tour in a week or two when this is over, my boy," he'd promised. "No sense in rushin' fences, don't ye know."

But when by mid-July it was apparent that their Lordships' burning ears were still to be assaulted by some weeks of sordid royal revelations, while from Redford Octavia Stanville wrote to propose another little summer visit to her dearest relative of Hadderton, David had come to realize that they must leave, and promptly, if they would ever leave at all. In March he had attained majority, and with it a more than adequate financial independence. He needed no parental guidance or permission, could draw immediately on funds at Lewes bank. He might as readily buy a carriage in Dieppe as ship one over from his father's coach-house, he discovered, or else hire a post-chaise to carry them to Paris. As for servants – what benefit could any common English fellow be, who knew nothing of Continental customs and spoke not a single word of French? '*The life of a man is but a little shadow thrown into the dust*,' quoth Sophocles. Or something very like it. And no good reason now, his impatient student told himself, to waste another flicker of it in prevarication.

He'd written and sealed three letters, accordingly. One to the French Consul in Poland Street, to request two passports by return. Another, to be sent on to his parents at their London mansion of St James's, and a third to his cousin Tavie at her father's house at Redford. A fourth more closely written document he himself delivered to the bailiff of the Hadderton estates – with notes upon their management until Lord Southbourne should return. Which done, he'd boldly ridden down to Brighton to find the master of a Channel packet that might expect to sail from thence within the next few days.

David straightened at the rail to rub his eyes and push up the dark hair from his forehead. So here they were already and in foreign waters. With Sary in the cabin, dependent now on his protection and his guidance, and only waiting to be told they had arrived in France. The tide was rising, the breeze onshore to carry them into the harbour of Dieppe. And in the young man's vision as he stared across the water, all of Europe, all their future life together, stretched out beyond it toward the rising sun.

Until the final moment of departure, when their boat ground off the shingle to row out to meet the *Eliza* packet, Sary herself had never quite believed that he would take her. Sary Snudden, harlot's brat and whore – to progress in princely style through Europe! To stay in grand hotels and see the sights, even to cross the Alps! And to return from their *hymeneal tour* a finished lady at the least, if not a titled Viscountess! Despite Davy's brave intentions to fly his gilded cage – despite her own bold statements of support, plain commonsense had told her not to pin her hopes to anything so frail and insubstantial as a lover's promise. No, not even to her David's. Willingly she had approved the *itinerarium* he drafted for the journey, the *cartes de visite* he had printed, and all the letters of introduction he'd assembled. She loved to listen to the extracts he'd read over to her from his 'Gentleman's Companion for Travelling into Foreign Parts'. Nor had she needed any second bidding to order for herself a brand new travelling-dress of cherry coloured merino, with a quadruple-caped pelisse to match, and the latest thing in scuttle bonnets bedecked with all the plumes and trimmings it could carry. But it was not in fact 'til Black Peg and Barbara had embraced her on the shore (and cried until the mastic

151

coursed in grimy channels through their rouge), 'til Hodge had pushed them off, and Mother Perrin shouted out a final caustic warning to 'be good, my lovely, just like Madge learned ye!', that Sary really could allow the dream to be reality – deliberately forgetting for the present her employer's earlier, more serious observations on the tour. To let out all the flood of triumph and excitement she'd been storing up through months of waiting for this moment.

"Will ye look there, Davy," she exclaimed. "For gracious sake, you'd a-thought they'd build a pier in Brighton, wouldn't you, the trouble that beach-loading gives 'em. Why, that raft 'longside the packet looks fit to dish its cargo in the drink – 'orses, coach and all! And ain't you glad now that you left your own at home?" Jiggling up and down upon her seat beside him in the lighter just like a boisterous child. "Oh Davy, duck, I can't 'ardly wait to get aboard, can you?" she cried. "And only fancy – this time tomorrow, if the wind holds true, you and I will be in France. *Abroad*! I wish poor Ma could see me now, I really do!" And not even the unfamiliar motion of the larger vessel, which confined her to the cabin through all the hours of crossing, could dampen Sary's spirit. She'd lain quietly in the darkness of her little shelf-like bunk, enduring cramp and nausea, yet trembling with excitement all the while. And when at last the creaking movements of the bulkheads became less violent, and she'd fallen into sleep, she dreamt of sailing on a lake of bright blue water. In sunny Italy, as she imagined, with ruined marble temples all along the shores. And David standing at the mast in golden coronet and robes of purple silk, beseeching his dearest Sary to be his consort. So that, when he'd woken her to say they were arrived in French Dieppe, she laughed aloud and told him that she'd passed it long before to take her crown as Queen of Italy!

* * *

Four decades later, the lady in her drawing-room of fashionable St James's was striving to impart some sense of what a girl like her had felt, and how she had reacted to her very first experience of Continental Europe.

"In the days before the steam-packets and the railways, Mr

Brown, I can only tell you that to cross the English Channel was still an adventure in geography, and of the human spirit." Her still handsome amber eyes unfocused, gazing inwardly at images too numerous and intimate to find a place within her narrative.

"These days," she said, "when any little office clerk with thirty pound in hand may take his holiday in Paris, and make the trip from Charing Cross within a single day, 'tis hard I think for anyone to appreciate quite how remote it all still seemed to us back then in 1820. All so utterly *original*, you understand. So wonderfully exciting! And from the moment that one first set foot on foreign soil . . ."

* * *

From the *Bureau de l'Octroi*, the crowded little custom-house beside the quay, a barefoot boy of nine or ten – his hand-barrow stacked high with their luggage – escorted them across a wooden bridge to where a flaking signboard proclaimed 'PRATTS HOTEL. Welcome to English'; and a woman in a high starched head-dress reserved for them a room without a second glance for Sary's vivid painting.

"The object of travelling," said David (who, although he'd never toured before, had read extensively about it, and carried in his pocket Martyn's *Gentleman's Guide Through France*), "is to leave our English prejudices behind, to break the bounds of our conventions and learn from all we see." And while the young philosopher himself set forth into the town, to find a barber and see about their transport through to Paris, Sary sat within the window of their room in Pratt's Hotel to put the theory into practice. The smells of fish and sewage that rose up to her from the river they'd already crossed, if not agreeable exactly, were certainly of powerful interest. Moreover, the houses reflected in it from the further bank seemed like to scrape the sky, she thought, so tall and straight they stood – six, seven, eight casements, one upon the other! Nothing like them ever to be seen in Seaford or in Brighton!

'And mayhap these Frenchies must always strive for height in everything?' she postulated, eager to discover all she could about them. For in their several doorways beneath this towering cliff of masonry, she'd noticed that the women sat to spin or weave their

153

lace, in head-dresses so monstrous tall they had to stoop to clear the lintels when they went indoors!

Nearer to the quayside, hidden from her neighbours by an angle of the street, another younger woman leant against the wall with hands on hips, her head inclined a little to one side. So still, it seemed to Sary that the colours of her dress had merged into the very stones behind, like streaks of red and black upon the wall. An unknown young woman of Dieppe. Yet one who now already shared a secret with the English girl who watched her from the hotel across the river. For beside her in the wall an open door gaped darkly. 'And if I'm a judge, at any moment now she'll slip inside,' thought Sary, 'and up 'er petticoats to order of the Tom that's standing in the 'allway casting 'er wet fortune. She will and all, or I'm a Dutchman's aunt.'

And so she very promptly had. The man himself glimpsed briefly as he closed the door behind the pair of them. One thing at least that was arranged the same way here in France, it would appear, as in old England!

The next morning following, the young English 'Milor' and his *fille de joie* (as everyone at Pratt's Hotel had instantly and accurately defined them) departed from Dieppe by public *diligence*, en route for Paris. In the course of his enquiries at the barber's, David had established that a private post-chaise might possibly be hired to convey them to the capital. But since the journey must in any case be broken twice, the couple would be advised, the barber thought, to travel in the greater comfort of the modern diligence that left at six from their hotel. And, moreover, at a fraction of the cost.

"What, in *that?*' cried Sary with a shout of laughter when she first beheld the monster from the gallery of their hotel. "They call that 'modern'? A whale on wheels, that's what I call it – a blessed wooden whale! And ropes to draw it, Davy, and fat old slugs of cattle! Dearie, we'd crawl to Paris quicker, that's eyeproof!"

At a lumbering average speed of just six miles an hour, the diligence was certainly no Brighton Flyer. And yet, inside the rear and principal compartment of this 'Gallic omnibus', the seats were quite as wide and comfortable as anyone could wish. Glass windows on both sides allowed fine views of all the passing landscape. And even Sary must eventually confess that its slower pace, its balanced suspension above the eight great wheels, made travelling *en diligence* a far from disagreeable experience.

From the top of the hill above the Channel port, Normandy stretched out before them to the horizon as a rolling agricultural plain. Huge undivided tracts of ripening oats and barley lapped the margins of a highway that was straighter, broader and, by far, more level than any Sussex turnpike. In place of English hedge-rows there were elm plantations and fruiting apple trees. Or else (to show no doubt how extra-high a Norman tree might be induced to grow) great avenues of lofty poplars. Here and there along the road, fields choked with dock and scarlet poppies, or empty barns and half-deserted villages attested to the years of war which had depopulated northern France. A number of noble châteaux that they passed were shuttered up or delapidating into ruin, with placards inscribed '*En vente*' beside their gates. And yet you never would imagine from the stout and smiling peasants at the roadside, or from the way in the *auberges* they spoke so proudly still of 'l'Empereur et la Gloire', that this French race had ever lost at Leipzig or at Waterloo.

The first stage of the journey overland to Rouen, being a distance of some forty miles, had taken until mid-afternoon to complete; with numerous halts along the way to take in sustenance and rest the horses. Twice while the other passengers tarried over meals or coffee at auberges, David and Sary walked on ahead along the Paris road. To view the wildflowers in the margins of the waving corn, and to indulge those lovers' tendencies to touch and mention things unmentionable, which the presence of two know-ing Frenchmen and an elderly *curé* must certainly inhibit within a six-seat diligence compartment. After their lengthy voyage across the Channel, they both had felt too weary when finally they lay together in their bed at Pratt's Hotel to do much more than pay love's courtesies to one another. And to sleep. But that was then. Now, thoroughly refreshed – triumphant in the knowledge of what they'd left behind them, thrilled by the prospect of all that lay ahead, and already hopelessly enamoured of the full-blown beauties of the Normandy *campagne* – it was only the risk of being overtaken prematurely by their transport, that prevented them from deviating to some wayside barn or granary to put an end to hours of delectable suspense.

155

But if David on the road to Rouen was reminded of the early days of his infatuation, when he'd ridden off to Brighton as erect and tumid as a lovesick satyr; for Sary the experience was something altogether new. Her love for Davy had been compounded hitherto of tenderness and something close akin to family affection. Emotions all bound up with the mother she had lost and the child she now might never have – and with her memories of that awkward 'Johnny-raw' who'd come to her for his initiation. Feelings more to do with giving than receiving, and dependent in no obvious way upon those amatory skills by which she'd earned her living. Now, for the first time in her life, Sary experienced an active, selfish longing for possession of a man, and for a man's possession of her. Nothing maternal now in what she felt for David. No Madge or Mary Price to keep tally on how many times, and in what mode, he had her. Now at last, without compulsion, calculation or any kind of haste, she found herself at liberty to love as other girls of two and twenty loved. Now her thoughts, as they strolled together through the golden summer countryside of Normandy, no longer dwelt upon the arts she would employ to bring her David pleasure. Instead she painted him in her imagination, from head to foot and without a stitch of clothing. She thought of how his mouth would taste and how his skin would smell. Of how that part of him would feel enfolded in her body this night in their hotel at Rouen. She stooped to pick a bunch of vivid poppies at the roadside. And lingered stooping, aware of how the muslin clung to her perspiring body, wanting him to look, and daring him to touch her. She climbed the steep steps of the diligence ahead of him, and slowly. And once inside, with three other passengers to witness it, she smiled into his eyes and sent a message through their dark dilated pupils which shortly had induced his Lordship to sit upright on the leather cushions of his seat and drop a casual glove across his thighs. While, as she saw her dart strike home in him, Sary's own flesh opened in a very sympathetic wound.

*　　*　　*

The glass bell which once more enclosed her little childhood doll, dripped like a syrup pudding with the molten yellow light from the gasolier above it. With Mr Brown's polite bewhiskered face reflected on its curving surface. And nothing but a scrap of faded taffeta, a protruding porcelain foot, to reveal the presence of its occupant. Poor Jemima – poor little lady! No shoes, no bows or plumes. Her rosy cheeks, her eyes, her painted mouth all rubbed away. No eyes to see – no mouth to tell what she had seen and heard that glorious night in Rouen!

Though Sary herself could see Jemima still as she'd been then when she retrieved her from amongst the crumpled scarves and handkerchiefs in her portmanteau. Faded and tattered even then; nose chipped, hair no longer braided. Sparse now and matted. But still with eyes, a face, a personality. A *dame de qualité* when Sary was a child. A muppet to amuse the cullys when Sary was a whore, an impassive witness to the acts she had performed with them. And now somehow in Rouen – and in some way the girl herself had barely understood – a witness to record for all their future this turning-point in her existence. The reason why, with trembling hands, she propped the little doll up on a chest in their hotel room and turned its painted eyes of blue toward the high French bed.

* * *

Their chamber in the Hôtel Vatel at Rouen was roughly furnished and far from clean, with lath and plaster walls and cobwebs hanging from the ceiling. But Sary barely noticed. While David settled the arrangements for the next stage of their journey, to Louviers and from thence to Paris, she swiftly checked the bed for bugs and other livestock, then waited at the open window. Watching the bustle of activity within the dusty courtyard down below. Watching swallows swoop and twitter against a cloudless evening sky. Looking out across the roofs to the cathedral, her weariness entirely gone. And when she heard his hand upon the door, she lifted up her own to grasp the flaking shutters either side. Determined not to turn to meet him, or at least not yet.

"That poor French maidy, Joan of Arc?" she called out to him. "Was it over there they burned 'er, did you say, in the marketplace near the cathedral?"

His footsteps – one, two, three, four – approaching her across the bare boards of the chamber . . .

"Four hundred years ago," he said, his voice unsteady. So close behind her now that she could feel the movement of the air between their bodies.

"Tall towers ain't they," she said inconsequentially, "on the cathedral." Staring, now unseeing, at the scene beyond the window. Her hands still on the shutters. And in a moment, any moment, he would touch her. His arms around her, and his hands . . . Oh God, already lifting the soft tresses of her hair – already sliding down toward her breasts . . .

"Over 'ere they seem to want to push up everything as high as it will go. 'Ave ye noticed, Davy?"

"I have, my love – and know the feeling all too well," his ardent Lordship whispered in her ear.

She felt it too behind her. And his hands caressing all the while. His lips, his tongue upon the warm skin of her shoulder. And in a little while she'd turn. (In just a little while. But not quite yet.) The agony of waiting too exquisite – or *almost* too exquisite – to relinquish.

Chapter Fifteen

Octavia Stanville had glimpsed the postman's red and blue from an upstairs window of her father's house at Redford, and heard his knock and saw his horse retreating down the gravel before she moved to intercept the footman with the letter. There was no way, to be sure, that she could know that it was David's. Her father regularly maintained a dozen correspondents, and the Midhurst postman was no stranger to their door. Yet somehow she *had* known.

Lord Southbourne, on 'Queen's business' in London still, was not at liberty to frank letters out of Hadderton. So Footman John must needs pay eightpence from the post-box for this one's safe delivery. David himself had superscribed her name and situation on the verso.

A narrow fold of paper. A blob of scarlet wax. The impression of the signet that he wore upon his little finger. Her own name in his impatient script. And inside? A few brief rows of words – too few, if she knew David – in the approved abbreviated manly style. With several crossed or overwritten. And, at the bottom, his formal signature scrawled half across the page to fill the space. Not much in essence to a letter, Octavia thought, when you reflected the power that it might have to elevate or to destroy a person's life.

For no especial reason she could think of, she bore his letter down the landing to the schoolroom that she shared with Charles before they'd both been sent away to board. To open it while seated at an old school table which still bore remembrances of Charlie's penknife, and the large inkstain where she herself had upset the standish in her efforts to retrieve a stolen ruler from her brother.

Hadderton
August 2nd 1820

My dear Octavia,

I must thank you for the favour of your letter of July 28th, which prompts me to a swift reply.

With regard to your coming to Hadderton, any such plan must be deferred, I fear, at least until the Queen's examination be completed and my parents may return from London. For, truth to tell, I myself will not be here to receive you, intending as I am to leave next week for my Continental Tour, the which I have been planning, as you know, these many weeks and months. We are to travel by packet to Dieppe and from thence to Paris (for which place we have been furnished with numerous introductions). And then, when we have exhausted the treasures and the pleasures of that city, we migrate south to Italy. To the Land of Art and True Romance!

You may have noticed, Cousin, that I use the plural personal pronoun. And I do not think it will amaze you quite to discover that Miss Snudden is to travel with me. For though I know my father intended me to go alone, I must tell you that I am unalterably attached to her, and cannot be separated from my beloved Sarah for near so long a period. You have been unjust in your own estimate of her, Octavia, depend upon it. And I flatter myself that I know you well enough to believe that in due time you will come to see things with quite another face. You have represented me as careless of my home, its reputation and its future. But be assured that I have Hadderton in mind as much as anything, when I say that I intend to marry Sarah on our return to England and to make her the mother of its heirs.

I write, as you may suppose, in high spirits and expectations. So wish me well. For I can also assure you that I am, and would wish ever to remain, your affectionate cousin,

Denton

P.S. Excuse the scrawl – scratched in a great hurry. D.

With one long polished fingernail Octavia traced the folioles of the ancient ink blot. A fragment of her own unguarded youth preserved forever on the schoolroom table. And years from now, with Lord Denton safe returned to Hadderton and his inheritance, proficient in self-government and cured of his infatuation (for to Octavia it was self-evident that no one of David's background could really love a whore), then might not his hasty letter come to represent no more than this? This forgotten inky ghost upon the table?

Hadderton in mind as much as anything – 'Oh Davy, you fool!' Octavia, who believed in the Divine Disposer and in His dispositions, prayed uncharitably that her cousin's illicit liaison might yield none but bitter fruit. Resisting her first impulse to screw up the traitorous letter and fling it in the schoolroom grate, she refolded it carefully instead. Forcing herself to rise and leave the room with all the injured dignity she would have presented to its writer, if he'd been there in the flesh, to watch her do it with those damnably dark and long-lashed eyes of his. If only she could be sure he'd weary of the trollop before he could get a child upon her! Before he made to *marry* her, the dunderhead! The small white hand which had so sensibly preserved his letter, now crushed it suddenly in reaction to a pernicious and unworthy afterthought. A thought that shocked and shamed its thinker even as it crept into her mind. 'If only *my beloved Sarah* would contrive to catch a fever on the Continent,' it whispered to Octavia, 'and conveniently to die there!'

Although, as it transpired, the only fever Sary Snudden caught in France, she caught from the Parisians. And for a girl of her bold tastes and vigorous constitution, it wasn't a distemper the least bit likely to prove fatal. Free now at last of all restrictions, in love with David and with France, and with every daily new experience that they brought to her, she'd come to Paris in the perfect frame to catch from it the fever of frivolity and dissipation with which that post-war city was so thoroughly infected.

Since his final defeat and exile to the lonely rock of St Helena – since the second restoration of the decapitated King's brother, Louis XVIII – Napoleon Buonaparte was nowhere mentioned by his name within the capital, as he still was without it. The faithless

161

Parisians referred to him obliquely as *Celui*, 'That One'. Or else as 'The Tyrant' or 'Usurper'. Royalist *émigrés*, who seemed to have learned nothing from their years abroad, now fluttered once again about the stolid person of a Bourbon king, like moths around a fat and freshly kindled flame. Returning exiles, to whom the licentious societies of Rome and London and St Petersburg had become as familiar as their native Paris, now rubbed shoulders in its salons and resorts with the English dandies and *tourists* who followed on the Allied Occupation. And with the ladies of the *demi-monde* who hung upon their arms and laughed at everything they said. After years of revolution, war and Napoleonic gravity, pleasure was now the *mot d'ordre* for all. And pleasure was to be found in more places and in greater variety in Paris than Sary had imagined in her wildest dreams of what the city might be like.

The building in the Faubourg St Germain to which the diligence from Louviers delivered them, seemed closer to the private mansion of some nobleman or minor royalty than to any mere hotel, with its marble vestibule and luxurious residential suites. Or so Sary had thought, until the invitation to a soirée in the Place Vendôme across the river showed her how such people really lived in Paris. Passing, as she and David had on that occasion, through no fewer than seven vast and richly decorated apartments. To find their hostess in a flowing robe of apricot cashmere, lounging in an exquisite oval bedchamber, blazing with candles and festooned all round with scarlet Lyons silk. Here in the gorgeous salons of Restoration Paris, and elsewhere within the city, David's status as an English Lord (and one whose family was known to many reinstated royalists) secured for the pair of them an automatic place. No sooner were his cards and introductory letters delivered and received than they'd been swept into a perpetual stream of entertainment. Driving, strolling, dancing, jumping in and out of carriages; constantly surrounded by the cream of French society. One morning some old acquaintance of the Southbournes would insist they join an expedition to his *château de plaisance* on the Seine or in the forest of Vincennes outside the city, for an informal fork-luncheon and a stroll around the gardens; before returning in a convoy of berlins and hired barouches for an evening at the opera. With a supper afterwards at Vérey's. On another afternoon there'd be a picnic in the Bois. Or a balloon ascent to witness from the gardens of the Tivoli – with fireworks to follow and dancing by the light of Japanese lanterns. Or a grand masked ball at the Embassy in the Rue St Honoré. Or gaming at Frascati's, where even women nowadays were welcomed.

To Sary the fascinations and contradictions of the place seemed inexhaustible. Like a child at a party, she was continually admiring, exclaiming, laughing with delight or begging explanations from those about her. Why was it, she demanded, that the great ladies of the salons were so gaily robed and painted while the whores on the *entresols* of the Palais Royal dressed plainly and wore crucifixes around their necks? Why were the theatres so dull and sober here in Paris and the church rituals so dramatic? And why was everyone so monstrous fond of dogs and careless of their children? And if Brighton was the very jewel of Europe, as its *habitués* so often claimed, why was it then they had no *boulevards* back there, not even round the Steine? Because, to Sary's way of thinking, quite the most wonderful thing about this entirely wonderful city must be those noble avenues which ringed it round, and separated one busy crowded *quartier* from another. The Paris boulevards! And, every evening they were free from other invitations and engagements, she insisted David take her there to stroll beneath the trees.

"What, stay indoors, in bed – and on a night like this?" she said. "Not I, my Lord. Not likely!" And on would go her tallest feathered bonnet, and out they'd sally into the soft sultry summer night. To join the crowds along the Champs Elysées or on the Boulevard of Montparnasse. To watch the clowns and conjurors perform, or listen to the strolling singers. And then to consume their coffee and their ices at little café tables, or on the lawns before the brightly lit pavilions of the *glaciers*, while all the world together with his wife, his children and their nursemaids passed by in grand procession.

"Oh Davy, see the monkey in the little soldier's hat! Just like your cousin Charlie! Ain't 'e though? And look how those moths and beetles beat against the lamp, poor things. And look – do look, My Lady in the carriage 'as just lost half 'er ice atwixt 'er diddy-bubbies! And serve 'er right, I say, for lacing 'em so mighty high. Why I declare, the silly totty can't hardly find 'er way around them to 'er mouth!"

And David, who'd never greatly cared for his own species in such superfluous numbers, could only sit as he was bidden and wait with whatever patience he could find for their return to the hotel (where, so far as he was concerned, the main enjoyments of the evening still awaited them). Sary, who'd spent her life amongst the barrack troops of Blatchington and Alfriston, the busy sisterhood at Mrs Perrin's and the promenading crowds of Brighton, could hardly hope to understand how much he already missed the solitude of Hadderton. Or what it was that drew him from the popular modern exhibition rooms of the Louvre to the sombre unfrequented Claudes and Poussins of the Grand Gallery. Or why it was that he should prefer a rural drive beyond Montmartre or through the Bois to walking through the seething gardens of the Palais Royal. Her ideal world as full of bustle as his was ordered, quiet and tranquil. And it was only in the bedroom of their grand suite at the Hôtel d'Orleans that they could find a recreation which delighted both of them in nearly equal measure.

By the time they'd viewed together all the treasures of the Louvre and Luxembourg galleries, and the interiors of a score of Paris churches, royal palaces and châteaux, David was entirely ready to press south to Lyons. And from thence across the Alps to Italy. Within a fortnight of their arrival in the Faubourg St Germain, the London mail had brought a curt, reproachful letter, upbraiding him for his impatience and recording his father's verdict that he'd broken their agreement by bringing Sary with him on the tour. 'Send her packing while there's time still,' Lord Southbourne urged. 'Or leave the baggage with our friends in Paris if you must, and go on to Rome alone. My boy, 'tis time you cut loose from the petticoats to make your own way through the world. For I tell you frankly that you'll never see things clearly else, nor make a fitting master for Hadderton. And if you won't, then damn me, you may stay abroad for aught I care . . .' A missive to be followed by a spate of letters from Lady Alethea (who'd never shared her husband's reluctance to set pen to paper). To beseech, cajole, demand or threaten David – according to the writer's mood – to oblige her very much by ridding himself of that 'dreadful vulgar girl', and returning immediately to civilized existence. And, although he had replied to both politely in the negative, repeating that he'd rather stay abroad forever than be parted from his Sary

164

for a single day, David, who'd learned to dread the weekly mails, began to feel that Paris was a deal too close to England still for comfort.

He was also all too conscious, as Sary clearly wasn't, of the essential shallowness of Restoration Paris. A society that used its pursuit of pleasure as a shield against reality. As if there'd never been a revolution or a war. He saw, as she did not, the looks that the *grandes dames* of the salons exchanged at her gaucheries of conversation and appearance, whilst smiling to her painted face and remarking how refreshingly amusing, how enchanting they considered her. Sincere as she was always, he resented every hour that Sary spent in such unworthy company. In the Grand Gallery of the Louvre he stood before that Poussin masterpiece, *Adam and Eve in Paradise*, and dreamed a wistful dream of *primavera*. Of himself and Sary far away from all these people. Alone together in some springtime Eden beyond the Alps, beyond the reach of Lady Southbourne's anxious pen. Alone in Shelley's 'paradise of exiles'. In Italy!

He only had to say the word, he knew, and Sary would willingly have followed him to the world's end. She'd said as much herself a score of times. And yet he hesitated. After the struggle and the degradation, as he saw it, of her life in Brighton – after the shameful subterfuge he'd forced her to at Hadderton, the delays and months of waiting for this tour – he so much wanted to make her reparation. To see his Sary free and happy, enjoying life. Which here in Paris demonstrably she was. And if he himself grew weary of the endless expeditions and amusements with which she delighted to cram her days, he had their summer nights still in the hotel, when she rewarded him unstintingly, delectably, for his forbearance. Those hours worth all the rest to David, and much more.

One Saturday morning of the early autumn, with the leaves from the double row of plane trees in the Boulevard of St Germain already rustling underfoot, he found himself embarked on yet another urban expedition of discovery, in the company of Sary and a noisy group of half a score of students from the Sorbonne and the Conservatoire. Young men they'd met within the salons, who claimed unblushingly to be acquainted with every useful branch of art and science in the capital; and begged to be permitted to share such knowledge with their English visitors. They were all aghast! Milord Denton had not yet visited the botanical collection of the Jardin des Plantes? Milady had yet to meet with the celebrated *caméléopard* in its menagerie? Without a doubt they must themselves repair the omission, they insisted, and with all speed. And if David suspected that Sary's scientific education concerned them something less perhaps than her existing assets, he was sure enough by then of her fidelity to feel some sense of pride in her effect on other males. Her arm in his, not one of theirs, for their perambulation down the quay to the menagerie. And however they competed to impress her, to make her laugh with their attempts at formal English – it was his eyes, his hands, not theirs, that knew the secrets of her body. His privilege, and his alone at last, to taste its sweetest fruits.

The Jardin des Plantes, as their young escort were all too eager to explain, had been laid out for Louis XIII two hundred years before; and to a plan that blended art with nature in forms that only Frenchmen could hope to understand. Within its formal herb-gardens, its hot-houses and orangeries, there were, they claimed, a greater variety of living plants than in any other garden in the world. Within its *musée* and Gallery of Natural History, more curiosities. In its library more botanical volumes . . .

But Sary, for whom flowerless plants with pompous Latin names did nothing whatsoever, ignored all else to beg they should be taken directly, and without a moment of delay, to see the famous camel-leopard. An outlandish animal, she had been told, that combined the features not only of the camel and the leopard of its name, but – as with the legendary and ancient Chimaera – those of a goat, a serpent and a lion besides. (And one which Sary hopefully credited with scaly wings and giant proportions, in the bargain.) "As high as three tall fellows standing on each other's shoulders, so's I've 'eard tell – and weighty as three bullocks set together," she excitedly exclaimed, hurrying past a grove of palm trees grown in wooden tubs and then a pair of goggling ostriches, with barely a remark to spare for their originality. "And see 'ere, Davy – 'ere's the sign marked 'Came-leo-par-dalis'," she read out. "And will you look at the *size* of the kennel they've built to 'ouse the beast! Why, that door alone would clear an elephant in pattens and a stove-pipe hat. I'll swear it would!"

For two francs extra they were each admitted through a further wicket gate to join a swelling crowd around the bars of the enclosure of 'Cameleopardalis'. And when the space was quite full up, with every bar supporting its fair complement of fists, and every gap between, a face; the keeper of the wicket shot his bolts and jumped upon his stool to shout in thunderous tones: "*Messieurs-dames! Voici le premier valet de chambre!*" At the same time pointing a dramatic finger to where his signal had called forth an entrant to the barred enclosure. A negro slave, as it appeared, extravagantly robed and turbaned and blacker than Black Peg herself in his complexion.

A ripple of excitement passed through the crowd. And as the black attendant moved to open up the double doors that hid the creature still from sight, all pressed forward for a better view.

"*Voyez!*" cried out the gatekeeper again, his voice obscuring some command or invitation which the negro, standing in the entrance of the building, spoke quietly to its occupant. "*Mes amis, il n'y a rien d'autre de pareil au monde! Regardez le caméléopard!*"

For a long moment of heavy-breathing silence nothing stirred within the dark interior. Then slowly, almost apologetically, there appeared high up around the door-post the distended nostrils and fringed lashes of a leopard-spotted camel, with goat's horns up above and flicking deer-like ears. To be followed by a long, immensely long, reticulated python of a neck; and finally – just when it seemed the thing must be some kind of camel-headed serpent – by a massive dappled shoulder.

"*Mon dieu!*" and "*Ça alors!*" exclaimed two awestruck voices in the crowd. And a child's high wail of fear had rent the air. But most, struck dumb, drew back instinctively from anything so large – while on the monster came, picking its way through the drifting leaves of its enclosure with outstretched neck and stiffly jointed shanks, like some almighty wading bird.

"There now, and didn't I 'ave the right of it at that?" said Sary boldly through the silence. "These French want height in every-thing, and no mistake about it!" The very calmness of her voice a signal for the others to push back toward the bars and recommence their own exclamations of amazement. While David, who'd seen the English specimen of *Giraffa cameleopardalis* in London, before the poor thing died, had felt a surge of pity for the tall and lonely captive in its cage.

167

With the beast now fully visible to all, the gatekeeper embarked at once upon her further introduction. A recital which the young student next to Sary most obligingly translated into English for her. "Her name, *Messieurs-dames*, I give you as 'Ursuline'. The first of all her species to reach the shores of France alive. Although the scholars of antiquity inform us that the Romans brought living cameleopards to the Colosseum and slew them there for sport . . ." And while he spoke, the gangling Ursuline attained the outer limit of her compound and halted there beside her black attendant. The crowd, convinced by now that she was harmless, were calling her by name, rattling on the bars and waving gloves and handkerchiefs to make her look their way.

"Like her relative the camel, the animal can live for months with only thorns to eat and scarcely any water," the gatekeeper was forced to shout against the rising din. "Our French naturalists attribute to the cameleopard the highest and the noblest moral qualities. It is remarkable, moreover, that this docile creature is entirely mute and cannot cry, not even when in pain . . ."

In a graceful, unexpected movement the lofty head swooped down at that moment toward a fluttering handkerchief a few feet down the bars from Sary and her group; and several of the crowd leapt back with shrieks of exaggerated terror and surprise. Leaving Sary, as the animal itself recoiled, with the lingering image of a pair of gentle and perplexed brown eyes, with a feeling of great sadness and forbearance. 'And just like this they must 'ave died, poor dumb defenceless beasts,' she thought with sudden sympathy, 'all in among them yelling 'eathens of the Roman Collyseeum.' Indignantly she turned to tell the persecuting French herself, in plain King's English, to hold their silly tongues. To encounter, with an even greater shock of recognition, a near identical long-suffering expression in another pair of fine brown eyes immediately behind her.

David! Her most noble Lord, her very own dear Johnny-raw. Here hemmed in all about with laughing, shoving, cheerfully unfeeling Parisians, just like the wretched camel-leopard! She saw in a flash how selfish she had been to delay him here for all this time against his natural inclination. And having seen, and being Sary Snudden, she hastened to repair the error by the most direct and obvious means at her disposal.

Chapter Sixteen

"By sole and special permit of His Majesty Victor Emanuel I, King of Sardinia, Jerusalem and Cyprus, Duke of Savoy, Piedmont and Genoa," David solemnly read out, translating the formal printed notice as he went, "Messrs Bonnafoux of the City of Lyons are pleased to run the ROYAL DILIGENCE twice weekly across the Alpine Mountains from Lyons to Turin, and at all seasons of the year. The vehicle will pass across the Col of Mount Cenis, resting overnight (unless otherwise stated) at Chambéry, St-Michel and Susa.

"Next diligence departs Hôtel du Nord, 7 p.m. March 6th, arrives Piazza del Castello, Turin, 5 p.m. March 10th," he added a moment later, from a separate handwritten announcement in another corner of the coaching-office window. "Interior seats 75 francs, Coupé 50 francs."

The young Lord Denton turned back toward his listener with a faint lifting of his blackly feathered brows. An expression to be followed shortly, as expected, by a grin. "Foul smells and suffocation in the belly of the beast? Or fresh air and frostbite in the coupé? So which is it to be then this time, Sary Ann, amore mio?" he demanded of his mistress.

In the event they'd booked the more expensive, warmer and less healthy seats inside. And if the conducteur's assurance that but three of the four remaining places were taken, at first had raised in them rash hopes of breathing-space and elbow-room, these soon were dashed upon uncomfortable reality. On boarding the vehicle (a four-wheeled diligence of an older, cruder type than they had yet encountered), the first thing to meet their gaze was an ungainly wicker cage, suspended from the ceiling. A contrivance shortly to be crammed full with all the beaver hats and muffs and gloves, the bearskins and the winter woollens, which the other passengers had brought to wear above the snowline, and in the process to block out the very maximum of light and air within the coach. Of the other inside passengers – one smoked *cigarros* constantly, another fortified himself from a flask of powerful-smelling brandy. And the third, a lady very near as wide as she was tall, not only contrived to occupy the entire sixth seat, but also carried with her a noxious little lapdog. Nor was there any lamp, or place to hang one from within. So that by the time the diligence was finally in train to leave the Place St Claire in Lyons for its journey through the Alps, the atmosphere inside it (as Sarah Snudden feelingly remarked from the folds of David's box-coat) was already close approaching something between the Black Hole of Calcutta, and Irish Bridie's bedroom at Madge Perrin's on any working night of the Brighton season.

In the end, and despite Sary's repeated expressions of willingness to leave the French capital for Italy whenever David wished, he'd allowed their friends in Paris to persuade him to postpone the journey to sometime in early spring. There was unrest in southern Italy, they pointed out, with the Bourbon King of Naples but recently deposed, and talk of counter-revolution, or even Austrian invasion, in the wind. It would be madness in any case, they all insisted, to attempt the Simplon or the Grand St Bernard in wintertime. While even for the lower Alpine route across the *Col du Mont Cenis*, there were real dangers of drifts or avalanches when undertaking the traverse too late or early in the year. Why, only the previous January a coach had overset there in a snowstorm, to force its passengers – the famous English painter, Turner, of their number – to complete the whole descent on foot! Lord Denton would be well advised, they told him in the salons, to wait at least 'til March. And Lord Denton (who, like any other man, was only blind to reason when it interfered with basic instinct) had seen the sense of what they said; confining his expeditions and adventures for the present to maps and travel journals from Galignani's Library, all spread out across the bed of their hotel in St Germain. (Or otherwise to Sary, in similar deployment.)

The *giro d' Italia* he'd mapped and planned for them that winter, from his vicarious experience of Smollett's, Piozzi's and Joseph Forsyth's travels, scaled the Alps and crossed the Plain of Lombardy. To journey from Turin to see the Duomo at Milan, the Scala Opera, and the tomb of Juliet in a convent garden at Verona. In Venice to encounter the romance of gondolas – to voyage down the watery streets to the Rialto, the Piazza di San Marco, the architecture of Palladio, and Titians by the score! In Paris in the winter, before a blazing fire or lying in their curtained bed, he'd painted all the famous scenes for Sary in the pristine, glowing colours of his own imagination. He'd borne her south with perfect ease and comfort on the wings of his descriptions – to view the masterworks of Michelangelo and Raphael in Florence, in an atmosphere untainted by heat or dust, or stench. Hand in hand and quite alone, untroubled by the strident voices of the *cicerones*, or by any other mortal interference, they'd strolled between the fractured columns of the Roman Forum. They'd sailed to Capri and climbed Vesuvius, and visited too many galleries of antique and Renaissance art ever to quite recall them all. Each day returning from their expeditions with further priceless souvenirs, to ship back eventually to England.

And Sary, watching David, hearing the excitement in his voice, had been glad to travel with him in his fantasies of Italy. Understanding, as all successful whores through time have understood, the very real importance of a good imagination.

Whether or not he was ready to admit it, it was the *giro*, truth to tell, and not the destination of *Italia* that most appealed to David. The road that stretched beyond Dieppe was what he'd looked to, not the port itself. The same essentially in Paris, and later on in Lyons. He longed to travel. Not primarily, as he'd maintained to Sary, to view the treasures of that legendary peninsula, but actually to put as many miles as possible between himself and Hadderton. To blur its memories and escape its hereditary obligations. And to find a place somewhere (why not in Italy?), where he could feel his life with Sary to be more real and solid, finally, than either of the lives they'd left behind them. As guilty in his way as the Parisians of running blindly from reality.

Near the end of October, the Paris papers had gleefully reported the final collapse in London of the new King George's case against Queen Caroline. Despite the months of hearings, the evidence against the wretched woman had never been conclusive. The

English House of Lords had passed the bill by which the King hoped to break his matrimonial bonds. But by too small a majority to risk a Commons vote. And London celebrated the Queen's 'acquittal' by illuminating the capital for three nights in succession. With the announcement of Prinny's plans for a lavish coronation the following July, however, poor Caroline's brief spell of popularity had ended. To cheer the cause of a persecuted Princess was one thing. To acclaim and crown a blowsy, incontinent and patently unfit Queen, quite another. And in January of 1821, Galignani's *Messenger* in Paris took pleasure in reprinting a scurrilous epigram at that time circulating across the Channel. To illustrate, as it maintained, the English persecution of Caroline of Brunswick-Wolfenbüttel in the year of her royal husband's coronation:

> *Most gracious Queen, we thee implore*
> *To go away and sin no more;*
> *But if that effort be too great,*
> *To go away at any rate!*

In February Lord Southbourne, now returned to Hadderton, had written for a second time to his son – to demand Lord Denton's unfailing return to England within a fivemonth, to attend the coronation of his monarch. An ill-timed injunction, which had served instead to remind David of all he wanted to escape, and to hasten his departure in a precisely contrary direction. For Italy.

The self-appointed *valet de place*, who'd attached himself to Lord Denton and his unlikely lady on their arrival in the French capital six months before, was loud in his insistence that no young Englishman of quality must even think of travelling south without a courier to see him safe. A fellow who knew the pitfalls of such journeys. A man to load and guard his baggage and bespeak his rooms at the auberges – to defend unto the death the bills of exchange or quantities of gold napoleons that he must carry with him for his needs. A Frenchman whom 'Milor' could trust implicitly. A man, in short, exactly such as he himself! And an offer which Lord Denton, to the valet's astonishment and chagrin, rejected out of hand. For David's dreams of journeying through Italy had always been *à deux*. He personally would see to all the details, he declared. He'd defend his own wallet and money-sac, if need be, with the pistol that he carried in his belt. And take pleasure in it too, he might have added, as a son and as a lover. To show them all that he was old enough to manage his own concerns. To guide his own destiny, and Sary's; in France, in Italy, or anywhere on earth that he saw fit to take her!

The journey down from Paris to the Alpine terminus of Lyons had taken them but six days to complete. By diligence as far as Châlon, and from thence by *coche d'eau* down the river Saône. A delightful mode of transport, even so early in the season; propelled by oars at scarcely more than drifting pace between hills rimed with frost, lace-patterned with the shadows of their leafless vines. With the dauntless Sary lavishly dispensing waves and greetings on all the passing traffic of the river. And David only happy to have come so far already, with their baggage and their persons and their love for one another all intact.

In near twelve hours of cramped and noisome blackness, from the last flaring of the porters' torches in the Place St Claire to the first faint signs of early dawning, the ROYAL DILIGENCE progressed by something less than twenty miles. So dark the night, so constant their ascent into the Alpine foothills.

By morning, David's neck was stiff and sore. His boots both felt as if they'd shrunken round his feet; and his right arm, where Sary leant upon it still, had long since lost its natural feeling. In the dim grey light that seeped around the outer curtains of the coach, he could see the mop-thrum tangle of the Frenchwoman's little dog asleep across her lap. A Barbet or an unshorn Poodle. From where he sat the sagging luggage-rack obscured its owner's face, but not the gusty snores that she emitted. And David pictured her with gaping mouth and trembling chins, a pair of them at least – dreaming dreams of Lyonnaise peach-omelettes or *Truffles à l'Italienne*. Beside the snoring woman, a young man of not a quarter her circumference – and quite unknown to her – slept nestled like a child against her padded Lyons-velvet breast. His hat dislodged and fallen to the straw, his dark head rolling on the pillow of her huge left mammary each time it rose and fell.

David smiled, despite his own discomfort. And as he did so caught a corresponding gleam of teeth across the top of Sary's bonnet. The fifth inside passenger was also wide awake, it would appear. "George Grévin, merchant of fine fabrics at your service!"

173

was how he'd introduced himself to them the previous night, in between cigarros. "Supplier of Lyons silks – plain, watered, figured or brocaded – and of velvets, plain or ramaged. Dealer also in Italian lustrings, tabbies, paduasoys and broglios; all of the first and finest quality." A type all too familiar to David from his months with Sary amid the drapers and mantua-makers of Paris. And one whose friendly smile he knew to be a pilot only for the sample-books and offers of reduction, which must follow it, as surely as this fresh new dawning followed their uncomfortable night upon the road.

A reflection reinforced just then by the sound of the conducteur's hobnails on the roof, and the raising of the outside leathern curtains to admit a sudden flood of daylight. The green-washed scene without, delightful and harmonious. Inside, less so, when the large lady had awoken to find her neighbour dribbling cognac-flavoured saliva across her velvet bosom.

At Pont Bonvoison, on the border of his Sardinian Majesty's Duchy of Savoy – and after several necessary halts for relief of one kind or another along the way – *les voyageurs* were bidden to step down at last for breakfast at a village inn.

"And thank the Lord for that, say I," Sary called out pleasantly to the other woman in the carriage – in the sure conviction still that English must be intelligible to even such as she, if only spoken with sufficient force and emphasis. "I vow the way my belly's been creating these past four hours, it must 'ave thought my blessed throat was cut!"

At a long scrubbed table in the kitchen of the inn, they breakfasted or dined (they scarce knew which) on chicken broth, with fresh-baked bread and quantities of tea. The fat woman's little dog, Chouchoutte, sitting by her chair throughout and yapping piercingly for scraps; and the cloth merchant, with sample-book to hand, most anxious so he said to compliment both ladies on their fortitude – and on their stylish mode of dressing. Meantime, along the street, on the outskirts of the frontier village, their luggage was uncorded and unloaded at the custom-house. And one by one the passengers were summoned from the inn to review its contents with the interested *douaniers*. David and Sary went down together, cheerfully and arm in arm – laughing at the sight of soldiers guarding rustic bridges over streams which any healthy child could leap, exclaiming at their first glimpse of the

174

Alps above the village roofs. The mountains' shining snowcaps floated unsupported, as it appeared to them, way up above the clouds.

Others of their company were less favourably impressed by Pont Bonvoison. For the next hour of their journey, the fat Lyonnaise complained constantly of the duties they had made her pay on clothes which she was taking to her son's wife down in Susa. Gifts, generous enough, God only knew, which now became extravagance itself! While, at her side, the dark young Piedmontese who'd so defiled her own vast velvet bodice sat cradling his brandy bottle and glowering savagely.

"They have taken from him his Histories of Guicciardini and Davila, and his volume on the Revolution in France by Mignet," explained the merchant through a cloud of pungent cigar smoke. "Young men like him, they think that their republican ideas may travel with them in their luggage through Royal Savoy and into Piedmont," he added scornfully, "although they know it cannot be. They think they only have to wish it, for the King's *censeurs* all to vanish – how do you say it? – up in steam."

"In smoke – I think the word you seek is 'smoke'," the young man snapped in perfect English, ignoring Sary's spontaneous snort of laughter. "Is that not so, signore?" His large, intense brown eyes now turned on David. "And when all the brutal laws and edicts of these despots are blazing in the piazzas of Torino and Novara, then you may believe that signor Grévin here will see some smoke!"

The merchant smiled uneasily, and glanced behind him at the wall which separated their compartment from the coupé occupied by the conducteur and his outside passengers. "*Un conseil, mon ami – gardez vos opinions pour vous,*" he murmured, pointing significantly with his lighted cigarro. "*Les murs ont des oreilles, vous savez*? The walls, my friend, have ears."

But nothing now it seemed could stop the youth from speaking out. And he applied at once to David and to Sary for support. "You English, with your Magna Carta and your Cromwell, you understand so well the Italian cause," he confidently assured them. "You know what freedom is about. And when you hear as I have, that last week in this same village we have passed, the Prince de la Cisterna was arrested on his return from Paris and taken under guard to Finistrella, then you will burn with indignation too, I think?"

"And I'd think that we might burn a good bit brighter," said

Sary amiably, "if we knew who the devil this 'Cistern' feller is, and what he's done, and what the 'Finistrella' is when it's at 'ome." Her carmine smile and roguish black-lashed wink all the encouragement the other needed, in the event, to reproduce for them the entire history of his people's trials and tribulations. A most romantic and exciting story too. And one that nicely filled (as Sary afterwards maintained) the many hours which it had taken them to trundle through the valleys to the pass of Les Echelles, where their next change of horses and postilions awaited.

The young man was himself returning from an uncle in Geneva, he informed them, to university in the city of Turin. Pietro Gemelli by name, he had the honour to be the firstborn son of il Conte Bartolomeo Gemelli of the Riviera di San Giulio in the Piedmontese province of Novara. (The very jewel, as anyone would tell them, of the Alpine crown of Italy. And a place where love of liberty had for centuries survived the rule of force.) Seven times within a hundred years Novara had been occupied by foreign troops, while through it all her people had retained their ancient vision of becoming part of a united 'Italy'. In the year Pietro was born, his homeland at the very least could call itself *Italian* – a title restored to it by Buonaparte, together with some small degree of independent government. But, following the French Emperor's abdication and the restoration of Piedmont to its Sardinian monarchs, the name, even the idea of an Italy united, was once again forbidden to the Piedmontese.

"And worse, far worse than that," Pietro Gemelli exclaimed despairingly, "they have turned the clock back to the Middle Ages! You English would not believe the antiquated laws we now must labour under." He leant forward, and they smelt the brandy on his breath. "They bring back flogging, quartering for criminals. Even breaking on the wheel! They have dismissed our magistrates, our professors of science and philosophy. The Jesuits now run our university. And everything advanced or liberal in Piedmont has now been set aside!"

"And yet King Victor Emanuel is a righteous and a generous man, who stands for order and for decency," the merchant thought it advisable to interject; and with sufficient loudness to carry his loyal sentiments clear through the coupé wall.

" '*Le Roi des Sardines*'?" the inebriated young Italian snorted, flaring his nostrils like a high-strung horse. "Righteous, generous, decent – and *blind*! And blindly married to an Austrian Hapsburg, withal!" he recklessly declared. "When even now our enemies the Austrians are marching to invade the Democratic State of Naples! And where pray was his righteous Majesty this January, when my student friends were cast in prison for wearing scarlet caps and cheering Neapolitans? Or when the military, with bayonets and with sabres, cut down so many at the university for daring to support them? Where now his royal generosity? To see a man as liberal and patriotic as Cisterna arrested and dragged in chains to the dungeons of the Finistrella fortress? And for no greater crime than voicing his affection for our great Italian cause?"

Rhetorical questions all, with no answer expected or provided by Gemelli's English listeners. The climax of an entertainment in keeping perfectly, so far as David and his Sary were concerned, with the dramatic unreality of the scenery now visible to them beyond the window of the diligence. At Echelles, where their road ascended through dark pine forests and shattered crags of chocolate-coloured granite, the young man's diatribe was interrupted by a summons from the conducteur to disembark. The suspension of the carriage and condition of the rope-tackle must be examined, he portentously informed them, in preparation for the Alpine traverse. And while the passengers stood watching, sipping hot spiced wine from earthen bowls, the four stout post-horses that had drawn them up from Bonvoison were replaced by four more, even stouter; with the addition of an extra pair of 'mountain leaders' – high-haunched and frost-shod, with sharp calk-spurs set in their shoes to give them purchase on the ice. Their postilions too, it seemed, were of some special mountain breed – swarthy and thickset, and made to look far more so by the massive sheepskin buntas that they wore, with enormous iron-bound boots like oyster barrels to prevent their legs from being crushed between the horses' milling flanks.

"Looks like we're in for some fierce climbing, eh *signore*?" said Sary, giving David's arm a squeeze in her excitement.

And yet the incline of the road that bore them up the famous mountain 'ladder' of Echelles was scarce steeper than the chalk-hill track at Winton Street, where years before she'd scaled the Sussex downs atop a carrier's cart on that first momentous journey into Brighton. When all at last was ready the postilions cracked their whips flamboyantly. *"Vif, vif! Allons!"* they cried. And with one accord the horses lumbered into motion, straining in their collars, jostling and colliding at neck and haunch and shoulder, as their riders urged them from a starting trot into a thundering hand-gallop. Their path a *chaussée* blasted through the solid rock, to carry them in gradually ascending loops through wild terrain which twenty years before had been impassable to all but mules and mountain porters.

"You are right, 'tis Buonaparte you have to thank for it," Gemelli confirmed in response to David's question. "But reflect *signore*, as you admire his work, that he has built it on the bodies of Italians! For all his promises of liberty and of Italian independence, the Corsican was no better, when it came to it, than any other tyrant with a crown upon his head. In Novara and San Giulio our people starved to feed his armies, to build his bridges and his chaussées. We actually ate cats and rats – can you believe it? – to finance roads like this! And now we hear our righteous and our generous King is ready to destroy the carriageway – to go back to the mules and porters of his earlier reign, only to spite the memory of the base-born Emperor!" The young man laughed a bitter, mirthless laugh. "And you still ask me why we seek a change of constitution?"

But not all the royal spite, not all the Imperial pride and peasant sacrifices and revolutionary plottings in the world, could diminish the achievement of Napoleon's engineers. At La Grotte their road plunged clear beneath the mountainside itself, into a tunnel of such mighty length that it required a series of rough-hewn 'windows' to admit some daylight. A rocky gallery that echoed deafeningly to the cries of the postilions and the percussion of two dozen hooves and four great iron-shod wheels. The luggage piled upon the carriage roof broke off enormous icicles, which clattered round it with the shrill sound of breaking glass. And when the diligence emerged from solid rock into the twilight of the Alpine evening, it was to wind through defiles hardly less dramatic, festooned on either side with snow and ice and steeped in purple shadows.

At Chambéry, the snow-shod lead-horses were dismissed with their postilion, to make their way back to Echelles. And for a day of relatively easy travel – through a corridor of frozen mountains, with hot meals, warm beds and neat Savoyard inns at either end of it – the ROYAL DILIGENCE progressed some eighty miles or more. To breakfast on the Friday at Lanslebourg, the last settlement of Savoy. Above the little town, at a military barrack against the lower slopes of Mont Cenis itself, the passports of all ongoing passengers were duly stamped for Susa and Torino. And once again a second postilion with an extra pair of horses was engaged for the ascent.

"And what say we take the coupé, darling, and ride forward to the top? Oh Davy, let's!" cried Sary on a sudden inspiration. "I won't be cold, I promise you, and only think what famous sights we'll see from there!

"We'll 'ave it to ourselves and all, now the other fellow's stopped off at Shomberie," she whispered, giving him a nudge through his thick box-coat. "With no one to see just what we're up to, eh, behind our little curtain!" And so enchanting had she looked, smiling up at him from the cocoon of brightly coloured scarves she'd wrapped around her bonnet, that David could no more have denied her, than his body beneath its insulating layers of beaver, wool and flannel could have failed to stir to her suggestion.

Aside from regarding them as if they'd taken leave of all five senses at a stroke, the conducteur and his remaining outside passenger made no difficulty about giving up their seats to *les voyageurs anglais*. And by mid-morning all were set to scale the mountain that divided His Sardinian Majesty's Duchies of Savoy and Piedmont; with the intrepid English couple riding up in solitary state behind the horses.

In design, the coupé of a diligence was not at all unlike a little three-seat hackney cab or chaise, perched up before the body of the vehicle and sprung quite independently of it. Just like a cab, it had no door in front, but only a leathern apron to protect its inmates' knees from damp – with a curtain of the same material to draw across above in case of driving rain or snow. Thus, not ideally suited to a journey through the Alps, the open view that it afforded across the horses' backs was nonetheless superb. And certainly superior in every way, as Sary happily averred, to anything that anyone could hope to see through the smirchy glass and smoky atmosphere of the interior!

From up above, each time they rumbled round an outer curve of Buonaparte's *grande chaussée*, the slated roofs of Lanslebourg were seen to have receded just a little more – until they'd shrunk

179

into a miniature, a perfect little model of an Alpine settlement. Twelve, thirteen, fourteen bends above the town – they'd long since ceased to count – they reached and crossed the snowline. The rumble and the clatter of their passage now muffled to a duller sound, a background only to the shouts of the postilions and the constant ringing music of the horses' bells. At frequent intervals along the way, stone-built refuges had been constructed – safe-houses to protect unlucky travellers from blizzards or avalanches – with ten-foot red-painted posts set up between them at the roadside to mark its whereabouts in case of drifting; a file of elongated scarlet soldiers marching down the mountainside to Lanslebourg.

"And look," said David, leaning out to point to Sary where a thin black track wound up the mountain by another route. "That's how they had to come before the road. Can you imagine? By mule, or carried up in osier baskets, or in chairs on poles!" His voice elated, his dark eyes brightly shining. "And look Sary, d'ye see those crags? 'Nature's fortifications', someone said, 'to protect her paradise of Italy'. Aren't they *magnificent*?"

And Sary looked, and looked again at David with the warm breath gusting out of him into the frosty air each time he spoke. The bluish stubble of a two-days' beard now shadowing his lower face.

"And over there – see there!" he cried. "D'ye see the eagle soaring down the cliff? My God, it makes me feel . . . It makes me wish that I could fly!"

"Well does it now?" she said, one hand now busy with his coat and trowser buttons, the other ready warming on the bag of heated semolina which the woman in the Lanslebourg inn had given her to carry in her muff. "To fly? Or maybe just to *feel* you're flying, Davy Stanville?"

The leading postilion, shouting back instructions to the other for the negotiation of an outside bend, could see the English female sitting up on Monsieur's lap behind their leather apron. Both smiling fondly, with their arms around each other. Pledging love without a doubt. The young woman rising gently on her lover's thighs to the rocking movement of the coupé on its straps. (Or to something very like it.)

Chapter Seventeen

It was snowing hard by the time they attained the col and started to descend. Large energetic flakes that patently meant business, gusting and swirling round the diligence to obscure the outline of the mountain peak above it and the little huddling buildings of the post-house, inn and barrack on the high plateau immediately below.

"*Ah, les belles horreurs des Alpes!*" The *aubergiste* was waiting ready to receive them with the sympathetic platitudes of her occupation and sufficient hot spiced wine and brandy to revive or incapacitate them all, according to their needs and constitutions. And amid the general mêlée of their arrival in the snowstorm, the wrongly fastened buttons of his English Lordship's box-coat were unremarked (by all but one postilion, that is).

For two whole hours the snow continued falling, blowing into drifts around the shuttered inn. Safe inside, the stranded travellers appeared to David like some Old Master's painting of the Nativity – sharing their warmth and firelight with a coop of hens, a huge great shaggy mountain-dog, a cat and two brown goats. With the fat woman's poodle, in the character of the infant Jesus, lying quietly on her vastly spreading lap, and pretending not to see what it dared not antagonize. While David himself sat close to Sary in the inglenook, chafing her hands and smiling inwardly a broad contented smile. By five the blizzard had at last abated. And following a hasty conference between the conducteur and his postilions, and a group of local post-house men who'd gone with them to view the downward chaussée, it was announced that the ROYAL DILIGENCE would be sent on ahead at once to Susa by way of

Molaretto. The snow was presently too deep, the travellers were told, for progress by the usual means. But at Mont Cenis *traineaux* were constantly available for such eventualities; with one great sledge on which to load the wheels and luggage of the diligence, and another to drag the dismembered vehicle itself down through the snow at least as far as Molaretto.

"And as for us, my darling Sary – shall I tell you what they now propose?" said David through the babel of excited voices that followed the conducteur's further elaboration of the scheme.

"To send us down on tin tea-trays?" she facetiously suggested. "Like we done as kiddies back home in Alfriston, whenever we 'ad the snow for it on 'Indover or Long Barrow hill?"

"That's *right* – well done!" He kissed her, grinning, and for quite the hundredth time. "That's it exactly!"

"On tea-trays? All down the blooming mountain?" She stared at him in patent disbelief. "You're 'aving me on, ye rogue!"

"Not I. *'Glisser sur plateau'*," he enunciated, " 'to slide on a tray', that's what they say themselves. They have these portable toboggan-affairs you see, called *'lezes'* . . . No really, Sary, 'tis true – I swear it! They've used them up here for centuries to carry travellers to Lanslebourg, or even down to Susa, when the snow prohibits any other form of passage. They're safer, so they say, and a great deal quicker than the big horse-sledges. Which means that for just a few francs extra we can stay and eat our evening meal up here in warmth and comfort, don't you see – while our friend and his postilions take on the diligence and trunks, to meet us later at the bottom."

Outside, when they emerged, the wind had dropped. Above them in the Alpine twilight the pale disc of a near-full moon played hide-and-seek through drifting banks of clouds. The thick snow wedged and squeaked beneath their feet as, following in the tracks of the great horse-traineaux which had passed on ahead some hours before, the onward travellers left the shelter of the buildings. Six passengers in all, with three stout *coulants*, or sled-men, to lead the way to their descent. Each man supporting on his back the wood and cow-hide 'leze' that was to bear them down to Italy.

"Look like little walking coffins, don't they?" said Sary brightly to the young Gemelli, nodding toward the coulants' elongated silhouettes ahead. "Let's 'ope they ain't then, eh? For me and Davy intend to see this 'bella Italia' of yours before we turn our toes up. And that's the truth!"

"And so you shall indeed, signorina," the young Piedmontese was at pains to reassure her. "These men, you must believe, are very skilled. You will not come to harm. Tonight we rest in Susa, tomorrow in Torino! And you shall see, signorina – it will be my pleasure to demonstrate to you – there is no other land in all the world to rival Italy in beauty."

Well fed and fortified, toasted without and glowing within from all the best effects of woodfire and alcohol, their little party set forth again in optimistic frame. The Lyons merchant loudly dwelling still on the excellence of the famous Cenis trout they'd sampled, from the frozen lake beyond the inn; while close behind him his very large compatriot waddled beneath a private mountain of cloaks and shawls, beseeching her poodle-dog repeatedly to urinate: *"Fais pipi pour Maman, Chouchoutte. Fais un effort, cherie – essaie pour Maman!"*

Shocked by the hostile, frozen nature of the stuff she'd been set down in, the little dog at first crouched shivering, and deaf to all encouragements. But not for long. Before 'Maman' could scoop her up again to try her on another patch of snow, Chouchoutte discovered for herself the delightful yielding texture of the substance, and capered off ahead along the sledge-tracks, yapping shrilly. A dingy-looking, highly animated dishmop frisking through the frozen landscape.

"Chouchoutte, cherie – viens ici!" cried out her mistress anxiously. But when the tiny creature turned to stare back wildly at her through the fading twilight, its face a white clown's mask of powdered snow, she'd laughed as readily as all the others. An indulgent parent delighting in the antics of a wayward child.

David never tired of watching the expressions of his Sary's face. When she laughed for instance, as she was laughing at the dog, she did it, as she did all things, without restraint. Head back, chin up, wide-open-mouthed to show her teeth – her golden eyes squeezed into little shining, swimming fantail fishes above her round pink cheeks. Her laughs, her smiles so slow to fade. The dimples and the fantail lines remaining after, like a visual echo. The gathering

shadows of a frown between her brushed and darkened brows at
first unable to displace the joy and humour that her face so readily
expressed.

Why frowning though, he wondered? And as he did so, became
aware of Sary's fingers gripping tightly on his arm. No trace now
upon her features of that slowly fading smile.

"There in the trees," she said unsteadily, pointing with her free
hand to where a wood of Alpine spruce pushed out a long black
tongue toward their track. "Davy, is that another dog – or . . .?"

The final word remained unspoken, as a long-legged shadow
slunk between the trunks, then crouched. Then moved again
decisively to leave their shelter some twenty yards or less from
where Chouchoutte still gambolled, unaware. A young wolf bound-
ing, breasting through the snow with unmistakable intent!

"*Au loup! Au loup!*" Pietro Gemelli, the first to find his voice,
now sounded the alarm. A warning which the pampered poodle,
nose-down, still snuffling in the snow, chose fatally to disregard.

"*Chouchoutte, attention! Mon Dieu!*" This time the little dog
had turned, but only with mild enquiry, toward its shrieking
mistress; facing wrongly, and too low besides within the sledge-
track to see or hear the fast approaching pads of death.

David, fumbling in his coat, at last reached out his pistol in the
very moment Chouchoutte looked up to see the wolf, bare-fanged,
immediately above her.

"*Non, Milord. Pas de pistolet!*" The merchant Grévin's well-
gloved hand pushed down the pistol barrel before David could
align it. He jerked his head towards the snow-clad peak above
them. "You kill the wolf, maybe. But maybe you start an
avalanche also. *Non, Monsieur, le risque est trop grand.*"

The poodle meanwhile, yipping and yapping in its terror, had
flung itself into the deeper snow beyond the track – where it now
floundered as an easy target for the larger predator. The young
wolf sprang. The woman screamed, and all seemed over for the
little dog. But then the woman screamed again – to see her beloved
pet leap free, propelled by an instinct for survival which for the
moment matched the wolf's. And then somehow to find the
strength to leap again. And then again. Each time into ever deeper
drifts of snow.

But then a canine bred for an accessory, to weigh no more upon

184

a lady's lap than would her muff or reticule, could have no chance against that member of her race which Nature had herself bred up for her own best uses. And when the wolf plunged in a third time on its victim, a single high-pitched yelp had finally proclaimed an end to Chouchoutte's struggles.

An end, indeed, to poor Chouchoutte.

The wolf emerged to cross the track and lope back to the shelter of the wood with almost casual ease. The small dog, in all likelihood already dead, still kicking feebly in its jaws.

"*Chouchoutte! Chouchoutte – mon pauvre bébé!*" The fat Lyonnaise, wailing most piteously, sank down upon her knees into the snow – with Sary crouched beside, her arms around as much of her as she could possibly encompass – and David and the others standing awkwardly around, unsure of what to say or how to act. The three coulants, meantime, had merely shrugged their heavy sledges at each other, casting up black eyes and weatherbeaten faces to the moon. "We will give *la grosse* five minutes to compose herself," they sensibly agreed in their patchwork-patois of dialectic French and Piedmontese-Italian. "Or ten at most," they added as another heartbroken wail rent the evening air. "And then we must descend, *subito*!"

The plateau of Mont Cenis, with its woods and trout lake, its little group of buildings and its wide expanse of snow, created the illusion somehow of a gently sloping valley amid the mountain peaks. And it was not until they reached the edge that David recalled how far in fact they'd climbed these last three days of travelling. As the coulants set down their burdens in a neat south-facing line along the snow, the moon likewise shook off her veil of cloud to show a vast and gaping void between the col on which they stood and the mountain range which previously had seemed to rise immediately beyond it. A descent far steeper than the way they'd come – a virtual precipice down which the carriageway to Molaretto and to Susa miraculously clung, doubling and re-doubling in white coils of moonlit snow, to disappear eventually in darkness!

"*Voila Madame, asseyez-vous! Et Monsieur, vous êtes debout ici!*" The 'leze' toboggans to which the travellers must now entrust their lives were made from single five-foot planks of wood, like

185

little flattened boats – curved up in front to show the dappled cow-hide facing which gave them speed in one direction and purchase in another; and each fitted with a hinged wooden seat some two-thirds down its length.

"And 'ard as rock, I don't mind telling ye," said Sary, settling down as she was bidden, nonetheless, with her arms clasped round her knees. "I won't be offering to change places, mind," she added, smiling back a little anxiously while David took his stance on the foot or so of wooden floor behind her, and grasped the loops of plaited leather in her seat-back. "They say a man will stand up for near anything in nature. Which I do 'ope's the truth, my duck – for 'tis a long way down from 'ere and no mistake!"

"Never fear, I'll be as right as rain back here," he told her with all the confidence that he could muster, and at the same time planting one furry finger of his glove on her uptilted nose. "You haven't lost me yet, you know. And nor are you about to, Sary Snudden. Not now or ever, do you hear?" he added, stooping down to whisper it and – whilst in the near vicinity – to kiss the soft skin underneath her very chilly ear-lobe.

A few feet away, the tearful Lyonnaise was refusing point-blank to entrust herself to anything so small and flimsy as her coulant's sled. "*Non, non! C'est trop périlleux!*" she cried. "*C'est trop idiot!*" And it was not until the exasperated Piedmontese had threatened to abandon her to the wolves and blizzards of Mont Cenis, that she reluctantly consented to lower her substantial rear on to the narrow seat. Behind her the young Pietro stepped bravely up to take his place – for all the world like one of Cinderella's little lizards, waiting behind the outsize pumpkin, to be changed into a footman. While on the furthest sled the merchant, George Grévin, was seen to be already seated, with the tall Lombard who'd ridden outside in the diligence as far as Lanslebourg, standing at his back.

"*Voila, ça va. Poussez!*" Without more ado the senior coulant cast a snowboot across the prow of his small craft; and squatting practically in Sary's lap, launched off with powerful arms and legs into the long descent – five thousand feet to Italy!

Travellers crossing Mont Cenis the other way, from Italy to France, might glide directly down the mountain cone to Lansle-bourg in times of heavy snow, so David had been told. But travelling in this direction, on the far steeper southern faces of the

Cottian Alps, it was only by the winding chaussée that their sleds could hope to pass. A restricted gradient in itself, and one which might have borne them gently to their destination, had not the coulants urged their 'lezes' forward so impatiently, using their hands like paddles to build momentum on the straights.

By the time they reached the first bend, hard against the shelving rock, they were already gathering speed. And when the second loomed – too soon, too sharply curving, too obviously projecting into empty space – it seemed impossible that they could hold it. Sary gave a little gasping cry and shut her eyes. David felt a stab of fear pierce through him as he braced himself for almost certain death. While from the front their coulant remarked politely, "*Tenez-bon Monsieur-dame. Maintenant nous allons virer sur la gauche,*" nonchalantly thrusting out an iron-spiked heel, to send an ice-spray high into the air and spin them round into the next descending straight.

Another shouted exclamation, another hissing spray of ice and snow, announced the second sled's arrival up behind. To be followed very shortly by a scream to curdle blood and turn all heads – and the sight, as they emerged around the bend, of the wretched little coulant who'd been set to man the final 'leze' struggling desperately to do so from beneath the clinging, shuddering, shrieking mass of velvet-covered fat that was the Lyonnaise.

Before the next bend they wisely called a halt to calm the woman yet again as best they might, and to tie a blindfold round her streaming eyes. And from thenceforth her screams had been more muted, at last subsiding into sounds inaudible to those aboard the leading sled. Not that either of its passengers had time or thought to spare for her, beyond those first few fearful minutes. So utterly absorbed were they become in the excitements of their own descent.

David, learning of necessity how best to brace and bend and lean into each curve, had felt, each time he did it and retained his feet, a thrill too pleasurable for fear. Yet still too sharp for mere enjoyment. His muscles ached with tension. The rushing air and stinging spray whitened his brows and lashes, froze into a stiff cold mask across his lower face. No joy without some little pain. No triumph without effort or achievement. That morning above Lanslebourg he'd coveted the power and freedom of an eagle.

Now he felt it, swooping down the road Napoleon had blasted through the granite of the Alps. His arms and shoulders braced, knees bent, feet placed apart. And Sary's head pressed back against him . . . Ahead the moonlit ribbon of the chaussée - beyond, the darkness of the void, of death itself – bend after bend on which the least slip could prove fatal. The most splendid stimulating way that David could imagine to enter in upon his dream of Italy!

Sary, never one before for dreams or useless flights of fancy, was like a girl bewitched. At Hadderton in another, English, moon-light, she had perceived the beauties of a world beyond her personal attainment. An English world, and David's own. But here they both of them were dwarfed, as any human form must be, within the savage grandeur of the landscape; their individualities, the differences of birth and education which always had divided them, their sexes even, here in this enchanted place become irrelevant.

No longer fearful for her life, or David's, as their sled flew down the spiral way, she felt released from all mundane restrictions and realities. As if her own bold spirit flew beside them through the hissing ice-spray – leaping chasms as the chaussée leapt them, passing cataracts of water frozen into sheets of pendant ice – flying through a mountain village, through a grove of slender pines, to reach the brink of yet another vast abyss. To begin another long descent through wreaths of drifting cloud. Through all eternity, it seemed to Sary. Down, down the winding silver springway of their road, to where, like ants, the traineaux with their baggage and their dislocated diligence were creeping slowly forward on the road to Susa and Turin.

Chapter Eighteen

"But, Mr Brown, your tea is cold entirely, I'm certain that it must be. I'll send for more hot water, shall I?"

"No. No, please do not." Impulsively the gentleman put out a hand to stop his hostess rising for the bell. And then as quickly drew it back, fearful clearly of an impropriety. "I am not really any sort of tea-drinker, you know," he said apologetically, "and wouldn't wish to put you to the trouble."

"Then may I bring you something else? Or let me ring at least to see if we can discover what it is that's detaining Octavia. I cannot think such lateness like her." The movement she made to rise this time no more than a suggestion, however, for the sake of form. "Unless, of course, you'd care to hear a little more of ancient history?" she added lightly. As if it scarcely mattered to her one way or the other. As if she wasn't longing now to tell him all the rest.

"Indeed, Ma'am, if you feel inclined to speak of it?" he said with grave politeness. As if he wasn't every bit as anxious to be told.

Her large soft hands moved in her lap like restless birds, pale against the blackness of her skirts. "Then let me ask you something, Mr Brown. Do you know Italy? Have you ever been there in your travels?" she enquired. And as her eyes met his, he saw how she had been. How she must have looked when she was young and beautiful, and passionate. A girl of three and twenty on her first venture to the Southern Kingdoms. "Sadly, no, Ma'am," he told her with a real regret. "Geneva is the furthest point that I've attained abroad, I must confess. The city, I collect, that your young revolutionary had come from when he joined your diligence at Lyons."

"Why yes, that's right – how clever of you to recall it! I believe

the headquarters of resistance to the Bourbon government o
Piedmont were situated at that time in Switzerland. And no doub
that's why Pietro went there. But we were speaking of Italy, M
Brown. I asked you if you'd been there. Because, if you have
not . . ." She smiled a deprecatory smile. "I've had so little forma
education. In the company of those who've been bred up to do so,
have learned in time to speak with tolerable correctness. Or so I
like to think. But still I lack the words, even the imagination
maybe, to paint a living picture for you of my Italy, as it then was ir
1821. Today our papers tell us the entire peninsula now has its
unity and independence for the first time since the Roman Empire
– that it has won at last the right to recognition as a country. But
even then, you see, before Cavour and Garibaldi, even then it had
its own identity. Pietro was right in that at least."

The lady sighed a reminiscent sigh. "David and I saw that at
once," she said. "We felt its Italian magic from the moment we
descended from the mountains. Perhaps even from before that –
from the time we left the Col of Mont Cenis for our exciting
glissade sur plateau. ITALY, Mr Brown – a place, an idea. A way of
life! Something . . . how can I describe it? . . . something come
together out of beauty and antiquity and passionate emotions.
Something quite unique!" She smiled again. "And there, you see,
the extravagant effect it has on me, even after all these years. I fear
I'm quite incurable!" She reached across to lay a hand on the black
sleeve of her solicitor's best London suit. The gesture he himself
had found too awkward to sustain in the reverse. "And just
imagine how we felt the day that we arrived there in Turin. In that
lovely little brick and terracotta city, all fenced in by hills and
snowcapped mountains – to find a revolution sparking up right
underneath our noses! Italian opera, Mr Brown – *molto dram-
matico* – Nothing in this world of ours to equal it!"

*　　*　　*

By noon the tension in the Piazza del Castello was almost visible.
The day was mild for March and overcast. The pennants ranged
along the roofs of the Royal Palace hung inert against their
ornamental poles. And beneath the arcades opposite, at the far
end of the square, the people stood in silence while the church bells

struck out the hours. Or talked in lowered voices. Waiting like an audience in a hushed and darkened auditorium. Staring down toward the palace with its drooping flags and ranks of rigid soldiers; beyond it to the chapel built to house the famous Holy Shroud. Staring at the baroque magnificence of it all, as if at any moment the whole thing might explode!

"But confound it, Pietro, if this revolutionary army of yours now means to march on Turin," David was saying to the young Gemelli, "then there will surely be a civil war in Piedmont? The people here in the capital are loyal to the King. Is that not so?"

"No, no, signore, you have not begun to understand!" Pietro's voice already hoarse from declaiming slogans at the students' demonstrations of the day before along the city ramparts. "We ask only for our King to join us in defending the democratic principles of our brother Italians down in Naples. To defend their constitution against Austrian invaders, and to establish like reforms in Piedmont." The young man's drink still stood untouched on the café table that he shared with the English couple in the arcade of the piazza. "Reforms, a democratic constitution, and an Italy united against the menace of Austrian Imperialism. That's all we seek." He spread his hands appealingly, as if such a reasonable formula must automatically commend itself to any self-respecting autocratic monarch married to an Austrian. "There is no need for bloodshed," he insisted.

'No need, no need for bloodshed!' The cry with which so many well-intentioned individuals have naïvely launched themselves into the wholesale carnage of a war or revolution. And hard for Sary, even now, to take Pietro's wild pronouncements seriously. Nothing here within her view of the Piazza del Castello – nor in the single day that they had spent within the city of Turin – nothing to contradict the sense of total unreality that she'd brought down with her from the Cottian Alps. Sary took another sip of the strange tasting herbal *vermouth* they had given her, and looked out to where a *carrozza* clattered with self-conscious consequence across the quiet piazza in the direction of the Opera House. Its horses gorgeously caparisoned with saddle-cloths of leopardskin and red morocco harness; its coachman clad in scarlet, its lady-passenger decked out in a small fortune of golden ornaments – around her neck and swinging from her ears, and combed and pinned and woven through her plaited hair. A rich woman riding out to see the troops formed up before the Palazzo Reale and all the waiting populace around it. Revolution seen merely as a form of entertainment.

Sary turned to ask Pietro if he knew the equipage. But, as she did so, a loud report rang out across the city. Then a second, and a third. The sound of cannon-fire, it could be nothing else!

"*Madre di Dio!*" Pietro's glass crashed down to spread a stain like blood across the tablecloth. Then all at once the vaults of the arcades began to echo to the sounds of scraping chairs and running feet and raised excited voices. People spilling out from all sides through the arches and into the piazza. A rippling movement like a great wind through a field of wheat, passing down the ranks of Royal troops standing to attention still across the palace frontage. Explanations shouted out in French, and in the guttural Piedmontese-Italian of the region, were filtered and translated for Sary's English understanding, by David and the flustered young Gemelli. Some said a hostile Austrian force had marched hotfoot from Modena and were even now about to enter by the *Porta Nuova*. The Austrian Queen, a second Marie Antoinette, had sent for fifty thousand of her countrymen to cross the Brenner and subjugate her husband's refractory Kingdom, was the claim of others. Or that the rebel troops had come to bombard the capital! Cannon-balls would soon be falling from the sky like rain!

But then word reached the Piazza del Castello that, in truth, the cannon were their own, sounded as a bold salute to independence from the very ramparts of the Citadel. A group of citizens and students had stormed this city stronghold to proclaim the Neapolitan Constitution and hoist the new Italian flag. And although that act proved nothing in itself, the excited crowd before the Royal Palace now seized upon it as a triumphant blow for liberty.

"*Viva la Constituzione!*" someone shouted. To be joined by others on the instant: "*Viva la Constituzione! Viva l'independenza d'Italia!*" And everywhere in the arcades and piazzas of the city, compatriots embraced and wrung each other's hands.

"Our country breathes at last the clean air of fraternity and peace!" Pietro Gemelli told his English friends, with tears of emotion rolling down his cheeks. While at the far end of the piazza a group of eager citizens were flinging insults, bread and well-cooked pasta at the nervous Palace Guards.

By mid-afternoon more than half the population of the *contradas* and piazzas of Turin had gravitated to the Citadel. Where (as later Italian histories would record) the Heir Presumptive to the throne, the most noble Prince of Carignano, was to be informed by those who held the revolutionary garrison: "Our hearts are faithful to King Victor Emanuel. But from this moment forward our people must withdraw from fatal counsels. War with Austria and the Neapolitan Constitution. That is our demand."

For those remaining in the arcades, meantime, in the cafés and *bottegas*, there were cigarros to be lit and toasts to drink to *l'Italia libera*; and countless pledges to be made to the King and to the Constitution. Until everyone was filled with patriotic fervour (or else with vermouth or with Asti wine). And even Gemelli's English guests were coming round to see, through the tobacco smoke, that a bloodless revolution might actually be possible.

Remarkably, Pietro himself showed little inclination to join the fervid masses round the Citadel – preferring café rhetoric to anything more risky it would seem. And, closing one eye to consider him the better across the dark red pool of vermouth in the glass she held against her cheek, Sary marked him for a *bragga-dacio*. A rabbit with a fox's bark! Not a thing she blamed him for, but just a fact. Just like the fact that everyone in the arcades had drunk too much. Herself included! She looked beyond him. Beyond her flush-faced, quietly drunken Davy, to where a girl sat much as she did at a table with two men, a glass of wine or vermouth at her elbow. A girl she envied with a desperate envy. Not for her jewelry, like the woman in the carriage. Nor for the gold threads in her bodice. But for its opening, for the ripeness of the breast that it disclosed – the darkened nipple and the little greedy working mouth that suckled it.

Sary watched the baby for a long time, feeding first from one breast then the other; thinking as she did so of the uses that grown men had put her paps to. So many men in all her weeks and months and years at Madge's, and so many uses. Every use that lust or ingenuity could find for female breasts. All but the correct one! And when the girl looked up to catch her watching, the proud and gentle smile she gave her struck poor Sary like a blow.

A new sound was already audible within the square by the time the girl had fed her child and buttoned up her bodice. A sound like the roaring of an ocean on some distant shore, or like the feet and voices of an enormous multitude of ten or fifteen thousand people (which in actual fact it was).

" . . . *Il Principe di Carignano!*" Through the acclamations of the approaching crowd the phrase was frequently repeated, in company with another: " . . . *La bandiera – la bandiera Italiana!*"

"The Prince of Carignano is returning to the Palazzo Reale with our flag!" cried out Pietro suddenly in English, flinging both arms dramatically into the air. "The flag is carried with him! Our country's hour of independence has arrived!" As he spoke, the first horsemen of the Prince's escort rode into view. From somewhere across the square a band struck up with frenzied enthusiasm; and shortly afterwards the Prince himself appeared, surrounded by his guards. A rigid young man in military uniform – his face very near as pale as the old-fashioned powdered peruke he wore beneath his hat – with, fluttering at his stirrup, the tricolour banner of the Neapolitan Revolution. *"La bandiera Italiana! Viva l'Italia independente!"* the people shouted wildly, surging through into the Piazza del Castello. A great river of humanity channelled in by the contrada – to be joined by groups and individuals in rivulets and trickles through the arches of the arcades that flanked the square – growing, as Sary looked on, fascinated, to the proportions of a flood. Like water through the arches of a bridge, sweeping ever wider up the sides of the piazza – until suddenly she realized with a shock that they too were going to be engulfed.

In the next moment the crowd was on them, running through between the café tables. Men with red sashes or scraps of scarlet cloth tied round their arms and necks, shouting and hooting like great big excited boys. Women with their hair about their shoulders, children anxious only to keep up. Chairs were upset and thrown aside. Then a table fell, its white cloth trampled underfoot. And, before Sary knew it, she was on her own feet, laughing, helpless, carried forward on the tide of human bodies that flooded the piazza – calling back to David and Pietro in the press behind her, as yet a deal too thoroughly well insulated by all the vermouth she'd consumed to understand the danger they were in.

"Hold on, I'm coming!" David shouted, abandoning his companion to leap and thrust and swim his way toward her through the sea of heads and shoulders that divided them. Arriving breathless

194

but triumphant at her side. Ahead, at the end of the long piazza, the Prince's escort and the revolutionary flag were already disappearing through the massive gateway in the centre of the palace. "They're counting on him to persuade the King to adopt the constitution that they want," explained David, supporting Sary with an arm around her waist; as once again the crowd surged forward, shouting out for Carignano and the Constitution.

She laughed. "I doubt 'e will though, Davy. Not once he's safe inside, with all those men and 'orses atwixt them and 'im."

The numbers of the Royal mounted guard were certainly increasing by the minute, trotting four-abreast out through the gateway, to form a double line across the palace frontage for the entire width of the square. "*Arrière! Arrière!*" they heard them shouting to the crowd in French and saw the rows of plumes upon the riders' helmets advancing slowly on the seething multitude. And, like the backwash of a gigantic wave, the forefront of the crowd pressed back on those behind, while others from the back were pressing onward still.

"Gawd above! They're going to squash us flat as bedbugs!" Sary cried in sudden panic, feeling bodies all around her – sweating, panting, gusting evil-smelling breath. Someone treading on her foot. Someone else's elbow in her back. No longer laughing. No longer now buoyed up by the alcohol; feeling sober, all too real, and frightened. "Help me, Davy!" she called out to him, as another lurching backward movement of the throng wrenched his arm away and lifted her clean off her sandalled feet. "Oh Davy, help me, darling, or they'll 'ave me down, I swear!"

Sary, his lovely Sary, with her French velvet bonnet on the skew and her coppery hair all coming down about her ears. And fearful, almost childlike, begging him to save her! If not a maiden in distress exactly, quite like enough to one to bring out all the Lancelot in young Lord Denton; as he reached to gather her into his arms, and to align one shoulder and one hip into the path he judged to offer least resistance. Then, using every ounce of strength that he possessed, he forced a passage, inch by painful inch – forwards and sideways in a long diagonal across the piazza to the arcades that abutted to the south and western elevations of the Palazzo Reale. By now the Royal cavalry had withdrawn to their original position beneath the palace windows, faced at a distance of some twenty yards by the uncertain vanguard of the crowd – a narrow strip of no-man's-land before a crowd that now stretched back to fill the whole piazza, overflowing through the arcades and into the other city squares. A population mobilized at last.

The horses of the guard tossed heads and shuffled feet upon the cobbles, plainly nervous. An officer barked out an order: "*Tenez ferme!*" And someone in the crowd threw back their own defiant slogan: "*Viva la Constituzione!*" "*Viva – viva la Constituzione!*" The multitude took up the cry at once.

And, "*Viva il Re!*" cried back the Royal guardsmen, breaking discipline to show their solidarity.

"*Viva la Constituzione! VIVA LA CONSTITUZIONE!!*" The crowd had found their weapon, chanting now as one. All individuality submerged. A monster eager to reveal its power to those inside the palace, listening. "*VIVA LA CONSTITUZIONE!!*"

"*Viva il Re!*" the guardsmen shouted bravely once again. The cry they used for battle. Or would use if they were called upon to charge. And in response, from somewhere in the centre of the crowd, another forward impulse, another wave began to build.

"Good God, they're going to push us right on to the horses!" David – near the front now, a few yards only from the archway of the sheltering arcade – felt the pressure, lost his line of exit, saw the arch sweep past him as he and Sary were carried forward irresistibly to the front edge of the crowd.

"*Sabres!*" The weapons hissed and clattered from their scabbards all along the line of guardsmen. Curved steel, held high in fists that trembled, razor edges faced directly to the wall of human flesh that still advanced toward them.

"*Madonna! Attenti!*" Those in front were struggling frantically to stem the tide – straining, bracing, scrabbling for a purchase on the paving flags before the palace, their hands held out submissively toward the champing horses.

Sary, gripped now so tight against her lover's body that she could scarcely breathe, heard the order: "*A l'attaque!*" Looked up to see the threatened horsemen charge. Two people only now between them and the first great horse, the upraised sabre of the nearest guard! And People screaming; and David shouting at her through

196

the din – straining sideways for the safety of an arch they'd never reach. To die this way in Italy! And for a cause she hardly understood!

At the moment of their impact with the heaving wall of terrified humanity, the horses turned their flanks or reared up, striking with their forefeet. Necks arched, eyes rolling whitely, nostrils widely dilated – their heads as fierce as dragons and their hooves packed hard with death. A woman fell. A boy let out a high-pitched scream as the sharp spur of a wheeling guardsman slashed across his arm. High up above them all a horse's body rose to block the light – standing, pawing air for what seemed an age of time to Sary, before the hammers of its iron-shod hooves crashed down. One hoof a yard from Sary's face. She felt the punch of wind it drove beneath it, saw and heard it strike. The short grey-headed man in front, who'd dodged back to avoid the other forefoot, received the blow full on his cranium. Dropped dead without a sound.

"Now!" shouted David, breaking through the strange slow dream in which Sary saw the act repeated – the driving hoof, the sharp crack of the skull, the falling man . . . "Now Sary," he repeated, "now, underneath its belly!" And before she realized what he meant, he'd forced her down to scramble through beneath the animal itself – all in amongst the moving legs, the blood, the smell of horse-sweat. And then across the slippery cobbles, stumbling toward the arch, leaping an open drain – to where willing hands reached out for them and dragged them into safety.

Looking back to see the fallen bodies, the black horses dancing backward, sideways, all along the ragged line. The guardsmen's sabres still, mercifully, upraised.

Chapter Nineteen

In their bedroom at the Pension suisse that night they'd boastfully compared their bruises. His on his back, his shoulders and his buttocks, already a satisfactory bluish-purple. Hers mostly where he'd gripped her round the ribs beneath her breasts – redder, angrier, more obviously in need of kissing better.

Of Pietro Gemelli's fate or whereabouts they had no certain information. "Though you can take a bet he's where the loudest talking is," said Sary, "and in the safest place. And we'll soon see 'im 'ere and all, unless I miss my guess – with all the latest on 'is precious revolution."

Her guess correct. At ten o'clock the morning following, Pietro came panting up the steps of their hostelry in his usual state of uncontrolled excitement; to confirm the news the girl had brought them with their morning coffee. The King had abdicated, he said, leaving the Prince of Carignano as Regent for an older cousin, who must first succeed to the Sardinian crown; and in whose absence he'd caused a proclamation to be posted on the doors of all the churches in Torino. Pietro himself had made a transcript on the back of an old menu, most carefully translated into English. And naturally no power on earth could prevent him reading it aloud to David and Sary within the little crowded parlour of their pension.

" 'PROCLAMATION OF THE PRINCE REGENT, CHARLES ALBERT OF SAVOY, PRINCE OF CARIGNANO.

We make known that His Majesty, King Victor Emanuel, in abdicating the crown has conferred his whole authority upon us, with the title of Regent. We invoke the Divine assistance; and in announcing that tomorrow we will make known our intentions in answer to the general wish, we order that all hostilities should cease.'

"Which can only mean two things," pronounced Pietro triumphantly, "the democratic Constitution that our friends the Neapolitans have embraced, and war with Austria! For what else *should* we wish? And, signore," he added earnestly, "I think you cannot now in safety escort the signorina on to Verona and Venezia, or even to Milano, with hostile forces in movement on the roadway. I think that you must stay now in Torino for the present, to witness with our people the consummation of this glorious Revolution!"

So they had stayed. To hear within a matter of mere hours the much vaunted democratic Constitution proclaimed, in the name of Carignano. To stay on, and witness in a further week the repudiation of that same Constitution by the new King of Sardinia; to be followed by even more disastrous news of the defeat by Austria of the democratic Neapolitans themselves.

"But all cannot be lost," bewailed poor Pietro. "The Prince is with us still. We have our code now – our Constitution. And our people here are firm behind it, every one."

Except (as he and all the people, every one, were shortly to discover) the noble Prince of Carignano already had abandoned them, to join the new King's forces at Novara; leaving behind him a second proclamation to restore the ancient order to Piedmont and Savoy, with all its feudal horrors. A revelation which had soon convinced the craven young Gemelli that a change of air was needed. He would take his English friends to see San Giulio, he asserted. With all the country so unsettled, his father's lakeside villa there assuredly would be the very place to stay. They'd rent a *cambiatura-chaise* at once, and travel up together by way of Ivrea and Borgomanero. No certainly, he must insist on it!

On the terrace of the Casa Gemelli, Sary stood barefoot and virtually unpainted – watching the lake-fishermen of San Giulio casting their nets. An early morning pleasure in which she'd frequently indulged herself these past six weeks (as once she had in Brighton at those times each month when nature ruled a necessary holiday for those of her profession).

The water at her feet stretched out a pale grey-green shot through with light, as smooth as polished glass – a mirror to reflect the boats, the red clay roofs and wooded slopes of Pella on the further shore, and the snowcapped peak of Monte Rosa up above it. A pair of twittering swallows crossed her line of vision, skimming inches from the surface, down to where the island floated like a lily on the lake. 'Isola di San Giulio'! Even its name was magical to Sary's Anglo-Saxon ear; the island heart of the community – with its *municipium* and church and cemetery, its cypresses and all its hanging gardens. She herself had not the delicacy of language to do her feelings for it justice, that little floating island. She only knew that when she'd first set eyes on it from the window of their bedroom in the Conte's villa, the perfection of its image, reflected double in the water, had robbed her for the moment of any words at all. Quite literally it took her breath away.

"Oh Davy you must take me out there – will you?" she began to agitate as soon as she refound her tongue. "Look, there's boats aplenty, I can see them now from 'ere. And Pietro or 'is father must know the best way to engage one – bound to. Oh, let's go down and ask them now! It can't surely do no harm to ask 'em can it?"

Nor, when she had made the trip, was Sary any less inclined to love the little island. St Julius himself, their boatman earnestly assured them, had sailed across the water on a cloak, to claim the rock for God and slay a fearsome dragon in His name there. In proof of which they had been shown a dragon's bone (since turned to stone), and in the crypt of the basilica the remnants of St Julius himself, uncomfortably crammed into a crystal urn. The place *was* magical – no other word for it. And not least when she and David had explored the single twisting lane that linked up the water-gates of its *palazzi* by way of stairs and arches, little sun-filled courtyards and towering creeper-covered walls. A town in miniature cast out into a lake!

"*Isola di San Giulio.*" Sary said its name again aloud, and slowly. The syllables like wavelets lapping on the shore. Then she kissed her hand to it, her lovely little island, and strode out through the villa garden gate. That the lakeside path was equally well known to her was obvious from the easy way in which she swung along it, humming to herself and calling out, "*Buon giorno!*" to a group of women kneeling at their washboards down by the water's edge – waving to their children on the beach.

"*Buon giorno. Buon giorno, signorina.*" And the fact that the mothers continued calmly with their work, even after Sary had passed by and out of earshot, revealed how well accepted she'd become herself along the Riviera.

Pietro's father, the Conte Bartolomeo Gemelli, had first greeted her in the charming manner of all well-bred Italian men. Her status as David's *amante* known to him, it must have been. He knew, he must have known, she was no lady. Yet when he took her hand, and when his deep-set eyes met hers, she'd felt no sense of criticism. His home, he said in wonderfully accented English, was hers and David's for as long as they required it. And without pretence of modesty or any kind of awkwardness, he had his housekeeper prepare for them the bedroom with the *letto matrimoniale* that he and Pietro's mother had shared until the day she died. Remarkably, their presence in his household seemed neither to disturb nor stimulate the Conte. He had his own routines. He read. He worked within his library on a history he was writing of the Savoyard victory at Col di Raus in 1793; and in which he'd played some part. Occasionally he crossed the lake to the municipium of the Isola di San Giulio, to sit upon the local Council of the Comunità. But through their luncheons and their dinners in the musty *sala* of his villa – while David and Sary caressed each other's feet beneath its long refectory table, and Pietro banged his fist upon its surface and talked of nothing else but disappointed revolution – his father sat and stared serenely at the wall, lost in some inner reflections of his own. Thoughts of a book he'd read, perhaps, or of the wife he'd lost. Or the shots he'd fired so long ago amid the Alpine peaks of Col di Raus.

On the far side of the beach the peasant women used for washing, the lakeside pathway wound beneath the gardens of a villa larger, newer and more ostentatious than the Casa Gemelli. The summer-time retreat of some wealthy Milanese who never saw the flowering of its vivid Japanese camellias. Sary plucked one waxlike crimson bloom from a branch that overhung the path, sniffed at it tentatively. And, finding not a trace of scent, flung it down to float upon the surface of the water. The blossoms that she'd come to find of quite another kind. Beyond the villa gardens, in a grove of twisted olives where grass was being grown between the trees for haymaking in June, wildflowers flourished in their thousands –

tens of thousands! Old friends all, from Sary's country childhood back in Sussex. Pink and white and blue and guinea-gold – lady's smock and ragged Robin, stitchwort, bluebells, dandelions and buttercups. All the best old favourites growing here for her beneath the olive trees of Italy! Standing barefoot in the long wet grass, listening to the birdsong and breathing in the perfume of spring flowers, it seemed to Sary Snudden that nothing in her life since childhood, since her Mamma had died, had ever been entirely real. Nothing until now, this very moment! As if she'd never really seen the world before in its true colours.

Out on the lake the fishermen were pulling in their nets already, singing as they did so. Their strong Italian voices carried to her clear across the water. Men's voices, resonant and loud, from thickened throats and deep chest cavities. And in the villa, even as she listened, her own man – her own beloved Davy, sleeping still – sprawled nude, face-down across the *letto matrimoniale*. David whose strength and bravery had saved her life in the Piazza del Castello of Turin. David who'd defied his parents, left his home to bring her here – to love her! How different to the gawky youth who'd come to her at Mrs Perrin's house in Brighton to learn his proper function as a male. From youth then, grown to manhood. And now almost become immortal. She saw him as he slept, as she had seen him when she rose that morning – saw every inch and hair and freckle of his body. Heard his breathing, felt and smelt the sweat upon his skin. Her worship for him fast becoming positive idolatry.

But then again the soaring tenor voice across the water of the lake . . .

"Di quell'amor, quell'amor ch'è palpito dell'universo, dell' universo intero . . ."

Though not those actual words, of course, for they'd come later on and in another place; long after the modern miracle that Saint Julius had worked on Sarah and on David. The fishermen out on the lake that morning may well have sung of love, the lady in her London drawing-room reflected. But not as Verdi wrote of it. Because in sober point of fact, Giuseppe Verdi in that year of 1821 had been but eight years old.

*   *   *

The miracle of San Giulio continued all through that spring and summer. By mid-April the 'Thirty Days Revolution' of Piedmont was over. And within a further month Pietro had received sufficient assurances from his friends at university, that Turin was once again become the dullest city, to feel safe himself to return there. (And to lay the groundwork, as he was anxious to assure Lord Denton and his mistress, for a second, more successful revolution!)

"But you remain – stay on, my friends," he had insisted grandly. "My father will be most pleased for you to reside here at the Casa Gemelli for as long as you may care to. *Papa*, is that not so? Will you not be glad to entertain them?" The Conte acquiesced. And if an amiable indifference was more apparent in his manner than actual enthusiasm for the scheme, he seemed at least quite ready to endorse it; graciously accepting David's payments for their bed and board, and placing no conditions or restrictions on their stay. His villa, gardens, boat-house, stable, servants, were theirs to order, *naturalmente*, as their own. He wished them joy of all of it.

And joy was what it brought to them, and in abundance; with David presently no keener than was Sary to continue with the tour he'd planned. In Milan, at the *Poste Restante*, there'd be English letters waiting. (Intrusive, carping letters from his parents and Octavia.) In Venice and in Florence more English news, and narrow English views and English tourists by the drove! But here – here in San Giulio was the very dream he'd dreamt in Paris, of Italian *primavera*. This was what they'd journeyed down through France and crossed the Alps to find! David realized that the moment he himself had first beheld the Isola framed within the villa window, and saw the rapt expression on his Sary's face as she turned to point it out to him. In Paris he'd felt excluded from the social pleasures she so patently enjoyed there. In England, Hadderton predictably rejected her for what she was and where she'd come from. But here in Italy and in this special place, where locals saw them only in the simplest terms, as *turisti* or *Inglesi* (and always as *amanti*); here on the Riviera di San Giulio their love for one another was surely all that counted? They bore it, wore it everywhere, this love of theirs, as blatantly as if it had been bound around their brows like Virgil's snow-white bands of recognition. And everywhere they went about the lake they were congratulated. The sentimental people of the Riviera smiled to see them strolling hand in hand across the *piazzetta* where the fishing-boats were moored, or down the narrow medieval street of houses clustered on the shore – reminded of their own adventures of the heart, or of the flesh. Or merely reassured, as any ancient people must be, by the fresh evidence of life's renewal which all young lovers represent.

"*Amore!*" cried out the fishermen, with grins and gestures to convey the most basic meaning of the word as they perceived it. "*Amore!*," sighed the women in the doorways, "*il fiore di amore,*" ('the flower of love'), whilst scanning Sary's belly with experienced eyes for tell-tale signs of fruit to come.

And, seeing how readily they all admired her, David found it easy to forget what Sary had been, might still be, back in England. Here in San Giulio all her glowing qualities were shown to their advantage. Her generous and open attitudes, the freedom of her movements and the ringing loudness of her laughter must surely have been made for Italy? As was her bold, high-coloured type of beauty. His Sary's rouge and carmine salve, her vivid taste in clothing – so startling in a muted English landscape, seemed right entirely against walls of terracotta or sienna and in Italian sunshine. Nor could her lover ever tire of seeing her in such a setting. His Titian Venus in her proper element at last!

One summer morning on the terrace of the Conte's villa, while Sary watched the fishing-boats and David simply watched her watching them, a butterfly had fluttered down to settle on the baking flagstones at their feet – its marbled rose and black and amber wings outstretched to catch the sun. She saw it first; and knowing less of insects than of wildflowers, proclaimed it instantly a 'Red King George'.

"Well in truth, my love, 'tis nothing of the sort." Having spent so many tedious hours rehearsing over with his tutor Linnaeus' Latin classifications for plants and beasts and butterflies, David felt bound to set her right. "*Vanessa atalanta* is I think the species you've in mind," he said a little pompously. "But this one you see, unless I'm much mistaken, is *Cynthia carduii*." (And although he also knew, and might have given her, its common English name as well – for some reason he thought perhaps he wouldn't.) "Would you believe they come from Africa, and fly each year right up

204

through Europe?" he offered her instead, whilst slowly reaching out a hand to catch the creature for her if he could. "This one could be bound for Switzerland or France. Or even for England. Just think, Sary my darling – it could be flying home to Sussex!"

"Then just you leave 'er be to fly there, Davy Stanville, if that's what she's about," Sary declared robustly, snatching at his stealthy hand and holding fast to it until the 'Painted Lady' butterfly was safe again beyond his grasp, flying strongly out across the water. "Life's plenty short enough for them poor things, Lord only knows, without you 'ave to go and make it any shorter!"

The transience of life a theme that Sary never had considered much before San Giulio – but now each day become so precious that, like the painted butterfly, it had to be safeguarded. Each day with David in the sun a treasure to be kept and stored within her memory against the coming rain. To be engraved upon her heart – knowing in her heart that happiness like this could never last. Not while Davy talked unconsciously of Sussex still as 'home'.

Sometimes in the early mornings while he slept, instead of gathering wildflowers by the lake she'd turn instead along the shallow cobbled stairway of the Via Corinna to light a votive candle in the church there. Sary, with a shawl to cover up her pale red hair, praying to a Blessed saint that she could feel at home with. A very handsome and Italianate Madonna draped in painted robes of blue and scarlet, crowned with gold, and flashing in the candlelight enormous gemstones of brightly coloured glass.

"Oh Lady, see your way to let me keep 'im. Make it as old Madge 'as got it wrong for once. It ain't a lot to ask you, is it? To spoil my shape for 'im and bear 'is child – just like any other girl who loved 'im would?"

Chapter Twenty

Repeated blows struck through the warm snake-coils of heat tha still constricted him. Bold hammer-blows of iron on bronze which even as he listened, weakened, faded into chimes. Coils tha gradually unwound to free his limbs, first lapping them like waves and then becoming waves in fact — the very ones that slapped the boat-house walls beneath their bedroom. Hot and drowsy, nc more than half awake, David lay and listened to them slapping a the bells of the basilica, watching their oblique reflections on the ceiling.

Later, yawning, stretching, padding naked to the window, he eased a shutter back to let in fresher air; and then to take advantage of its aspect to loose some water of his own into the greater flood below. Hot urine, tingling pleasantly through still-tumescent flesh — arching golden in the sunlight, splashing silver where it struck the surface of the lake. And something faintly wicked still in such an action, however popular and commonplace it might have been amongst the locals. Like taking *coolers*, David thought, up on the roofs of Hadderton. And having thought it, cheerfully compounded the offence by turning back toward the bed, still holding fast to all he valued most, to see if she was watching. Hoping, naturally, she was.

But sadly, Sary too had been backturned, shrouded in the sheeting he'd thrown off him in his sleep. One shoulder only showed above it against a sweep of tawny hair, the sole of one pink foot beneath; and in between, great whorls of crumpled linen spilling out from her across the bed and down on to the floor. A twisted tail of it lay on the tiles just near his feet. And before he thought, David already had it in his hand – and then both hands, gently, slowly pulling it towards him. Unveiling her to view, or trying to unveil her, while she slept still. Something that he'd never done before.

"Let me tell you something about us women, duck; and something else about you men," she'd told him gently, one afternoon like this in the *siesta*, when David had expected her to feel as he did, and was disappointed. "A woman can't turn it on to order, ye know – not even for the fellow that she loves – and there's the difference. A man remembers how 'e felt the time before, and *what* 'e felt, and wants it all again as soon as 'e can get it. Same as any other barnyard cock. 'Tis how it 'as to be, no doubt of that. But with a woman now, and even with a girl like me who's always liked 'er stiff-and-stout, with a woman 'tis the feelings in 'er heart and not 'er blessed quim that she remembers after. And where she is within 'er courses, that makes a difference, and what's so special in the way 'e treats 'er – what's different, do you see, and not what's just the same!"

David gingerly drew in the tail of linen, one hand passing to the other. The sheet took up the slack and then began to move, sliding slowly down across her shoulder to lie within the incurve of her waist – her back exposed, its silken skin indented with a long blue shadow. As David saw it, the natural pathway for a lover's finger – just now frustratingly obstructed by the heavy swags of sheeting draped about her hips. He tugged again, a little harder, thinking as he did so of the last time she'd agreed to find him 'special', up in the chestnut woods above the lake . . .

One forenoon of the week before, they'd climbed the hill behind the town to see its famous *Sacro Monte*. An expedition by then overdue – and now a living memory as clear and sharp in David's mind as if it happened half an hour before. (Exactly as she'd told him, unable to forget the pleasures of his body, just like any male!) They climbed by flagged and cobbled passageways that morning – up between high walls, around gardens and through orchards where trees were linked with ropes of grapevine, like dancers holding hands. A friendly dog escorted them part-way, chasing cats and lizards from their path. And they'd held hands as well, to scramble through the rocky beds of springs long since dried-up –

pausing only where the walls allowed a view down to the chaotic roof-tops of San Giulio, or out to the magic little island on the lake beyond.

And at the summit, when they reached it, they'd come upon the chapels, the *cappelle*, of the Sacro Monte; a little hilltop village of a score of stone pavilions set amongst the trees. And in the chapels, crowds of lifesize figures acting out the life of good St Francis – dusty dolls of painted terracotta grouped in operatic tableaux behind their gates and grills. Monks and soldiers, well-dressed ladies, Eastern potentates in turbans, projecting useless gestures into empty shadows. The Pope himself with all his cardinals – children, horses, donkeys and at least one camel; near four hundred figures, so the Conte claimed, and most of them two centuries old or more.

"And *look* it – every day of it, I'm sure," said Sary, unimpressed as ever by mere numbers. "Give me the creeps they do, standing there all dust and gloom like ghosties out of 'istory. You can keep your statues, and give me something real of flesh and blood, is what I say. And a nice little wood like this, my darling, and somewhere snug and private in it for the two of us. Then I'll show you how I fancy your 'Sackry-Monty', and there's a promise!"

And so she had done. Sary never one for idle boasts or broken promises. In an accommodating coppice on the landward side of the hill she knelt before him like the Eve in Michelangelo's depiction of *Temptation* – her wide straw hat pushed back on its ribbons round her neck, her bare head dappled red and gold to match the fallen leaves beneath her knees. His breeches open and his hands upon her shoulders, pushing down – hard down . . .

"Now then, Davy, what ye playing at, you devil?"

He'd pulled the sheet too hard, he must have. Or else she'd lain on it and felt it moving. In any case she was awake – now lying on her back with one hand firmly clenched upon the linen at her waist, her face turned full towards him and her eyebrows raised in mock surprise. "What you up to then?" she repeated softly.

"Nothing very much. Not yet at least," he said. And as his eyes met hers and found in them the sanction he was seeking, he felt a sharp stab like a pain hard in the centre of his chest. A pang of pure desire that shot and shivered through into his vitals – made him gasp with pleasure.

Deliberately, symbolically, she raised her hand to free the sheet. And he raised his, to drag it from her slowly and at arm's length. To let her see as much of him as he intended shortly to reveal of her. Their smiles beginning at the very corners of their mouths, broadening gradually until their eyes became involved. And no need now for further words with everything in train. The linen gliding smoothly now across her belly. Restraint at once a torment and delight. The blood now pulsing strongly in his heart and temples, heavy now between his thighs. Her hips already rising in response, pressed up to meet the rustling fabric. His heartbeats clearly visible in movement and increased dimension, jerking out and upward, pulse by pulse – as finally the sheet pulled free of her to fall upon the floor.

This time it would be special too, no doubt of that in either mind. And much the best time surely, for loving and for being loved – in the drowsy warmth of a Piedmont summer afternoon, and after the *siesta*. An opportunity unknown, or very largely so, to chilly unromantic Northern Europeans; but here an institution that no Italian in his senses would forgo, not even to order of the Pope of Rome himself! The promise of this afternoon and this occasion already now become a certainty for David and for Sary, inherent in the open invitation of her posture on the bed, and the force of his spontaneous (and from where she lay near-vertical) reaction. A certainty, but not an urgency. Not yet by any means, if David had his way.

And, if David continued to display his masculine endowment with something in the nature of a craftsman's pride in workmanlike essentials, then Sary now revealed herself a very artist in the ways she found to rearrange her loveliness for his delight. A woman certain of her female beauty, with all the languor of a sunning cat she yawned and stretched her arms above her head – the sunlight from the window falling in a dusty band across her tautened belly, incandescent in the scut of soft red hair beneath it. A natural focal point that curved and lifted slightly as she raised one knee, its living brilliance thrown into relief against the milky column of her thigh. Her hands, meantime, descending to her breasts in proxy for his hands – to cup them and caress them, and to tease the pink buds of her nipples into darker, harder contours. Her hair spread on the pillow in a tumbling tangled silken mass. Her smile now slight, yet more intense – her black-smudged eyelids heavy, drooping now with something more than sleep.

Loveliness which David longed to hold – not only in his arms, but for eternity. If he could, he would have caught it as he'd tried to catch the painted butterfly out on the terrace. Or he'd have had her sculpted for him as the Duke of Dorset did for his Italian mistress, Gianetta Baccelli, lying naked on his rumpled sheets. To raise a monument not only to her youth and female beauty, but to something even stronger and more elusive: to its effect on him. As it was though, the very best that he could hope to do must be to hold and to extend the feelings of the moment – to pursue those butterflies of sight and touch and all the other senses for as long as they would fly for him and Sary; accepting that in the instant of their final capture, like all mortality they too must die.

In spite of which intention, his next voluntary movement was a swift one. Looking clumsy as he supposed in his priapic state, David crossed the room in three long strides, to kneel to her as she had knelt to him within the chestnut coppice. His breathing quick and shallow, already burning in his throat. His head already bending down – eyes closed and searching blindly with that old, primordial instinct for the waiting nipple. Hungry for its shape and texture, flesh to flesh – pressing, sucking, softly squeezing with his lips; while Sary, sighing, tweaked his ears, massaged his neck and dragged her fingers slowly through his thick dark hair.

"Oh darling, that feels as if you're drawing out my soul through there!" she told him in a voice as soft and warm as melting butter. "Give us your hand, my love, and if ye like I'll show you where 'tis anchored to." Groping for it, kissing it and pushing down his hand, palm-downward, to her lower belly. "Through 'ere, way down through 'ere you're drawing at it, love – and then on some, d'ye see – to where it can't go down no more."

But his fingertips were there already and without the need for guidance, sensitive as eelskin – parting tendrils, grooving down through soft and swollen portals, ever deeper, to where his Sary liked to think her soul was anchored. Then up again and backward, delicately teasing. And down again, deep down – to free it for her if he could. On his feet now, standing, his body tensely arched above her. His tongue already restless in his mouth – sliding from her breast and downward, tracking down the lustrous satin skin and avid now for taste.

210

Then to this earthen bowl did I adjourn
My lip the secret well of life to learn
And lip to lip, it murmured, 'While you live
Drink! – for once dead you never shall return.'

With Sary opening beneath him like a flower, and at the same time reaching up between his thighs to grasp him, pull him down to kneel astride her pillow, above her wide, so wide, soft mouth. To raise her strong white neck and take him in a second time. Their bodies now a circle. His flesh enclosed and hers now doubly enclosing. To taste the salty essence of her being, and let her taste of his.

One moment in annihilation's waste –
One moment at the well of life to taste!

Too softly circumfused as yet within her mouth to take from her a fraction of the pleasure he could give, with agile and insinuating tongue and wetly dipping fingers. Until he felt her shudder and contract around them – and gasp and clasp and close again, and then again. Moaning now, now crying out aloud as he'd intended from the first she should. The further affirmation that he needed to turn himself about, and then turn her. To raise her up until the satin cushions of her buttocks parted crimson. Soft-arsed and wetly parted, to admit him where he longed and had to be.

To enter in, not as a conqueror, but as a natural lover who had earned the right to savour to the final moment all she offered. One hand to bend and guide his own proud flesh. To find the mark and plough the yielding furrow – smoothly, slowly, infinitely slowly, inch by inch – until their bodies were again conjoined. Pressed close, as close as human bodies could be. But then once more dividing. Both smiling now with mouths wide open, panting through their smiles – like happy children in some guiltless recreation – as backward ploughed the share again with that same smooth-sliding stroke. To linger at the very portal, just barely lodged within her. Poised there, trembling, while his hands reached out to lift and stroke her swinging breasts. Then once again to slip into its slow, voluptuous descent. One hand, intent to meet it, pressing back and down once more, through moist red hair to share with her the feeling of his own engorgement, to feel his own wet shaft glide through his fingers. And then to find the springhead where he knew that she most keenly felt it – gently coaxing, sensing her response, as he drew back to enter in again – and then again; mounting her each time more surely and securely.

And all the while with something still outside him listening to the slapping, lapping of the lake below. Slapping with his own flesh, with the muscles of his thighs – lapping with his fingers. Battering at her with a gentle violence, now building to a rhythm of its own. With something tight, and tightening inside him now at last – drawing back and drawing taut, as she cried out again beneath him. Something now beyond his own control or hers. Feeling now his strength and force, his length and breadth and every inch of his dimension. A man about his natural business with the woman of his choice. Plunging, sheathing now. Not like a sword, but like a rod of thick lubricious velvet corded through with heat. A weapon to degrade and yet exalt her – to force his love and everything he was, or might be, deep into her body. The cord within the rod too taut, too burning hot with friction now possibly to hold. Yet rubbing hotter, jerking tighter still – molten, ready to be jerked asunder . . .

Jerking, breaking – breaking seals and jerking out from him in red hot fountains of incredible sensation.

And Sary afterwards had lain beside him with her fingers interlaced through his. Wet palms pressed tight together. Wet legs pressed tight as well. And with a pillow tucked in underneath her tingling buttocks – to help the precious Stanville seed, as she supposed, to run back inward to her waiting womb.

Chapter Twenty-One

So sure, she felt, so certain this time it would take. No sowing ever more complete or thorough. So hard he'd pushed, so deep inside her; to fetch his milt for her so many times (five times at least that Sary counted). And shouting out so loud while he was doing it that she felt sure the Conte must have heard. And loving her, cherishing her so sweetly afterward. The perfect, perfect husbandman! And yet her course had come before the month was out, as regular as usual. And then twice more before the autumn, despite David's lavish husbanding and all her lighted candles in the church.

"But Sary, darling, there's no reason yet for any great concern," he'd hastened to assure her each time she dolefully announced the coming of *the reds*. "God knows, we've time enough ahead of us for all that business in the future. And I for one am more than tolerably happy with your belly in the shape it is just now, I don't mind telling you!"

And no one, surely, but a perfect fool would argue with a man so obviously contented – with Hadderton still so far removed in time and space from all they had here in San Giulio? Why not pretend like him; pretend it didn't matter if she never had a child? As if this perfect lovers' paradise of theirs, and their enjoyment of each other here, was truly all they needed to be happy ever afterward. Honesty now at last become for Sary Snudden a luxury that she no longer could afford. Or so she'd come to think.

But this supposed that she and David and San Giulio, that life as they had lived it there, would remain unchanged forever. (A thing which life, as has been noted, refuses consistently to do.) To begin with, no one in the north of Italy, or elsewhere in the hemisphere, could hope to feel the same in autumn as they felt in summer. Or in summer as they felt in spring. In spring, David and Sary's love had blossomed with the wildflowers and camellias of the lakeside; to soak in the heat of a hundred perfect summer mornings from June until September, and expend it in their bedroom through near as many torrid afternoons. But in the autumn, mist and cloud had robbed the sun of its intensity, to veil the pristine views across the lake and smudge the colours of its floating island. Rain sometimes in the afternoon had woken them from their siesta to feelings more nostalgic than erotic. Green leaves faded, turned to gold. Swallows, which a week or two before had swooped with careless grace across the water, now twittered on the eaves and down the ridges of the old town roofs, like nervous children assembling for an outing. The lazy, sultry days of summer now departed – change was in the air and all about them. And David, patently, was restless

*   *   *

"Our host, the Conte, was too much the gentleman to speak of our departure, Mr Brown. And Lord Denton only ever mentioned his old home of Hadderton in relation to a sculpture and some paintings that he wanted to commission for it from the local artists of San Giulio. But his year in Europe now was over – the twelvemonth he'd agreed with old Lord Southbourne. And I knew. I knew of course that he was thinking of returning, from the way he spoke and moved and looked that autumn. Even from the way he loved me, Mr Brown, if you'll believe it. The spell was broken, do you see? Even before Pietro brought the English letters from Milan."

And, when the lady rose this time, it was without an obvious object; the curtains drawn already, the offer of a second cup of tea declined. Restless now herself, as she described Lord Denton's restlessness in that Italian autumn of 1821, she steered her crinoline toward the fireplace to poke irresolutely at the coals and turn her broad back on the ticking clock.

"They didn't have no time to make that little statue of me in the end," she said distractedly, her grammar less than perfect for the first time in his hearing. "Which was just as well, maybe, considering the pose he had in mind. But they did the paintings for him of our precious little island; and very fine they are as well." She pointed to the trio of unsuitably framed watercolours on the wall beside the window. "Lovely, aren't they? And so full of memories for me, just like Jemima. I've always kept 'em by me."

"But you were saying that the young Gemelli brought some letters from Milan?" her listener tentatively prompted, unable any longer to suppress his lawyer's habit of returning wandering clients to the point. "Important news from England, I imagine?"

Her face confirming it before she'd even spoken. "That October there were executions in Turin," she said, "and the *carabinieri* were very active, so we heard, preparing for the new King's ceremonial entry to the capital. So much so indeed, that Pietro thought it might be prudent to spend a little time with friends of his in Milan that month. And, as he had Lord Denton's authority to fetch the mail for us if ever he was there, he brought it with him naturally, when he came up to see his father in San Giulio."

She paused and drew a little breath. "There were letters in the bag from David's mother and from both his cousins, all written in July. And one from the attorney to the Hadderton estate as well. His father, they informed him, had died suddenly in London and on Coronation Day. He was now Lord Southbourne, in other words, and had been for the past three months." The lady smiled a brave but unconvincing smile. "So that was it," she said. "The attorney's letter confirmed his succession to both title and estate; and all the others begged him, upon the most urgent necessity, to return to England and his responsibilities. As if by then he needed begging, Mr Brown!"

*   *   *

"Dad! Dad! 'Is Lordship's 'ome with all 'is bags and baggage! And Dad – he's got 'is *Lady* with 'im and all, up there 'longside of 'im in the kerridge!"

David had jumped down himself to rap upon the gatehouse window and stir that idle Bobby Fielder to admit them; to bid him 'Good afternoon', and see the recognition dawn in his astonished face. And now, driving in between the rampant wyverns, listening to the gate-boy's voice behind, imploring his old father to come

215

and see his Lordship pass up the drive, he felt at last that he was well and truly home. With every revolution of the wheels another dear familiar sight! The bare limbs of a beech or chestnut that he'd climbed in as a child. A glimpse of the Seventh Earl's ruined hermit's tower through the trunks. The fallow deer still working through the autumn flush, with noisy gangs of starlings picking insects from the cropped grass in their wake. A smell of dampness and of fallen leaves, which in a single whiff had brought him years of memories.

'*Do you think I could be happy for any length of time in any other landscape? Do you, Tavie?*' True then, and still true now, despite all that had happened to him since he said it. Something he'd realized finally himself, even before Pietro placed the fateful letters in his hand. His love for Sary, strong as it was, in the end no stronger than the sense of place and duty – of belonging – that comprised his love of Hadderton. So that truly, when he read what they had written in the letters and saw how things now stood here, he'd been all for starting out at once for home; waiting only for a *cambiatura* to be sent up from Gozzano, before departing for Novara on the first stage of their journey. An epic of nine hundred miles, which by travelling *post-haste* all the way, they'd remarkably completed in a bare three weeks.

And here they were already at the bridge across the stream. The place where Cousin Tavie had stepped out to intercept him three years before, and to make her bid for his renewed attention. As if he ever could have looked at her in that way once he'd met with Sarah Snudden on her near-new working mattress! David stole a glance at her, his Sary; so upright and controlled beside him in the rented chaise, so pale and solemn-looking without her vivid painting. A lady, surely, in the making! He transferred the reins into his other hand and slipped an arm about her. "Home, Sary – we're home at last!" he told her in a quiet voice, carefully controlled. "Your home as well as mine, my dear. And nothing in the world now that anyone can do or say to stop me wedding with you, and making you my Lady Southbourne! Do you hear me, Sary? You'll soon be mistress of all this, and of our place up in St James's; of everything, my darling, that is mine!" And even as he spoke, with Sary leaning silently against his shoulder – the famous, glorious, north-west front of Hadderton itself sailed into view against the dark blue bastion of the downland wall. The sight whose contemplation had sustained him through all the frustrations and discomforts of their weeks upon the road.

'And poor Papa,' thought David in the moment that he felt his father's mantle of possession fall upon him, 'to have to die away from all of this, in London.' A man who should have breathed his last hallooing after foxes on the hunting field, or in his own bed in the house his ancestors had built; to have his heart give out instead within the crowded cloisters of Westminster, at the termination of a suffocating five-hour ceremony inside the Abbey. Prinny's coronation, like his Pavilion down in Brighton, an ostentatious and enduring epic of bad taste. Papa one casualty of his anointing. And poor fat Queen Caroline another; turned away in her regalia from the Abbey doors, to die herself a fortnight later, some said of a broken heart.

But now already they'd attained the *porte cochère*, with the pediment above it that Cousin Charlie once had sat astride, the Stanville arms in marble and the naked flagpole where the Southbourne banner last had flown half-mast. 'And soon will fly again for me,' thought David with a satisfactory thrill of pride, as he drove the chaise beneath the arch to enter in on his inheritance.

"But not today, my duck," she'd begged him. "We don't surely 'ave to leave until tomorrow, do we darling?"

So foolish of her even to have tried to hold him in San Giulio. As if another day with him beside the lake could make the slightest difference to what had happened, or what was now to be. As if another night of lying in his arms and listening to the lapping of the water, or another morning of opening the shutters to view the floating island out beyond, could have brought back the enchantment. For Hadderton was there already, in the letters. His heart already flying on ahead. With nothing to be gained now from pretence, or from delay. And so she'd pasted on a smile and made the best of their departure, grateful that the lake was grey that afternoon, the clouds pressed down to hide the shining peak of Monte Rosa. She bravely put San Giulio behind her to go with him to meet his destiny – uncomplaining of their bustling days and sleepless nights upon the road. Too utterly in love, too anxious now to keep him and at any price, to let him know how much she truly dreaded this homecoming.

Lady Southbourne in the White Saloon scarce knew whether to rejoice or weep at the sudden unexpectedness of her son's return and in fact did both. Before Sary stepped into view to freeze her demonstrations into silence. Then she wept again, and a great deal more in earnest, when David impressed on her their firm determination to be married. Finally retiring to her bedroom with her vinaigrette, and the announcement that she never would emerge so long as Hadderton contained 'that odious creature' within its walls. Contriving still to monopolize the upstairs servants, with her continuous demands and overactive bell-pull; and leaving Sary to the tender mercies of a downstairs staff she knew to be united in contempt for her.

Nothing here had changed, in other words. The expression in the butler's eye had made that clear to Sary the first moment she again set foot in his domain. In David's presence his employees were careful to accord her all the deference that he expected. But inevitably the new Lord Southbourne was in much demand himself those first few days of his return. There were letters to be written and legal matters to discuss with his attorney and his man of affairs; inspections to be made around the house with Mrs Graham, and with the bailiff round the park and tenant farms. Wings to spread that he'd been exercising in his year of independence on the Continent. And with his young Lordship out of sight and earshot and otherwise engaged, the servants' attitude toward the woman of his choice had undergone an obvious transformation. They attended when she rang the bell, but never promptly. The maids' bob-curtsies and the footmen's bows reduced themselves to merest sketches. The eyes they lowered in his Lordship's presence met Sary Snudden's in his absence with a bold defiance. And if she asked for aught beyond the barest necessaries, they instantly referred her to their mistress:

"No, Miss, 'er Ladyship 'as charge of all the journals and the monthlies. She won't 'ave no one read 'em but 'erself."

"No, Miss. Can't serve tea without 'er Ladyship gives up the caddy-keys. You'd best to ask 'er for them if you want it." Knowing that she never would.

Not that Sary cared a snap, she told herself, what any of them thought. So long as David loved her. So long as David came to her room each night to show how *much* he loved her, she'd face them own, the lot of them! And in due time, when she was David's Countess, she'd have them all dismissed, the ones who'd treated er so scurvily. Starting with the haughty butler, Tillotson! But here were those who Sary never could dismiss; the ancestral tanvilles in the portraits on the walls of the saloons, and on the tairs and in the crowded picture-gallery. Rows of faintly elevated yebrows and scornful, disapproving stares. 'And what exactly loes she think that she's about?' they seemed to ask of one mother. 'A trollopy-wench like that dressed up to ape her betters, parading in her silks and satins – when 'tis plain as day to anyone hat she's a common whore! Sary, Sary Snudden, that's who she is, hat's all – a fire-shipped slut who cannot even bear a child! Sary inudden, who'll never be the ancestress of any man; who'll never nake a lady, however hard she tries!'

"But that's where you're so wrong, my Lords and Ladies," she old them stoutly to their supercilious faces – the First Earl with his tarchy ruff around his ears, the Fifth Earl's Ainslie Countess with er towering *fontage* and rigid cast-iron busk. "Because my love's vorth more to 'im, I'll tell ye, than all your perishing pedigrees set ogether. And to prove it 'e will marry me, you'll see, no matter vhat!" And having said it out aloud, she almost could believe it rue herself, that within three weeks they would be married. That ;ary Snudden would be Sarah, Lady Southbourne, Countess to the Vinth Earl; and qualified to take her place up there amongst the others in a brand new po-faced portrait by Lawrence or by Hayter! David had already had the first banns bawled in the little church of Hadderton across the park. And invitations to a small informal vedding had been sent out to various of his friends and relatives.

Charles Stanville was the first to make the journey from the Western County, together with his wife and two small infants, the children's nurse, and his sister Octavia – who'd insisted on taking ip the final seat in his barouche.

"But darling Sary – confound it, there's not the slightest occasion to feel awkward with my cousins, now that things are so 'ar settled," said David with all the wishful confidence of his new status. A rich and very slightly spoiled young man, who'd tasted power and now quite failed to see the reason why he shouldn't have his cake and eat it daily. "Cousin Charlie's a man of the world, as

219

we've both good cause to know. And Fanny's sure to do or sa
whatever Charlie tells her. As for Octavia – why, she is only thre
and twenty you know, no older than yourself. Years in which she'
seen a good deal less of life than you have, of that you may be sure
for all her boarding academies and London seasons. No, Tavie's i
no case for handing out advice to such as you, my dear. And if she
has the nerve to try to do so, you're hardly bound to listen, are
you?"

'Nor am I, neither,' Sary reassured herself, when on the firs
afternoon of their arrival Charles had challenged David to a
billiards match, and left her to entertain his wife and sister in the
candlelit saloon. 'You're not a coward, after all, and never 'ave
been, Sary Snudden,' she told herself with perfect justice, seeing
the conspiratorial glance that Charlie gave his sister as he proposed
the game. 'And whatever 'tis that they've agreed for 'er to say, i
can't change nothing now, that's certain sure.'

Charlie, the rogue, had bowed to her as he went out the door
The soul of courtesy, as ever; with, in his eyes, that little dancing
flame a man will always burn there for a woman that he's bedded
And Davy, the darling duck, had come up before them all to stoop
and kiss her on the neck. His lips as warm as ever on her skin. His
love and confidence the shield he left her with, to fend away
Octavia's best-aimed missiles.

They sat in silence at the first. As unlike in person and in
temperament as any three young Englishwomen could be. Frances
Stanville more unhandsome, dull and ovine even than she'd been
the last time that they met here, two pregnancies before. Octavia,
all smooth surfaces and inward self-possession. And Sary, even
without her paint in her most muted mulberry gown, as obviously,
unsuitably coarse-grained and ill-at-ease in these surroundings, as
she'd been suited admirably to those of Italy.

"Miss Snudden, you must realize that none of us can possibly
support this crazy scheme of marriage." Octavia, the first to break
the silence, came directly to the point and with a brisk determination that even Sary could respect. "I doubt you hardly know what
is at stake. Nothing of this sort has ever happened to the Earls of
Southbourne since their creation in the sixteenth century." (Her
sister-in-law, meantime, stitching at the patchwork in her lap as if
her life might possibly depend on it.) "Youthful lapses, petty

scandals, yes," the other girl inexorably continued. "But marriage to a person of your background, Ma'am; a woman totally without the breeding or the training to fulfil the role she's elevated to. A woman whose own history is too notorious, to put it charitably, ever to be forgiven or forgotten. You must see it for yourself –good heavens, the thing is totally impossible!"

'*And sticks and stones may bruise my bones,*' thought Sary, recalling in that moment the old childhood rhyme of her early days at dame-school, '*but words cannot molest me!*' "Impossible, is it?" she said defensively. "Impossible for Davy to be the first to go against tradition? Is that what you're saying, Ma'am? Because 'is dusty old ancestors never 'ad the knackers for it?"

"No indeed, that's not at all what I am saying, if you would only listen." Octavia, sitting very upright in her chair, was struggling not to show her real confusion at the other's outrageously explicit reference to the crucial masculine anatomies. " 'Tis not our traditions but your own shortcomings that disqualify you; your reputation, your lack of any kind of grasp on how to act in civilized society. Why, even the servants here despise you and defy you, that's obvious to us all. And believe me, Ma'am, they'll be the very least of all your critics."

"And are you so sure the trick of being Lords and Ladies is so desperate difficult to learn? Because if you are, Ma'am, then let me tell you I've known Ladies who couldn't even dress themselves without a girl to 'elp them, and Lords so stupid that they'd open up their collar for a piss," said Sary, instinctively taking refuge in vulgarity again. "And if *they* can act right in Society, well I wouldn't think I'd 'ave no trouble learning how!"

Octavia flushed. "*Au contraire*, Miss Snudden, your language shows too clearly how impossibly ill-equipped you are to learn."

"Impossible again? You like that word, now don't ye? *Impossible* to learn. *Impossible* to marry out of love instead of stiff-necked pride and duty?"

"And you talk of love as if it answers everything. As if it lasts forever," said Octavia. "But nothing lasts forever – love least of all. You talk of learning how to act the lady as if you might achieve it overnight. Well let me tell you what I think; I think that it will take you twenty years to make an even half-convincing lady. By which time you'll be forty-three, and fat. By which time you'll have robbed Lord Southbourne of his standing in the world and all his self-esteem, and in the process lost whatever love there was between you. And what will you have then to offer him? The tawdry imitation only of the lady he might have married if you'd given him the leave to do so!"

"By which, I collect you mean yourself, My Lady?"

That was the Parthian shot that won the skirmish. For Octavia could in no wise answer her without revealing more than she intended, or wished her sister-in-law to hear. But lying in her bed that night, waiting for David's familiar knock upon the door connecting their two rooms, Sary knew she had more battles yet to fight before the war was truly won. Not least within herself. Life after all was not a fairy-tale in which the prince had only to declare his love to elevate the goose-girl to a princess. In that Octavia had been right enough – with so much more than love alone to take into account. He loved her now. But would he if she failed him as a wife, and as a mistress for his precious Hadderton? And if Madge Perrin's calculations proved correct? What then, without an heir? Could love survive? And was it even fair to ask it to? Could she ever have enough to offer him in compensation – five years, ten years hence? And through all the years thereafter?

Alternatives, conflicting thoughts, jostled one another in Sary's mind, confusing her intentions. And yet at heart she knew, had always known, what she would do – had known it when she faced Octavia's dark-eyed stare, and all the time she lay there waiting for David's knock upon the door, waiting for the door to open . . .

*   *   *

The knock was merely a convention, two light raps of the knuckle delivered as the doors themselves swung back on well-oiled hinges.

"Octavia, my dear!" The lady left the fireplace in her tilting hoops, hurrying to slip a friendly arm around the female in the doorway and to draw her in to meet the gentleman, now standing awkwardly before the sofa.

"Well here she is at last then, Mr Brown. Octavia is come – and I think you will agree that she's well worth the wait? Such hair and eyes! Now did you ever see such living beauty?"

The girl she turned about for the solicitor's inspection, no more than sixteen years of age at most – her hair quite obviously dyed, and plaited like a drummer's at the back. Her eyes made-up with mastic and *Briançon*, her neck cut low enough to reveal a little glimpse of both her nipples; her lower limbs clad, not in a crinoline, but in Turkish bloomers of some diaphanous material that contrived to show a great deal more than it concealed.

The girl flashed a brilliant carmine-painted smile. "And how's my favourite gentleman today?" she asked him roguishly. "In starting trim, I 'ope?"

The greeting of a practised whore.

Chapter Twenty-Two

"That's right, my dears, enjoy yourselves! And take your time, Sir, if you will. Octavia has no other bookings, I am assured, 'til something after half past six."

Sarah escorted the unlikely couple out to the stairs in quite the manner of an indulgent auntie sending children out to play. "And, Mr Brown," she called up after the solicitor's stiffly retreating figure, "if I should chance to miss you when you leave, do please accept from me – from all of us at Number Fifteen – the season's greetings for a very happy Christmas!"

Back inside the intimate little drawing salon where she herself received and entertained the waiting clients, Sarah closed the double doors again and smiled. Poor Mr Brown – how very difficult he found it. Trying to maintain the pompous dignity that all men of law cultivated, whilst waiting in the salon of a nugging-house to meet his chosen *fille de joie*! And how he'd coughed and fidgeted, poor man, while she embarrassed him with all the details of her own nefarious past! She chuckled richly. Really, the hypocrisy of Victorian gentlemen would never cease to astonish her!

Still smiling, Sarah crossed the room to ring to have the tea things cleared away; then stood to check her own appearance in the chimney glass. Behind her on the back wall of the room the copy of the famous Boucher 'Portrait of Louisa' straddled its velvet couch with naked and voluptuous abandon. A pose Octavia was perhaps adopting even now for Mr Brown upstairs, preparatory to her main assault on that professional dignity of his! 'A good girl, Octavia,' Sarah thought, whilst considering if the rouging on her own cheeks was in need of restitution, 'and what a difference in a name!' When she was working at Kate Hamilton's in Prince's Street the trull had called herself plain 'Lizzie', and dressed accordingly. But now, with Lady Southbourne's borrowed appellation, and a somewhat more exotic wardrobe – well, she made a better class of trading-pullet altogether. That no one could deny.

Sarah bent closer to the mirror to check for grey along the central parting of her smoothly oiled and brightly hennaed hair. She started slightly as the maid knocked on the door, conscious of her status. And when the girl had duly bobbed, accorded her her honorary title of 'Milady', and cleared away the debris of her tea with Mr Brown, she thought again of David knocking on that other door, and in that other time and place. The last time that he'd come to her at Hadderton, the very last . . .

*   *   *

That night Sary clung to him as she had never clung. Trying not to think of her decision, or of what she had to do tomorrow. Trying not to think at all. And in the morning, while David rode across to Lower Tilton to see about some tenant's leaking roof, she deliberately sought out Octavia in her own room down the hallway and above the White Saloon.

"All right," she said without preamble, "I'll make a deal with you, Miss Stanville. I'll leave our Davy 'ere for you, and for this place, and for the proper heirs that 'e deserves – if you'll only let 'im come to me for those things that you'll never 'ave the heart or skill to give 'im. 'Ave ye got me? Or do I 'ave to spell it out?"

Octavia Stanville, sitting in her curling papers at her dressing glass, turned to face her with heroic self-containment. "I understand you perfectly, Miss Snudden," she said. "But not why you've changed your mind."

"No, and I daresay you never will at that. So let's just say I've come to see things your way, shall we? That I prefer to give Davy what I'm best at giving – and leave for you to give 'im what I ain't no turn for, and likely never will 'ave."

Octavia stared at her in silence for a moment, with one small hand steadily unravelling the white silk fringing of her dressing-table cloth. "Let me understand this rightly," she said at last. "Are

225

you asking me to *share* Lord Southbourne with you?"

"Not quite, My Lady. As I see it I'm offering you a share of 'im you wouldn't otherwise get sight of. But only on condition that ye do your duty by 'im as a wife and mother, and let 'im come to me whenever 'e so wishes. For Davy needs me and my love, Miss Stanville, and you'd be a fool to yourself to see it otherwise."

"And if I refuse to that – that last condition?"

"Well then, I'll stay and marry 'im next week. Nothing simpler! And see to it that you don't get to set so much as one of your dainty little feet inside this park of 'Adderton, so long as I'm its mistress!"

Their eyes met then and locked, and held; each finding in her adversary a strength of purpose to match her own. And more – to find in each, brown in gold and gold in brown, a reluctant glint of admiration.

"And if I agree," Octavia said. "What will you do then?"

"Why then I'll ask your noble brother to take me back again to where 'e took me first in Brighton – to Mother Perrin's. Charlie knows the way aright, and so do I. Ye may be sure of that!"

To walk down to the carriage at Captain Stanville's side. To force her feet to place themselves, one foot behind the other – just to walk, with Charlie's strong arm to support her. To sit blank-faced, ignoring Tillotson and the grinning footmen who threw up her luggage, uncaring of their petty triumph. To ride out through the dragon gates, beneath the wall of cobbled flint that she had peered across six years before to wish herself inside the park. And so to cross the Reach at Beddingham – she and Charlie, side by side in sympathetic silence. Then on to Lewes town, and down through Moulsecombe into Brighton.

Knowing that he'd come to find her. Striding in through Madge's door as if she'd never been away. Cutting short the noisy welcome they had given her. To find an empty bed, and on it to embrace the first spare cull that offered. Amazing and delighting the poor fool with her enthusiasm – so eager had she been to take him in, that first man after David. So eager to reduce the act to what it had been once, before Rouen, Paris and San Giulio. And in the process to return herself to what she'd been as well – an honest working whore.

226

And when he came to find her, as she knew he would – to take his suffering face between her hands and explain it to him in the only way she could. "It never could 'ave 'appened," she said simply. "Davy, I never could 'ave made the wife ye need for 'Adderton. In our own little world in Italy it might 'ave worked, p'raps. But that ain't the world Lord Southbourne lives in, is it?"

"But that's confounded nonsense! And hang it all, we've been over all of that before a hundred times!" He sprang up angrily to pace about through her discarded clothes on the floor. "I don't understand you, Sary, really I do not! You've never cared what other people think. Well, have you? And yesternight I thought that nothing ever again could stand between us and all the things we've wanted. I thought at last that you and I could face the world together, and as we are. Then *this*! You simply up and leave without a single word of explanation!"

"Because you never would 'ave let me go, my duck, that's why," she told him gently. "And Davy, think about it, honestly. Can you really see me as your Countess? Sary Snudden – the girl who's pleasured 'arf of Brighton in 'er time? And likely too fire-shipped by now, my love, ever to make you feet for little Stanville slippers."

"But that isn't what I care about, surely you must see? Charlie has a son now. If the worst came, he could be my heir." David stooped to her, then knelt to take her hands, both hands, into his own. "Oh, Sary – Sary, you are all I care about! I *love* you, do you hear me? I need you and I want you back. You'll break my heart if you do this to me!"

"Strong hearts don't break, my dear – and you ain't lost me." She kissed him on his furrowed brow, and then again full on the lips. "I'm 'ere for you whenever you may need me, Davy, and always will be."

"But here in this place, and with other . . .?"

"With other men, that's right," she said with a calm she was far from feeling. "And never any harm to that, I'm sure."

"No *harm?*" He stared at her, his face held stiff by shock. "To love me, yet give yourself to other men?" An involuntary and entirely nervous smile twitching at the corners of his mouth, the thing afterwards that she remembered with the most compassion. She took her cue from it, and laughed. Forced herself to laugh at him – knowing the effect that it would have.

227

"But, duck, you 'ave my heart," she said. "That's safe enough? And you may be sure that all the others want from me's my body. The which, God knows, they don't get as no gift. Not the way old Madge is charging now!"

For three weeks from the day he'd flung away from her so furiously, declaring never to return, David remained a celibate at Hadderton – in the company of relatives who never ceased to tell him how very right he'd been to change his mind, and send the wretched girl about her business. Sary on the other hand, and within approximately the same space of time, embraced (and satisfied to varying degrees) a good two hundred men; while thinking all the time of only one. The very one in fact, who'd ridden back to Brighton in the fourth week – to forgive her, and to return a little comfort to both their empty lives.

A little more than three years later, in 1825, Mrs Margery Perrin unaccountably decided to retire from honest trade and buy a little house in Rottingdean; where she and Hodge, as Madge herself had put it, might keep to better hours and contrive to make old bones in some degree of ease. And, if Lord Southbourne knew aught more about her motives or her future source of income, he kept the information to himself, admitting only to the freehold purchase of her house in Brighton. (His gift to Sary on her twenty-seventh birthday – made on the conditions that she wore his ring thereafter, and bent her energies within the house exclusively toward its management.) Later in the same year, in October, the *Weekly Advertiser* announced the alliance of the Ninth Earl of Southbourne to his cousin, Octavia Stanville, at a marriage solemnized in London, in the Royal Chapel of St James's. A disloyalty keenly felt by all true Sussex folk. And only finally forgiven when his Lordship's firstborn daughter, Lady Caroline, was christened the August following, in the village church of St Peter ad. Vincula outside the walls of Hadderton.

During the next decade (which saw out Prinny and his brother, King William, and saw in the new Queen, Alexandrina Victoria), the population of Brighton almost doubled. And with the coming of the London railway, in 1840, Sarah had declared the place entirely ruined for quality tail-trading. The town was full of riff-raff. The young Queen, disliking the Pavilion, seldom brought her court there. And in the Season the beaches, promenades and lanes were overrun with cheap gay-girls down from Marylebone and the Haymarket; undercutting, lowering standards, and spreading every kind of genital disease.

No, the only places these days where decent, clean and gentlemanly trade could still be guaranteed, said Sary, after due consideration of the case, were up in London's Mayfair and St James's. At which Lord Southbourne had generously obliged by finding her the ideal venue for her new establishment, within easy walking distance of his own town house just off St James's Street.

'Palaces fit for the dwellings of noblemen and persons of quality,' was indeed the brief to which the mansions of St James's Square were first erected. And if in actual usage the definition was expanded to embrace the pleasures and diversions of nobility, then that was no surprise to anyone. In its early days of residence the Square had housed no fewer than three of King Charles's mistresses. Later, the celebrated Mrs Charlotte Hayes had entertained a titled audience at Number Twenty-One to re-creations of 'Cook's Voyages to the South Seas', complete with native virgins and rampant English sailors. And later still, at Number Twelve, Lord Baltimore maintained his own seraglio. The profession of the latest residents of Number Fifteen was more a matter for private celebration therefore, than for open scandal – so long as their pursuit of it remained discreet.

Through his London solicitors, Eustace, Smithson and Brown, David had purchased the house in Sarah's name, and helped to furnish her personal apartments there with favourite items of his own from Hadderton. (With or without his wife's acquiescence? Sary never knew.) The girls, she brought from Brighton or recruited from the better London houses in Albany and Prince's Street; engaging a reliable physician to attend them, and charging high to keep the clientele exclusive. And within five years the profits she accrued enabled her to repay David every penny he'd invested in her. A condition she imposed on their continuing relationship as lovers. The price for Sary of her self-respect.

In May of 1856, Verdi's controversial opera, *La Traviata*, was first performed in London at Her Majesty's Theatre, Haymarket; three hundred yards or less from the centre of St James's Square. And Sarah Snudden, who never missed a new Italian opera, leave alone one on her doorstep, was amongst the first night audience in the pit. It was a production, besides, whose history had to be of special interest to one of Sary's character and background. Based on the famous Dumas novel, *La Dame aux Camélias*, in truth it owed its origin to that author's youthful affair with the notorious Marie Duplessis. (A *grande cocotte* who sported red camellias at those times when monthly courses put her *hors de combat*; and who'd died in Paris of consumption at the age of twenty-three.) A sordid little tale, some said, of an unworthy and immoral woman deservedly balked of her lover and her life. "The story of a dying whore", as others even more unkindly put it. Banned as a play on the London stage, condemned in advance by *The Times* as "full of foul and hideous horrors" – it had to be instructive at the least, thought Sary, to see just how Polite Society would view the elevation of a draggle-tail to the status of romantic heroine!

Polite Society, meantime, was very much on view itself within the gilt and velvet jewel-case of the famous London playhouse; eager, as ever, for any opportunity of showing off its finery so early in the Season. Tiers of boxes and balconies, and rows and rows of stalls, rioted with moving colours and reflected lights. Diamonds sparkled everywhere – at throats, on wrists and studded through white shirt-fronts. Silk rustled, flounced and gleamed as patrons pressed into their places. Laughter and excited exclamation drowned out the orchestra's attempts at tuning. Fans snapped open. Tailcoats parted. And, in a side-box three tiers up, Lord Southbourne and his party took their seats.

She knew of course that he was likely to be there. The little shock of his appearance no more than she expected. The thrill no less, when David's eyes met hers and crinkled at the corners – the fingers of his white-gloved hand just faintly waving at her from the velvet ledge on which they rested. Grey-haired, grey-whiskered now, her Davy. But young still where it counted. Young in a way his Countess never had been, so thin and upright at his side in green shot-silk and pearls, so dignified and cold. Yet Lady Southbourne had fulfilled her part of their agreement to the letter; and not only in her tolerance of Sarah. For youth, real youth, was at their back and all around them – in the characters of three junior

230

daughters emerging from a billowing silken sea of crinolines, and of one much-cherished son, standing behind his mother's chair. A darkly elegant young man with easy manners and a charming smile. A noble Johnny-raw, maybe; and certainly a stranger still to Sary and her house, for all that his existence meant to her.

To think he might have been her son! (And in a way he was, perhaps. Not of the body, naturally – but of the character and spirit. Because without her spirit and decision that boy could never have been conceived. Of that much she was certain.) 'And all the rest of you,' she thought. 'You sit up there so proud and pretty, so much entitled to respect. And no one's pointing, no one's laughing at you, are they? Or whispering behind their fans about your false pretensions. And *that* you owe to Sary Snudden – that and all. Whether you know aught about it or you don't!'

And peering down into the pit just as the lights began to dim, the young man in Lord Southbourne's box nudged his sister Alice to regard the over-painted red haired woman sitting four rows from the front. To see how familiarly she smiled at them, as if they all were known to her. As if they could be!

But now the orchestra had launched into the overture – into a rising wave of wonderful violins. So many of them, and so sad! To be followed shortly by the famous *Traviata* waltz. Then as the curtain rose at last to display the lavish decoration and brilliant gaieties of Violetta's Paris salon, Sary straightway lost her hold upon the present – as she always did in any kind of drama – to concentrate entirely on the story. She needed no translation of Italian to understand Alfredo's love for Violetta. And when signor Calzolari's soaring tenor proclaimed its theme to her with such alive, romantic passion, Sary's eyes filled with tears. '*Di quell'amor, quell'amor ch'è palpito dell'universo, dell'universo intero . . .!*'

And, when in the second act the heroine abandoned the poor man to free him for another, the tears had come again; and having come, refused to stop. She wept all through the little trader's subsequent debasement and rejection. Sitting dumbly weeping through two intervals, through all the harrowing scene of Violetta's death, throughout the audience's acclamations for the youthful *prima donna* who had sung her. Unable to look up at David, uncaring of her running paint, unable to do anything but weep.

* * *

She'd seen the opera three more times between that year and this; and wept each time afresh as soon as those sweet soulful violins began to play.

"He died last year. But of course you know that, Mr Brown," she said aloud, imagining the nervous client sitting where he'd sat so long upon her salon sofa. "Died in my arms, just how he always wanted to. He came to me you see, when they told him that his heart was weak, asked me to – to love him into death.

"Yes, in the end he came to me, and not to Hadderton, you see . . ."

The barrier between life and death sometimes seemingly no more than but a hairbreadth. At others like a mile, a hundred miles across. Yet always impenetrable. The one great mystery. He on the one side and she the other. She had his portrait and his letters – the characters he'd formed on paper to the dictates of his heart. She'd kept them all, just as she kept her battered little doll and the watercolours of that lake in Italy. She had his house still in the square, and everything within it.

All she did not have, was David.

She picked up his miniature from where it leant against the chimney glass – stared at it, as Alfredo in the last act of the opera gazed at his painted Violetta. Then Sarah turned again toward her own reflection in the mirror. The image of an ageing, painted woman, in mourning for a royal prince. A woman who was growing old beside the portrait of the fine young man who represented all her youth and happiness. Images, faces. One living and one dead, with forty years to separate them. Yet neither one more real to her than the other.

Di quell'amor, quell'amor ch'è palpito dell'universo, dell'universo intero . . . Love – our love is the impulse of creation, at the heart of all creation . . .

She thought of Marietta Piccolomini, who'd sung so beautifully on that first night of *Traviata*. A little wraith in white, singing herself to death for love.

232

'And Sary Snudden? Has this one true love of yours proved your undoing?' She looked the painted lady of the mirror in the eye, and smiled. 'A character of your strength and standing? A woman of your extensive memories? The very idea!'